TOWER HAMLETS

D0519244

BRITAIN AND IRELAND'S
TOP 100
RACEHORSES
OF ALL TIME

BRITAIN AND IRELAND'S
TOP 100
RACEHORSES
OF ALL TIME

ROBIN OAKLEY

With a foreword by Henrietta Knight

CORINTHIAN BOOKS

Published in the UK in 2012 by
Corinthian Books, an imprint of
Icon Books Ltd, Omnibus Business Centre,
39–41 North Road, London N7 9DP
email: info@iconbooks.co.uk
www.iconbooks.co.uk

Sold in the UK, Europe, South Africa and Asia
by Faber & Faber Ltd, Bloomsbury House,
74–77 Great Russell Street,
London WC1B 3DA or their agents

Distributed in the UK, Europe, South Africa and Asia
by TBS Ltd, TBS Distribution Centre, Colchester Road,
Frating Green, Colchester CO7 7DW

Published in Australia in 2012
by Allen & Unwin Pty Ltd,
PO Box 8500, 83 Alexander Street,
Crows Nest, NSW 2065

Distributed in Canada by
Penguin Books Canada,
90 Eglinton Avenue East, Suite 700,
Toronto, Ontario M4P 2YE

ISBN: 978-190685-042-5

Typeset in New Baskerville by Marie Doherty

Printed and bound in the UK by
CPI Group (UK) Ltd, Croydon CR0 4YY

To Carolyn, always my No. 1

CONTENTS

CONTENTS

CONTENTS

CONTENTS

ABOUT THE AUTHOR

Robin Oakley was European Political Editor at CNN International and before that Political Editor of the BBC and of *The Times*. The author of numerous books on horseracing, he has been the *Spectator*'s Turf correspondent for almost 20 years. His most recent book is *Clive Brittain, the Smiling Pioneer* (Racing Post, 2011).

ACKNOWLEDGEMENTS

I am, as ever, deeply grateful to my wife Carolyn who has supported my efforts tirelessly while overseeing the often frantic restoration of our crumbled home. Special thanks go too to Ian Marshall and Duncan Heath of Icon Books for their help, encouragement and meticulous editing. Any remaining errors are, of course, all mine. Yet again I am indebted to the sagacious Tim Cox for his generosity in allowing me access to his superb racing library and excellent coffee. And thanks finally to those fellow racegoers and *Spectator* readers who have come up with their own ideas on the horses deserving of a place in this volume. I doubt if any of them will agree totally with my rather unscientific rankings but I hope they will still enjoy reading about some of those moments that have given us all intense pleasure.

FOREWORD

It is a great honour to be asked to write the foreword to *Britain and Ireland's Top 100 Racehorses of All Time*. It is the most fascinating book and beautifully written. What else would one expect from such a distinguished writer?

Robin Oakley is a perfectionist and has that rare ability to capture the imagination of his readers. I have always loved his racing articles in the *Spectator*. He cleverly summarises situations and events. He writes with feeling and his points are meaningful. Yet how could anybody choose their top 100 racehorses and place them into an order? It is a bit like judging 100 horses in the show ring. Nobody will ever agree with the judge's choice and many will dispute the final decision.

The book comprises a wonderful mixture of the best ever Flat racehorses together with the cream of the jumpers. As a child, I adored Petite Etoile and yet she is only rated 49th, but even Noel Murless may have found it difficult to have placed his wonderful filly in the correct order. This book is full of intimate racing details. It is certainly one to treasure and a must for anybody's equestrian library. Don't miss it!

Henrietta Knight

INTRODUCTION

How would you set about choosing the top 100 British racehorses? It has been fun, but it has also involved many sleepless nights trying to rank in any kind of meaningful order, for example, sprinters such as Mumtaz Mahal and Lochsong and Cheltenham Gold Cup heroes like Golden Miller or Dawn Run.

This is not a book for the purist. You will not read here detailed analyses of precise handicap ratings or fractional race timings. Improvements in racing surfaces and inconsistencies in watering practices for me make the stop-watch alone an unreliable guide to the relative ability of horses from different generations. Go for one kind of quality alone and you would simply have to list the top 30 Derby, Arc and Cheltenham Gold Cup winners, which would be rather too predictable.

I respect the job handicappers do – we wouldn't have our sport without them – but my approach is a less mechanistic one: the crucial factor for a horse's inclusion in this book is my perception of its impact on the watching public. Great races make great horses, and the fabulous contests we all remember such as Grundy vs. Bustino, Arkle vs. Mill House, Monksfield vs. Night Nurse, and Galileo vs. Fantastic Light made their selection imperative.

For me, racing is the simplest form of sporting contest involving man and beast: who gets there first. It is about colour and excitement, athleticism and bravery, and, yes, it is about sentiment and emotion. This is a book for those who find the little hairs on the backs of their necks prickling as a Frankel walks from the saddling boxes into the parade ring; it is for those not ashamed of having wept a tear as Best Mate adapted from equine athlete to street fighter to clinch his third Cheltenham Gold Cup. It is for those who stood and applauded Charlie Swan when he pulled up the favourite Istabraq after only two obstacles in his final Champion Hurdle. Most of them had done their money, but they didn't care. They could see something was amiss and what mattered was that no risk should be taken with a great horse who had given us all so much pleasure.

Here and there, an approach based on the watchability factor has meant jettisoning some impressive but virtually forgotten Derby or Oaks winners in favour of gritty old handicappers who have been loved by the public and cheered home by people who followed them as they support their local football club.

If the anoraks reckon that takes me down the wrong route, I can live with that, taking solace from the *Racing Post*'s poll in 2004 in which the public then rated their top ten favourite racehorses as: Arkle, Desert Orchid, Red Rum, Istabraq, Brigadier Gerard, One Man, Persian Punch, Dancing Brave, Sea Pigeon and Nijinsky. Now, you could reasonably expect that Kauto Star, Sea The Stars, Frankel and Denman would be vying with those. But the lesson is clear: to the average punter, character and visibility count just as much as sheer talent.

Some other ground rules of this collection – or rather the lack of such rules: the publishers asked initially for the 100 greatest 'British' horses. But nationality itself is a problem in racing. When Godolphin's Sakhee won the Prix de l'Arc de Triomphe with Frankie Dettori they played 'God Save the Queen'. But Sakhee was bred by Americans, owned and trained by Arabs and ridden by an Italian ...

I have taken liberties with the term 'British', because

the English and Irish racing worlds are so intertwined. Many top horses trained in Ireland have raced pretty sparingly on home territory but have appeared frequently this side of the Irish Sea: it would not only be churlish to exclude them, it would make the collection meaningless. Nijinsky may have been prepared in Ireland, but he was the last horse to win the British Triple Crown of the 2,000 Guineas, Derby and St Leger. You can hardly have more impact on the British racing public than that. But while Cottage Rake and Flyingbolt won crucial British races and are included, the great Prince Regent is not, simply because wartime restrictions meant that he did virtually all of his racing in Ireland.

Some French horses, while they have made a brief impact in Britain, haven't appeared here often enough to deserve a place, like Montjeu. I had even wondered if I should exclude the mighty Sea-Bird on the grounds that only once in his eight-race career did he cross the Channel to contest a race in Britain. But since on that one occasion he won the Derby with a majestic ease never experienced by racegoers before or since, to exclude him would have been plain pernickety.

Inevitably, this is a personal choice and we are all conditioned by the era in which we have watched most racing. Those who rate horses simply on speed, on the prize money collected in their careers or on their breeding record will probably feel that I have included too many jumpers. I plead guilty. One reason why jumping attendances have continued to boom while Flat racing keeps trying to talk itself to death is simply that the jumpers are with us for so much longer, racing from four years old to 12 or more. We get to know them as characters, with their likes and dislikes, their track and distance preferences in a way we rarely do with their sleeker cousins on the Flat.

If a bias has crept into this volume, it is probably to do with the number of older 'Cup' horses included from the Flat – the Swains, Pilsudskis and Fantastic Lights – who have not been rushed off to the breeding sheds immediately after their three-year-old Classic careers. Hurrah for the late developers: they do a lot for Flat racing, allowing character and individuality to emerge.

Among the Flat heroes who have made it, there is probably a slight skew to horses of the Classic generation, simply because that is where maximum effort is expended by so many, where so many dreams are directed and on which so many millions are spent.

Some horses, such as Lammtarra, make it after comparatively short racing careers. Is that unfair? Not really, I feel, if the quality was unquestionable. The longevity of a Flat racing career is a less realistic concern now that the breeding world has been changed by 'shuttle stallions' serving six months of the year in each of the southern and northern hemispheres. As Mill Reef's trainer Ian Balding put it on Sea The Stars' departure, it was not surprising that he was retired after two seasons: 'These days you can understand why it happens because they can make so much money. In Mill Reef's day that wasn't an issue, because you didn't cover more than forty mares per year. Now, if you want to, you can cover a hundred and fifty here and a hundred and fifty in Australia.'

One complication in assessing the relative merits of horses from different decades is the internationalisation of racing. The King George, now the crucial mid-season European competition for middle-distance horses, was instituted only in 1951. The Breeders' Cup series began in 1984, Dubai's World Cup only in 1996. A top European horse's racing programme may take a very different shape nowadays.

Do not, therefore, expect perfect order and reasoned justification for every choice. Consistency, someone once said, is the refuge of small minds, and if some horses are included here on a pretty sparse racing record, then so be it.

Others, such as Persian Punch, make it simply because win or lose, he was always a courageous battler: horses who came up against him knew they had been in a race. I have to confess that I even thought of including old Willie Wumpkins, the ex-invalid who made a noise like the Penzance express pulling out of Paddington and who won only seven of his 65 races, but who defied the handicapper by winning the Coral Golden Hurdle at the Cheltenham Festival on three separate occasions.

Everyone reading this book will disagree at some point with my chosen order. Everyone will have candidates whom I have left out and will wonder, 'Why on earth did he include that one?' Why are Fantastic Light, Swain and Pilsudski in and Kalanisi not, for example? One answer is that Kalanisi (like Bustino) figures in the stories about the others, just as that excellent stayer Le Moss gets a mention in connection with Ardross. Another is that there simply is not room for everybody. If Frankel had not come on the scene, then Canford Cliffs would be in.

I am well aware, too, that things are changing even as I write. I have, for example, omitted Long Run. If he fulfils his earlier promise, he will be pushing for a place, possibly quite a high one, in future editions. But the list had to stop somewhere, and hopefully there will be reminders of some happy moments for every racing fan. Perhaps, too, some who have not yet gone racing will start to see from this collection what binds us all together in the racing tribe.

BRITAIN AND IRELAND'S

TOP 100

RACEHORSES

OF ALL TIME

100. MELD

Being by the top-class stayer Alycidon out of the four-times winner Daily Double, the Classic-winning filly Meld was beautifully bred. You could probably say the same of her owner-breeder, Lady Zia Wernher, who was previously Countess Anastasia Mikhailovna de Torby. She was the elder daughter of the Russian Tsar Nicholas's grandson Grand Duke Michael Mikhailovic, her mother Countess Sophie of Merenberg. Her parents were banned from Russia after eloping to San Remo and she married Major General Sir Harold Wernher, whose father had made a fortune in South African diamonds.

Lady Zia's outstanding filly was trained at Newmarket by Sir Cecil Boyd-Rochfort. Boyd-Rochfort's assistant and key participant in his success, Bruce Hobbs, was excited when in 1954 the big filly arrived in the yard, full of quality and power, and she soon showed her talent on the gallops. Unfortunately, she split a pastern at exercise and had to be kept in her box for two months, not seeing a racecourse until the autumn.

When she did, she ran her stable companion Queen's Corporal to a length, the only time she was ever beaten, and when the two fillies came back it was the runner-up that Hobbs went to unsaddle, provoking Lord Derby's racing manager to declare: 'My word, you've chosen the right one.' On her next outing, Meld won an 18-runner maiden at Newmarket as she pleased.

A kind filly with a wonderful temperament, Meld wintered well. Jockey Harry Carr, then 39, was still for various reasons without a Classic winner after nine years with the yard and he was so keen to get to know Meld perfectly that he rode her at exercise every day, and even gave up his New Year holiday to keep on doing so. The filly moved like a ballet dancer, but could whip around on a sixpence and Carr's devotion was rewarded. She won the 1,000 Guineas comfortably without a preparatory race.

Meld then went to Epsom having never run publicly over more than a mile, and beat the classy filly Ark Royal by six lengths over the 12 furlongs of the Oaks. She then reverted to a mile at Ascot, winning the Coronation Stakes from Gloria Nicky by five lengths.

Her final test in that unbeaten Classic year was to take on the colts in the St Leger, effectively the only Classic in which both sexes compete regularly. Bruce Hobbs, who adored the filly and was determined she should earn a deserved place in history with a Fillies' Triple Crown, was worried because Newmarket had been hit by a bad coughing epidemic. When she headed for Doncaster 49 of the 52 horses in the Boyd-Rochfort yard were clearly affected. Meld had been exercised apart from the others as far as they could, and every precaution had been taken. Hobbs was, he told his biographer, 'up to my arms in disinfectant'.

The third leg of the Fillies' Triple Crown in 1955 proved the hardest task Meld had faced. She was ailing herself – she coughed in the parade ring – and Harry Carr, who had felt she was not herself on the way to the

Meld, with Harry Carr in the saddle, wins the Oaks by six lengths from Ark Royal, May 1955.

post, gave her the easiest race he could. Meld won by just under a length from Nucleus and then had to survive an objection (unprecedented then in a Classic race) from Lester Piggott, who had ridden the runner-up. The stewards not only threw out Lester's objection, they made him forfeit his £10 deposit, which would not have pleased a man well known for being careful with his money.

Meld's victory in the St Leger was harder-won than it looked and showed her courage: when she returned from Doncaster she had a high temperature and lay on the floor of her box for 48 hours. It was a measure of the times that Meld's earnings of £43,051 in 1955 remained an all-time record for fillies for some years and her victory in the St Leger made Boyd-Rochfort the first trainer to have won more than £1 million in stakes for his patrons.

Career highlights:
1955: 1,000 Guineas, Oaks, Coronation Stakes, St Leger

99. NATIONAL SPIRIT

Here is a pub quiz question for you: which horse ran in Cheltenham's Champion Hurdle and the Prix de l'Arc de Triomphe the same year? The answer is the five-year-old Le Paillon, trained by Willie Head, who not only ran in the Arc in 1947 but won it in the hands of Fernand Rochetti. Le Paillon probably should have won at Cheltenham too, but finished a close second. His jockey, Alec Head, later to be a great trainer himself and the father of trainers Freddie Head and Criquette Head-Marek, was only 22 and had not ridden at Cheltenham before. He went all the way round on the outside while the canny Danny Morgan, who was about to retire and who had picked up National Spirit as a chance ride when his intended jockey was injured, hugged the running rail on his mount, who came home the winner by a length having taken a much shorter course.

Trained by Vic Smyth, National Spirit was a public favourite, perhaps not surprisingly in post-war years with a name like that (although he had originally been called Avago), and he returned to Cheltenham to defend his title successfully in 1948, this time ridden by Ron Smyth, another of the Epsom dynasty. The big 17 hands horse, whose appearance was not improved by his regular wearing of a hood and protective bandages, was a spectacular jumper of hurdles, although he had been an expensive failure over fences first. He not only won again in 1948, but took five seconds off the record time, bringing it well under four minutes, in doing so.

Nobody much noticed at the time, but in fifth place behind him was a scruffy little gelding called Hatton's Grace, who was then transferred by his owners to the care of one Vincent O'Brien. Hatton's Grace won the next

National Spirit (*right*) falls at the last, allowing Hatton's
Grace (*left*) to win his third consecutive Champion Hurdle,
Cheltenham, March 1951.

three runnings of the Champion Hurdle, but the eagerly
anticipated duels between him and National Spirit helped
to establish the Champion Hurdle as a major attraction
and to popularise hurdling with the racing public.

In 1949, National Spirit was a hot favourite to collect
his third title, but his new jockey Bryan Marshall elected
to ride a waiting race on him and was hampered by a
horse who made a mistake in front of him when beginning his effort. Many punters blamed the jockey for
National Spirit's defeat – in fact he finished only fourth
– but Hatton's Grace had sprinted away so effectively that
it is doubtful if he could have won anyway.

In 1950, National Spirit was the first of four horses
racing virtually abreast to touch down over the last, but

again it was Hatton's Grace who forged ahead of his field on the run-in. Even in 1951, National Spirit, who ran again as an 11-year-old in 1952, led at the second last, but on that occasion Tim Molony came with such a rattle to jump the last beside him on Hatton's Grace that National Spirit seemed to be unsettled and fell without touching the obstacle.

His second victory in 1948, though, meant that trainer Vic Smyth had won the Champion Hurdle four times in six attempts, and Ron Smyth had ridden his third Champion winner on three different horses. National Spirit, who won 16 of his 20 hurdles from 1946 to 1950, ran 85 times in his career and won 19 hurdles and 13 Flat races.

Career highlights:
1947: Champion Hurdle
1948: Champion Hurdle

98. SHAHRASTANI

It was most unfair to a good horse that the 1986 Derby is always remembered for the horse who didn't win it, Dancing Brave, rather than the one who did. As his big-race jockey Walter Swinburn said on Shahrastani's death in 2011: 'He was the perfect Epsom horse. He had speed, stamina and mentally was well-equipped for the occasion. He deserved to win the Derby that day. I'll never forget the press conference afterwards, when all people wanted to do was to talk about Dancing Brave.'

As Swinburn says with some feeling, there wasn't much he could contribute to that conversation: Dancing Brave didn't handle the hill and got too far back and, although he was gaining on him at the end, the winner's rider

The Aga Khan leads Shahrastani into the winners' enclosure
with jockey Walter Swinburn aboard after winning the Derby,
June 1986.

never saw him in the whole race. Shahrastani, by con-
trast, not only had the serene temperament to cope with
the Epsom hullabaloo, he also handled Epsom's undulations perfectly. On the day, Swinburn and Shahrastani did
everything better than Dancing Brave did and they were
worthy winners.

Because so many felt that Dancing Brave was the vic-
tim of pilot error at Epsom, Shahrastani was effectively
left in the curious position of being a Derby winner who
was still required to prove himself. He did so emphatically in his next outing in the Irish Derby at the Curragh.

It wasn't a matter of squeaking home either – the son of Nijinsky won by eight lengths.

Shahrastani had two more outings after that, one in the King George VI and Queen Elizabeth Stakes and the other in the Prix de l'Arc de Triomphe. Both races were won by Dancing Brave, but the Aga Khan's horse showed his consistency by finishing fourth on each occasion among some of the hottest middle-distance horses seen for years. The tussle in the latter stages of the Arc that year between Shardari, Triptych, Bering and Shahrastani, before Dancing Brave cut them all down, was a real treat for racegoers.

Career highlights:
1986: Derby, Irish Derby

97. TIME CHARTER

When she was good she was very, very good. Time Charter didn't have a totally consistent record, but on her day she was as good a filly as we have seen.

Trained by Henry Candy, her juvenile form was nothing special, but her first race as a three-year-old, the Masaka Stakes at Kempton, revealed that Time Charter had trained on with a vengeance: she made every yard and finished five lengths clear of the field, earning herself a run in the 1,000 Guineas of 1982.

In that first Classic, she kept on well for second place, but was easy to back at 12-1 nonetheless for the Oaks, largely because her sire, Saritamer, had been campaigned only in sprints by Vincent O'Brien. Time Charter, though, must have inherited stamina from the female line, because at Epsom she showed herself a natural middle-distance performer. Demonstrating a real ability to accelerate, she improved from three furlongs out, reeled in Last Feather and Slightly Dangerous and won by a length with something in hand.

At Goodwood she was unable to concede 7lb to Dancing Rocks, and an infection kept her out of the Yorkshire Oaks. Re-emerging in the 1m 2f Sun Chariot Stakes in October, she had to give weight to all, including older fillies, but she scored a smooth victory from Stanera. Then came the cherry on the top – Time Charter's eye-catching end-of-season display in the Champion Stakes as the only filly in a field of 14.

On the descent into the Dip, she was going best of all but every route to the front seemed to be blocked. They were on the rising ground before jockey Billy Newnes found the smallest gap, but when she saw daylight she was through it like a minnow through the weeds. By the time they reached the winning post, her nearest pursuer was seven lengths behind.

Kept in training as a four-year-old, Time Charter still had her winter coat on when contesting the Jockey Club Cup and lost by a head. A stone bruise kept her out of the Coronation Cup and she was unsuited by the slow pace in the Eclipse, so expectations had been dulled before she ran in the 1983 King George VI and Queen Elizabeth Stakes, especially since she was facing the Prix du Jockey Club winner Caerleon and that year's Oaks winner Sun Princess. Under Joe Mercer she produced a performance to still any doubters: Diamond Shoal had been kicked clear by Lester Piggott, but Time Charter quickened to get to him at the furlong pole and ran out the winner by three-quarters of a length. The next filly or mare to win the race was Danedream in 2012. Joe Mercer, who said 'I don't ring up for rides', partnered Time Charter only

Time Charter, ridden by Billy Newnes in the Champion Stakes,
Newmarket, October 1982.

because his wife rang Henry Candy and asked for him to
have the opportunity.

Time Charter then won her prep race for the Arc, taking the Prix Foy, but although it was a triumphal year for
the distaff side in the big race, with the first three home
being All Along, Sun Princess and Luth Enchantee, Time
Charter was only fourth, albeit by a length, a short neck
and a nose.

Unusually, Time Charter was kept in training for one
more year and, while there was only one victory from her
four appearances, it was one that marked her once again
as a racemare of the very highest quality. The previous
year, Sun Princess had won the Oaks by ten lengths. In

the Coronation Cup of 1984, Time Charter coasted up to her a furlong out and then shot away from her fellow Classic-winning filly as if she had been parked on the spot.

In the Eclipse that year, Time Charter went under by a neck to Sadlers Wells. She was fourth in the King George and her career concluded with a lacklustre 11th place in the Arc. It was her Epsom performances, though, that will be long remembered.

Career highlights:
1982: Oaks, Sun Chariot Stakes, Champion Stakes
1983: King George VI and Queen Elizabeth Stakes, Prix Foy
1984: Coronation Cup

96. MASTER MINDED

Owner Clive Smith, his pockets full of Kauto Star's winnings, and trainer Paul Nicholls, always on the lookout for winners, were constantly pushing to acquire Master Minded when he was in Guillaume Macaire's yard in France. Finally, they got him for 300,000 euros, a decent chunk of which was repaid when he finished second in a big French chase before leaving.

When an over-bold Master Minded fell at the third at Exeter on his British debut, that must have seemed a lot of money. He was brave but silly, said Nicholls, and it was back to basics with his jumping. But then Master Minded ran decently in a Sandown handicap, began improving faster than any horse Nicholls had seen and shocked the Ditcheat team by out-powering Kauto Star in a gallop.

Nicholls was emboldened to run him in the Game Spirit Chase against the then two-mile champion, Voy Por Ustedes, in February 2008 and his French recruit gave

Master Minded and Tony McCoy jump the last fence before going on to win the Tingle Creek Chase at Sandown, December 2008.

an exhibition round of jumping to win by five lengths. He went on to Cheltenham and, at the age of only five, astonished the jumping cognoscenti by winning the Queen Mother Champion Chase that year by 19 lengths. On that form, he could have won any race at the Festival, said the normally restrained John Francome, and Master Minded finished the season as the highest-rated chaser in the world. Despite having Kauto Star, Denman and Big Buck's in his yard, Nicholls called Master Minded in January 2009 the best he had trained.

In the 2008–09 season, Master Minded scored an effortless victory in the Tingle Creek Chase at Sandown and as a six-year-old, only 75 per cent fit after sustaining an injury, he successfully defended his crown in the Queen Mother Champion Chase at the Cheltenham Festival. But I remember then Paul Nicholls sounding a note of caution about whether such flamboyant success could last for ever, and in the 2009 Champion Chase Master Minded was beaten by Big Zeb.

He continued to win a string of top chases – the Victor Chandler, the Melling Chase at Aintree, another contest with Big Zeb at Punchestown – but the aura of invincibility was chipped away.

For the first time ever, Master Minded was allowed to compete with Kauto Star in public, over three miles in the King George VI Chase on Boxing Day 2011, and while that day ended in triumph for Kauto with a fifth victory in the race, poor Master Minded cut into himself during the race and was pulled up with a career-ending injury.

In his prime Master Minded was spectacular, a horse who seemed at his best when bowling along in front and who gave his fences air, clearing them majestically, yet without losing momentum. He was a gentleman in his box, an asset when he suffered his major injury, and one of the most exciting presences I have encountered on the racecourse. In all, he won 13 of the 20 chases he contested in Britain. Clive Smith may have paid plenty for him, but Master Minded won his connections more than £500,000 before his retirement.

Career highlights:
2008: Game Spirit Chase, Queen Mother Champion Chase, Tingle Creek Chase
2009: Victor Chandler Chase, Queen Mother Champion Chase, Kerrygold Champion Chase Punchestown
2010: Game Spirit Chase, Tingle Creek Chase
2011: Melling Chase

95. PERSIAN PUNCH

If he had been a boxer not a horse, Persian Punch wouldn't have been a sleek Cassius Clay, he would have been a bare-knuckle fairground battler, the only one left standing in the ring when the rest of the bloodied challengers had cried enough. He was big, he had the heart of a lion and, so rarely for a Flat-racer, he thrilled us for nine great seasons.

Form-book purists probably wouldn't have Persian Punch in their top 300 horses. He lost too many races to satisfy them and he never won a Group One contest. But I have no hesitation in including him in my top 100 – and not just because I would run the risk of dire retribution from his thousands of admirers if I didn't. Persian Punch forces his way into the list because of his courage, his character and his sheer watchability.

I defy anyone to look at the videos of Persian Punch racing and say that horses are not brave or courageous or competitive animals, that it is only humans who make them battle. Sure, Persian Punch was a hard ride for a jockey through most of his races. He had to be pushed and driven and coaxed to get into his racing rhythm. Said his most successful partner, Martin Dwyer: 'Before our first race together, I spoke to a few of the boys who had ridden him and they told me to take an oxygen tank … he's a hard ride as you are pushing him from a mile and a quarter out and you have to keep both yourself and the horse going. You have to really stretch him and make his stamina come into play.' But once Persian Punch was racing, there was nothing he loved more than a scrap. When other horses came at him and tried to pass him, he would lower his head, thrust out his neck and do his damnedest to defy them. That was why crowds used to applaud him

Persian Punch, ridden by Richard Hughes, wins the first of his
three Jockey Club Cups at Newmarket, October 2000.

into the ring and out of the winners' enclosure, as well as
through the last two furlongs of the long stayers' races he
used to contest.

He was famous not for swooping from the clouds to
snatch a race, but for eyeballing his opponents and slug-
ging it out with them through the last two or three furlongs of epic stamina tests. In contests such as the Gold
Cup at Ascot, a race he contested on seven occasions, he
simply never gave up. In 2001, Royal Rebel passed him
fully one and a half furlongs out, but Persian Punch
fought back every yard of the way to the line, going under
by merely a head at the post. On their next two meetings,
it was Persian Punch who won.

He didn't have an exhilarating burst of speed: he won his races by grinding out a pace that eventually wore out the others, or by responding virtually every time a horse came at him and tried to pass him with a resolution that often, though not always, beat them off. Passing Persian Punch seemed to stimulate him: time and again, he responded by clawing his way ferociously back to the front, often getting there on the line, as he did in an epic Jockey Club Cup against his old rival Millenary in 2003. A hundred yards out, Persian Punch had been fourth, but he never stopped trying and he got there.

If ever there was a horse where the statistics don't tell you the full story, it was Persian Punch. He was owned by Jeff Smith and trained by David Elsworth, who also handled that other heartstring-puller, the jumper Desert Orchid. Persian Punch faced the starter 63 times, winning 20 races and being placed in 19 others. A total of 14 jockeys rode him in races, his most regular partners being Richard Quinn, Ray Cochrane, Richard Hughes and Martin Dwyer. What the statistics don't tell you is that Persian Punch was, in his prime, the most popular racehorse in the country. In the *Racing Post* poll of the greatest horses conducted in 2004, Persian Punch figured at number seven.

He may not have won a Group One, but he won 13 Pattern races including three Jockey Club Cups, three Henry II Stakes, two Goodwood Cups, a Doncaster Cup, a Sagaro Stakes, and a Prix Kergorlay. He also finished second in the Irish St Leger and was twice placed in the Melbourne Cup. In that race in 1998, he was beaten a neck and half a length, trying to give almost a stone to the pair who beat him. Persian Punch also won more than £1 million in prize money. In the debates about how to get more people to go racing, one senior official declared that the answer was simple: 'Run Persian Punch every day.'

Jumping folk are more used to the tragic moments, but there has probably never been such an outpouring of grief on a British racecourse as when the great old battler met his end at Ascot in 2004. Running in the two-mile Sagaro Stakes, one of his regular contests, Persian Punch suffered a massive heart attack and collapsed and died 100 yards from the line. Owner Jeff Smith, trainer David Elsworth and jockey Martin Dwyer were all in tears, as were many in the crowd.

Career highlights:
1997: Henry II Stakes
1998: Henry II Stakes, Sagaro Stakes
2000: Henry II Stakes, Jockey Club Cup, Prix Kergorlay
2001: Goodwood Cup
2002: Jockey Club Cup
2003: Goodwood Cup, Jockey Club Cup, Doncaster Cup

94. HALLING

Halling was a late developer, so much so that he did not make it to a racecourse as a two-year-old. Handled initially by John Gosden, this son of Diesis out of Dance Machine had his first run in the July of his three-year-old career and still took time to learn the game, running unplaced in three maidens. That hardly looked like the start of a stellar career, but Halling was to go on to become a dual winner both of the Eclipse and the Juddmonte International and a highly successful sire.

Halling did not win until he took the Harrogate Handicap over ten furlongs at Ripon in August 1994,

Frankie Dettori rides Halling home to his second victory in
the Juddmonte International at York, August 1996.

but once he had acquired the habit it stuck. Three weeks
later, Halling won the Ladbroke Handicap at Doncaster
and then, with Frankie Dettori riding, he concluded
his English season by carrying 8st 8lb to victory in the
Cambridgeshire, beating Hunters Of Brora and 28 others. At that point, Halling was taken over by Godolphin
and sent to Hilal Ibrahim in Dubai, who won a three-
runner handicap with him there.

Back in England for the 1995 season, the former
handicapper took a significant step up in class, contesting the Coral Eclipse against a tough field including
Muhtarram and Eltish, who had been first and second
in the Prince of Wales Stakes at Ascot, Red Bishop, who
had won the Queen Elizabeth II Cup in Hong Kong, and
Singspiel, who had finished a close second in the Grand
Prix de Paris. In the hands of that expert judge of pace

Walter Swinburn, Halling set out in front from Singspiel and Red Bishop and that was the way it stayed until they passed the jamstick. Mick Kinane had a momentary glimmer of hope when Swinburn dropped his whip inside the final furlong, but confessed afterwards: 'I felt we were always on the losing end unless Halling didn't get home.'

After that, it was on to the Juddmonte International at York, for which Halling was made the favourite. Again ridden by Walter Swinburn, he was opposed by St James's Palace Stakes winner Bahri and by Annus Mirabilis, who had been third in the Irish Derby. They proved no match for the Godolphin colt: Halling was set alight by Swinburn two furlongs out and drew clear.

It had been intended that Halling would run in the Queen Elizabeth II Stakes and the Champion Stakes, but he missed both of those through injury and finished his season with an unsuccessful foray to America to run on dirt in the Breeders' Cup, where he finished tailed off.

Halling's next season started again in Dubai, where in March he won the ten-furlong Al Futtain trophy by eight lengths. He took on the great Cigar in the Dubai World Cup, but again faded to finish last. After that, Godolphin determined he would never again be asked to run on dirt. The colt was given a rest until May, when he was sent over to Longchamp for the Prix d'Ispahan in which he led all the way to beat Gunboat Diplomacy.

The next target was a repeat run in the Eclipse. This time Pentire, who had won the Irish Champion Stakes the previous back-end, was the favourite, with Bijou d'Inde, winner of the St James's Palace Stakes, and Valanour, winner of the Prix Ganay, also in the field. Ridden by John Reid, Halling set the pace. He was challenged in the final furlong by Bijou d'Inde and Pentire, but held on to win by a neck.

Halling's next contest, too, was to defend a crown, this time in the Juddmonte International. It was the race of the season, with four other Group One winners in contention. Halling was again opposed by Bijou d'Inde and also by the Sussex Stakes winner First Island. Again he made the running, clearly enjoying himself, and in the straight his jockey, Frankie Dettori, steadily wound up the tempo for an imposing victory. Halling, he said, had more pace than Lammtarra, and they went on to beat First Island by three lengths with Bijou d'Inde one and a half lengths away in third.

Halling's final contest was in Newmarket's Champion Stakes, but perhaps the length of his season was telling by then, as he was well beaten by the 1,000 Guineas winner Bosra Sham. His key seasons may have ended tamely, but no other horse has won two Eclipses and two Juddmonte Internationals.

Career highlights:
1994: Cambridgeshire Handicap
1995: Eclipse Stakes, Juddmonte International
1996: Eclipse Stakes, Juddmonte International

93. DOUBLE TRIGGER

Double Trigger raced for as long as many of the jumping horses who are more easily taken to the hearts of the racing public. But it wasn't just the length of his career that made him, as Timeform put it, 'the people's horse', it was his attitude. 'Always Trying' is the motto of Mark's Johnston's stable, and the dogged, honest Double Trigger was the epitome of that slogan.

He was the stayer who stayed for ever, longer even than

Jockey Darryll Holland salutes Double Trigger as he wins
the Doncaster Cup for the third time, September 1998.

the mother-in-law. They loved him in the north, where he
won three Doncaster Cups and where his statue stands on
the racecourse today. They loved him in the south, where
he won three Goodwood Cups and a memorable Gold
Cup at Ascot, and it is fair to say that Double Trigger's
career helped to swing back the pendulum in the years
when fashion-followers were trying to put the squeeze on
true stayers' races and reduce their distance.

The way Double Trigger won his final race, the last of
those Doncaster Cups, was typical. With Darryll Holland
aboard, he led all the way against Henry Cecil's Canon
Can, John Gosden's Three Cheers and Barry Hills's Busy
Flight. Busy Flight stayed on his heels, but when he came
for him, Double Trigger shot him down and went away

again. As his proud trainer said: 'Now he's finished we can tell them: don't try and beat him for stamina. If they wait there until tanks are on empty they can't beat him.' Only by breaking him early on could Double Trigger be beaten, said Mark Johnston: 'You can't beat him late in the race, that's when he is at his best.'

Double Trigger's career began with a ten-length success in a Redcar maiden in 1993 and victory a month later in the Listed Zetland Stakes at Newmarket. At three, he ran fifth in the Great Voltigeur and third in the St Leger. In 1994, he won the St Leger Italiano but ran only seventh in the inaugural Hong Kong Vase at Sha Tin.

Obviously there was middle-distance potential, but it was as a true stayer over long distances, two miles or more, that Double Trigger made his career. In 1995, he was the champion stayer, winning the Sagaro Stakes and Henry II Stakes in the spring and then going on to take the Stayers' Triple Crown by winning the Gold Cup at Ascot in an epic battle with the St Leger winner Moonax, and the Goodwood and Doncaster Cups. The Goodwood race was a special thriller and the horse he beat by a neck was his brother Double Eclipse. The disappointment of the year came after the British season: Double Trigger headed to Australia for the Melbourne Cup and was sent off favourite despite his 9st 7lb. He ran a stinker, finishing only 17th, but a dope test found nothing to explain why.

Double Trigger was never quite such a cock of the roost again back home and suffered several injury setbacks, but he still won plenty of top-distance races, and in capturing the 1996 Doncaster Cup seemed to have recovered all his old resolution. There was another all-the-way success in the Goodwood Cup in 1997.

The 1998 season began poorly, but then Double Trigger showed his true quality again by running the all-out Kayf Tara to a neck in the Gold Cup at Ascot. Perhaps he had become aware that he was being offered at an insulting 25-1.

Mark and Deirdre Johnston and their team kept Double Trigger going for six seasons, and the 14 victories from his 29 starts included 12 Group races and one Listed. Writing about racing you never stop learning, and I was intrigued to discover the things they changed in Double Trigger's final year to help retain his enthusiasm for racing. He wintered at Bill Gredley's stud farm instead of in Middleham, he was excused the duty of leading out the Johnston string, and it was decided to leave his tail unplaited in his races in a bid to relax him more. A twist in the tale, indeed.

Career highlights:
1993: Zetland Stakes
1994: St Leger Italiano
1995: Sagaro Stakes, Henry II Stakes, Gold Cup (Ascot),
*   Goodwood Cup, Doncaster Cup*
1996: Sagaro Stakes, Henry II Stakes, Doncaster Cup
1997: Goodwood Cup
1998: Goodwood Cup, Doncaster Cup

92. TULYAR

Jockeys are not always the most loquacious of sportspeople in celebrating success. Perhaps it is the strain imposed by the constant battle with the scales, perhaps it is fear of saying a word out of turn and upsetting the owners on whom they depend for their rides. There are glorious exceptions, such as the exuberant Frankie Dettori, and I have never forgotten the first example of racing humour that I

The Aga Khan's Tulyar, winner of the Derby, May 1952.

encountered: when he came into the winners' enclosure after winning the 1952 Derby, Charlie Smirke lived up to his name and beamingly appealed to all and sundry: 'What did I Tulyar?'

Tulyar was bred by the third Aga Khan, Sultan Sir Mahomed Shah, the spiritual leader in those days of the Shia Muslims, and his son Prince Aly Khan. The brown colt, who was trained at Newmarket by Marcus Marsh, took a while to reach his best. In his two-year-old season, he was beaten three times before opening his account in a nursery stakes over a mile. He won once more before coming second in the Horris Hill Stakes at Newbury, but was still rated 19lb behind the best of his year in the Free Handicap.

As a boy living next door to the old Hurst Park track near Hampton Court – sadly long since redeveloped as a Wates housing estate – I used to prop my bicycle against the fence, stand on the saddle and watch the horses gal-loping past, their hooves thudding into the turf and their jockeys shouting for room. That was how I became hooked on racing, and I like to think I would probably have caught a flash of Tulyar hurtling by on his way to win the Henry VIII Stakes when he opened his three-year-old career. I went on to live in Epsom, within dog-walking distance of the Derby course, for over 20 years, and have rarely missed a Derby since.

The backward two-year-old baby Tulyar had matured over the winter into a significant racing machine, and he went on from his Hurst Park victory to win both the Ormonde Stakes at Chester and the Lingfield Derby Trial. A flood of late money on the day installed him as the 11-2 favourite to win a Derby contested by 33 runners.

At Epsom that year, Chavey Down, H.V.C. and Bob Major were racing up the straight in a line abreast until, at the two-furlong marker, Smirke and Tulyar swept past them with an irresistible momentum. Gay Time, who was Lester Piggott's second Derby mount, followed him to challenge, but could not sustain his effort, and Tulyar won by three-quarters of a length. Soon after the win-ning post, Gay Time stumbled and unseated Piggott. His mount having disappeared down Chalk Lane until he was caught and returned by a local stable lad, Lester was unable to weigh out for a further 20 minutes. The delay also meant he was too late to launch an official objection to the result.

After that success, Tulyar went on to contest the Eclipse at Sandown, where as the 1-3 favourite and with the aid of a pair of pacemakers, he scored another success, beating one of them, Mehmandar, by three lengths. Only a week later, he triumphed at Ascot in the King George VI and Queen Elizabeth Stakes, again beating Gay Time. Before being sold to the Irish National Stud, he concluded his successful career by winning the St Leger by a comfortable three lengths, drawing away from Kingsfold in the last furlong.

It is a comment on an inflationary century that for those successes, Tulyar retired with a record prize money total of £76,577.

Career highlights:
1952: Derby, King George VI and Queen Elizabeth Stakes, St Leger

91. TRESPASSER

Trespasser should be in the record books as a Champion Hurdle winner. There was only one reason he is not: while he was at his peak there was no Champion Hurdle, a race introduced at the Cheltenham Festival only in 1927.

Trespasser, who was trained at Epsom by Jimmy Bell, was the best hurdler of his time by far, the best seen out before the Second World War, and he was ridden in most of his races by the best hurdles jockey of pre-war years, George Duller, who in 1922 brought home 97 winners from just 239 mounts.

Known as 'The Croucher', Duller revolutionised the art of riding over timber, keeping his weight well forward and not shifting his position on take-off. He was said to be almost impossible to dislodge, however hard a horse hit an obstacle. Horses ridden his way lost less momentum over the obstacles, and Duller was all about speed – he flew his own aeroplane and later became a motor racing driver at Brooklands.

Until well into the 1930s, the Cheltenham Gold Cup

Trespasser, the best hurdler of the 1920s and a stayer
on the Flat too.

very much played second fiddle to the Grand National,
being seen merely as a prep race for the Aintree spectacular, and in Duller's time the hurdle race that mattered was the Imperial Cup, the big handicap at Sandown
Park. Duller won it seven times and three of those victories were scored on Trespasser. An entire horse (that is
not gelded like most jumpers), he was unbeaten in his
six races over hurdles and twice he carried the massive
burden of 12st 7lb to victory in the Imperial Cup, still
winning by ten lengths in 1921 and three in 1922. He was
also an effective stayer on the Flat, winning races like the
Queen's Prize at Kempton and the Bibury Cup.

Career highlights:
1920: Imperial Cup, Two Thousand Hurdle
1921: Imperial Cup, Queen's Prize
1922: Imperial Cup, Bibury Cup

90. BADSWORTH BOY

There was a period in the 1980s when the two-mile Champion Chase at the Cheltenham Festival threatened to become the private preserve of one famous Yorkshire racing family. In 1982, it was won by Rathgorman, trained by the perfectionist former jump jockey Michael Dickinson, who next year won undying fame by producing the first five home in the Cheltenham Gold Cup.

In 1983, Rathgorman was favourite to win the two-mile event again, but this time he was beaten by a stable-mate. The nine-year-old Badsworth Boy, ridden by Robert Earnshaw, gave a spectacular display of speed jumping and was still on the bridle when he went clear three out to beat Artifice by 'a distance' (30 lengths or more). It was Badsworth Boy's fifth consecutive victory that season.

In 1984, Badsworth Boy, who had been trained in his time both by Michael and his father Tony Dickinson, was handled by Michael's revered mother Monica Dickinson. At the second last this time, once again ridden by Robert Earnshaw, he went right away from his field to beat Little Bay by ten lengths. At the same Festival, Monica Dickinson also took the Cathcart Challenge Cup by ten lengths with Mighty Mac.

In 1985, Badsworth Boy was back again to win the Queen Mother Champion Chase by the same emphatic margin of ten lengths, this time with Far Bridge toiling behind him. Jockey Robert Earnshaw too completed the treble.

Few horses have jumped fences at the same speed as Badsworth Boy, but the price he paid for his exhilarating pace was that he was not always foot perfect. Nevertheless, he won eight hurdle races and 18 chases in his career. Part of his claim to fame is that he was handled in turn by

Badsworth Boy, winner of the Queen Mother Champion Chase,
with jockey Robert Earnshaw, Cheltenham, March 1985.

three members of the remarkable Yorkshire dynasty led
by the woman known to all as 'Mrs D'.

A hardworking and forthright woman who had been
a champion showjumper, Monica Dickinson was the hub
of the Harewood stables. She would have made history by
becoming the first woman trainer to be champion had
not her Browne's Gazette, ridden by Dermot Browne,
veered violently left at the start of the 1985 Champion
Hurdle, for which he was odds-on favourite, forfeiting
his chance in the race. Top jockey Graham Bradley, who

rode for the Dickinsons for ten years, declared: 'The boss [Tony] used to do all the buying, Monica used to do all the feeding and Michael did the training – they were a great team.' There was no better example of their team effort than Badsworth Boy.

Career highlights:
1983, 1984, 1985: Champion Chase

89. GENEROUS

Generous, the best colt in England, thrilled racing crowds in the summer of 1991 as he duelled with Suave Dancer, the pride of France, and they came out with the honours even. Trained by Paul Cole at Whatcombe for Fahd Salman, Generous was a son of Caerleon whose looks were the equine equivalent of a matinee idol, definitely on the flashy side. But there was nothing much wrong with his performance.

The famous trainer Atty Persse once said that horses which attracted a trainer's eye as potential Classic contenders shouldn't be run often as two-year-olds, but Paul Cole did things a different way with the best horse he ever trained: Generous showed a lot of speed at home and he ran on six occasions as a two-year-old, beginning his career with a win over a mere five furlongs at Ascot in May.

He was back at the Berkshire track to run second in the Coventry Stakes to Mac's Imp, but not all his races as a juvenile were impressive, including a failed trip to France, and when it came to the Dewhurst at the end of the season, his starting price was a whopping 50-1. At that stage, Richard Quinn was still Salman's rider. Pressing through

Generous, with Alan Munro in the saddle, enters the winners'
enclosure after victory in the Derby, June 1991.

the second half of the race, he went ahead only in the
final furlong to beat Bog Trotter by three-quarters of a
length.

Staying was always going to be Generous's real business, and in the 2,000 Guineas the next year he finished
fourth to Mystiko. He had run like a Derby colt and that
was what he proved to be. With Alan Munro now the
retained rider in the Salman green, Generous demonstrated how a Derby winner needs both pace and staying

power. Well positioned throughout behind Mystiko and then Arokat and Hector Protector, Generous moved up smoothly in the straight, taking command at the two-furlong pole. There Munro drove him clear and he won by five lengths from Marju.

Meanwhile, a late-developing colt, who did not race until November of the previous season, had been catching the eye in France. Suave Dancer, who had been bought as a yearling for his owner by American jockey Cash Asmussen, won the Prix Greffulhe and then romped away with the Prix du Jockey Club, the French Derby, by four lengths. The must-see race that summer therefore was the Irish Derby in which the two colts were to clash.

Generous won his races by injecting pace three or four furlongs out and grinding the opposition into the track as they tried to catch him. Suave Dancer, trained at Chantilly by John Hammond, was a late swooper and, with Asmussen injured, he had the perfect big-race substitute in Walter Swinburn. In a small field on 30 June the clash took place.

The pace was poor up front and Munro was forced to take Generous into the lead much earlier than he would have wished. It was going to be all about pace judgement and courage in the finish. Munro gradually wound things up on Generous, Swinburn waited for the moment on Suave Dancer. Two furlongs out, Suave Dancer was told to go and get Generous. He quickened, but so did Generous on whom Alan Munro had husbanded some reserves. Suave Dancer narrowed the gap but he never closed it and within the last furlong his effort faltered.

Generous, the evens favourite to Suave Dancer's 9-4, had beaten off the challenge and went on to win by three lengths. Generous went on from that victory to a smashing success in the King George VI and Queen Elizabeth

Stakes, where he had seven lengths between him and Sanglamore in second. Suave Dancer went back to Ireland for a four-length victory in the Irish Champion Stakes. It was game-on once more, but in the final round, the Prix de l'Arc de Triomphe, it was a far more one-sided affair.

It had been a long season for Generous and he finished eighth, never really in the reckoning. Suave Dancer came from last to first to win on home territory by two lengths. Cash Asmussen, back in the saddle, famously declared: 'We were so far back you needed a searchlight to find us.' For the big two, the series was an honourable 1-1 draw.

Career highlights:
1991: Derby, Irish Derby, King George VI and Queen Elizabeth
*   Stakes*

88. INGLIS DREVER

When Inglis Drever won his third World Hurdle at the Cheltenham Festival in 2008, the then Cheltenham chairman, Lord Vestey, opened several bottles of champagne to aid the celebrations. Not only were his then owners, Graham and Andrea Wylie, present, but so were Bobby McAlpine, Inglis Drever's breeder and first owner, and his second owner, Piers Pottinger.

Piers, as cheerful a cove as you will ever meet on the racecourse, is not the kind to let anything get him down, but he must have had mixed feelings that day. After Inglis Drever's Flat career with trainer Sir Mark Prescott, he had planned to put him into training over hurdles himself, with Nicky Henderson; instead, he was advised by a vet to send him to the sales where northern trainer Howard

Inglis Drever, ridden by Paddy Brennan, runs on to win
the World Hurdle, Cheltenham, March 2007.

Johnson acquired him for the Wylies. To the Newmarket
trainer's solid profit, several of Prescott's former Flat
horses followed the same route and Sir Mark was said
to drink a toast every New Year to the continued good
health of Mr Wylie.

Inglis Drever won four of his 12 races on the Flat for
Sir Mark, but it was in the tough stamina-sapping world
of the three-mile hurdlers that he truly blossomed in
the capable hands of Howard Johnson, a man who collected his own headlines from time to time, once losing
£100,000 in cash when armed men raided his house, and
retiring in 2011 after being banned for four years by the
racing authorities after an illegal 'de-nerving' procedure
was carried out on one of his horses.

Inglis Drever was the first horse ever to win the World
Hurdle, an event that became the hyped highlight of one
Festival day when Cheltenham expanded the meeting

from three days to four, on three occasions. What the crowd enjoyed most was that Inglis Drever usually made it look hard work on the way before he powered up the final hill to secure his victories. Surely this time he is done for, we would think to ourselves three hurdles out, and then once again he would reassert with that final surge.

Inglis Drever secured his first World Hurdle victory in 2005, de-throning France's Festival hero Baracouda, who had won the race under its former title for the two previous years and was himself something of a Festival hero. In 2006, Howard Johnson's charge was injured, but in 2007 he was back to out-battle Mighty Man up the final hill and wrest back his crown. In 2008, it was Kasbah Bliss whom he overhauled in the latter stages. In all, he won 17 of his 35 races.

Career highlights:
2005: Kingwell Hurdle, World Hurdle, John Smith's Hurdle, Long Distance Hurdle
2006: Long Distance Hurdle
2007: World Hurdle, Long Distance Hurdle
2008: Cleeve Hurdle, World Hurdle

87. DAYJUR

Dayjur was one of the fastest things ever seen on four legs, but tragically he is remembered more for a race he lost than for his seven scintillating victories in an 11-race career.

The Danzig colt was owned by Sheikh Hamdan al-Maktoum and trained by Dick Hern, and it took even those experienced horsemen a while to establish his true *métier.* After finishing seventh in the Free Handicap at the start of his three-year-old career, Dayjur was dropped back first to six furlongs then to five. He won a small race at Nottingham, finished second at Newbury and then, in the Temple Stakes at Sandown in 1990, his true quality showed when they abandoned all attempts to hold him up and he scorched home the winner.

Next time out in the Nunthorpe at York, he was soon motoring and had all his rivals bar Statoblest trailing. Shaken up at the furlong pole, Dayjur went clear to win by four lengths, lowering the course record. Two weeks later, moving back up to six furlongs, he took on the July Cup winner Royal Academy in the Ladbroke Sprint Cup at Haydock, and gave another stunning display of front-running under his regular pilot Willie Carson, surging five lengths clear at halfway. Royal Academy mounted a late effort, but the unchallenged Dayjur could have doubled his length-and-a-half margin with no trouble.

It was next stop Paris for the Prix de l'Abbaye at Longchamp on Arc day, and so impressed had the critics been with Dayjur's summer efforts that he started as a 1-10 favourite on the Pari-Mutuel. He took the first two furlongs easier than normal, but when Willie Carson then asked for an effort his acceleration was electric and he went from a length ahead to five. Well clear, Dayjur then spotted a shadow across the track and shied at it, losing his concentration.

'He was reading the noticeboards', said Willie Carson, who took his mount on to a two-length victory over Lugana Beach despite easing off. Nobody made too much of the shadow-shying at the time, but it was to be remembered after Dayjur's next dramatic race, which took place in America.

Such was this speedster's reputation that although he was running round a bend for the first time, running on a dirt surface for the first time and running against the

Willie Carson brings Dayjur home in record time to win
the Nunthorpe Stakes at York, August 1990.

crack American sprinters who had never yet been worsted
in the race by anything from Europe, Dayjur was made
favourite for the Breeders' Cup Sprint at Belmont Park,
Long Island, that October. What made it even harder was
that he had the worst draw on the outside, number 13.

Dayjur handled the flight to the US well, his head
never out of his haynet, and took well to the dirt surface,
posting extraordinary practice times, so Hern was quietly
confident, declaring: 'Dayjur is by far and away the fastest
horse I've ever trained. This is my best chance ever of winning a Breeders' Cup event.'

It was certainly an eventful race. Early on, two
American contestants fell. From his wide draw, Dayjur
missed the trouble but had to be pushed along because,
like so many British runners, he had not been able to

match the starting speed of the US horses. Soon, though, he was up with the quickly away mare Safely Kept, and into the straight the two went clear of Glitterman and the rest to stage an epic battle, nostril to nostril. Dayjur looked the stronger and was a neck up, when suddenly within the final furlong he glimpsed a shadow across the track and tried to jump it. Willie Carson stayed aboard, but Dayjur's breaking of his stride cost him crucial momentum and Safely Kept won by a neck, with Dayjur jumping another shadow on the line itself. It was a scene reminiscent of Devon Loch's collapse between the last post and the finishing line in the Grand National.

It was a freak accident, an accident that might with hindsight have been prevented by the wearing of a sheepskin noseband (what the Americans call a 'shadow roll') to aid concentration, and it was cruel luck for Willie and for the horse's connections.

Career highlights:
1990: Temple Stakes, Nunthorpe Stakes, Ladbroke Sprint Cup,
Prix de l'Abbaye

86. CRISP

Before he ever came to England to join Fred Winter's successful Lambourn yard, the almost-black Crisp had enjoyed a successful career back home in Australia, where he won two Flat races, five hurdles and a couple of chases, including the Melbourne Cup Chase. En route to Britain Sir Chester Manifold's horse had also won the Carolina Hunt Cup.

Crisp had scarcely had time to acclimatise from his winter arrival when he ran in the Champion Chase of

Crisp, ridden by Richard Pitman and owned by
Sir Chester Manifold, November 1971.

1971 and yet, ridden by Paul Kelleway, he won the two-mile championship by 25 lengths on tacky ground.

That was a phenomenal display by the horse once labelled as 'the black kangaroo'. But the performance for which Crisp will be never be forgotten came at Aintree in the 1973 Grand National. In the days before handicappers began compressing the Grand National weights to give quality horses a chance, he was set to carry 12st against the 10st 5lb given to Red Rum, who was to prove the greatest Grand National horse of all time.

Ridden at the head of the field by Richard Pitman, Crisp soared into the lead over Becher's Brook and proceeded to give a demonstration of jumping Aintree's formidable fences that has never been bettered. Watchers were awestruck as he not only soared over the obstacles, but did so at two-mile champion speed, a speed that took him not just 20 lengths but probably 100 yards clear of his field.

'He can't go on like this', said the watchers in the stands, but the big black Crisp kept on doing so, stretching out the field behind him. It was exciting for his rider, exhilarating for the watching nation and exhausting for those in the race with him. But it was taxing for Crisp himself. As Brough Scott wrote, he must have built up the biggest oxygen debt in racing history. Two fences out, it still looked as though he could do it, but there just the smallest hesitation on landing showed the strain.

When Pitman and partner reached the last fence, Crisp still led by maybe 20 lengths but suddenly the distress signals were blinking as he ran out of stamina. His reserves drained to the last drop, the gallant Crisp began to wander about on that implacable 494-yard run-in and slowed almost to a walk. Pitman, one of the nicest men ever to ride Aintree and never a 'whip jockey', blames himself unfairly for using his 'persuader' in the wrong hand. He gave Crisp one crack with the whip, but soon discovered that that only hindered the steering as he veered away from the line to the post.

There was no momentum left. It was as if Crisp was rocking up and down on the spot in slow motion, while behind him Red Rum was remorselessly encroaching. Along the last 100 yards of white-railed run-in, Crisp, all energy gone, was ground down by his pursuer. In the last few yards, he was caught and passed by Ginger McCain's Aintree phenomenon. Red Rum won the first of his three Grand Nationals in record time by three-quarters of a length. The dual Gold Cup winner L'Escargot, who was himself to win a National, was a distant third. But if the day belonged to Red Rum, the memories belong to Crisp.

The only race Crisp ran after the Grand National was what turned out to be a two-horse match at Doncaster with Red Rum, which Crisp won. He was then hunted for eight seasons and when he died a cherry tree was planted on his grave. Appropriately, it flowers at Grand National time.

Career highlights:
1969, 1970: Hiskens Cup (Australia)
1970: Carolina Hunt Cup
1971: Champion Chase, Cheltenham

85. HATTON'S GRACE

It was extraordinary enough that Vincent O'Brien launched his Cheltenham Festival career by winning three consecutive Gold Cups with Cottage Rake, but the Irish genius was not content with that. In the same period, he trained Hatton's Grace to win three Champion Hurdles on the go as well.

At least Cottage Rake was something to look at. Hatton's Grace was not. There was always something scruffy about him, and he was only the size of a pony. Hatton's Grace appeared at Cheltenham for the first time trained by O'Brien in 1949, the year of Cottage Rake's second Gold Cup. His trainer not yet being the name he was to become on the English side of the water, he was allowed to start at 100-7, but whatever he looked like he dominated the Champion Hurdle field from the moment he headed it at the top of the hill, winning by six lengths.

O'Brien had enlisted the help of English trainer Fred Rimell in finding somewhere for him and his horses to stay, bringing a fine Irish salmon as a thank you. Mercy Rimell told me she was less than impressed with the hurdler who came to stay. 'He was a miserable-looking little thing walking round the paddock, and I thought: "I don't

Hatton's Grace (*left*), ridden by Tim Molony, on the way to his
third consecutive Champion Hurdle victory, Cheltenham,
March 1951.

think much of that." But Hatton's Grace promptly trotted
up and ours finished in the ruck.'

It was a similar story the next year. Of the four horses
who touched down at the last together in 1950, it was
Hatton's Grace who then forged ahead on the run-in to
win by four lengths.

Rough and woolly, the trace-clipped Hatton's Grace
was back again in 1951, Festival of Britain year. Available
at 4-1, despite his two previous victories, he made it more
of a Festival of Ireland down in Gloucestershire. The
ground on Champion Hurdle day was badly waterlogged
and the rest of the meeting was to be postponed. By the
turn at the top, Hatton's Grace and National Spirit, like
him a former champion, had seen off the challenge of
two French horses. National Spirit, England's hero, led
over the second last, but Hatton's Grace, who had had
the speed to win on the Flat, was closing rapidly. Timing

his challenge perfectly, Tim Molony had him jump the last with great momentum close beside National Spirit. The English horse appeared unnerved and fell without having touched the obstacle at all. The race was over and, like Cottage Rake, Hatton's Grace became a three-time champion, a quite extraordinary feat for his trainer.

Hatton's Grace, who won 11 of his 27 hurdle races, didn't see a racetrack until he was six because of wartime restrictions. He was owned by Colonel Dan Corry, an international showjumper, and was trained by him and by Barney Nugent before he passed into the hands of O'Brien. He was nine when he won his first Champion Hurdle and less than a month later showed his versatility by winning the Irish Lincoln Handicap over just a mile on the Flat. The O'Brien team were probably rather less delighted by Hatton's Grace's victory that November in the Irish Cesarewitch. On that occasion, they had their money down for his stablemate Knock Hard.

Career highlights:
1949, 1950, 1951: Champion Hurdle
1949: Irish Lincoln, Irish Cesarewitch

84. BALANCHINE

Godolphin is the mightiest racing empire we have ever seen or ever will see, and so Balanchine earns her place in this volume partly as the first Group One winner Godolphin ever had. But there was no doubting her quality anyway: not only did she win the 1994 Oaks, she then scored an epic victory against the colts in the Irish Derby. But for an illness later in her three-year-old career, she might have developed into one of the truly greats.

Bred by Robert Sangster at his Swettenham Stud, Balanchine was originally trained for him at Manton by Peter Chapple-Hyam. As a juvenile in 1993, she ran twice in September, winning a Salisbury maiden by three lengths and a minor stakes event at Newbury by seven, before being purchased by Maktoum al-Maktoum and sent to winter in Dubai, one of the first to test the Godolphin theory that horses would benefit from being prepared in a warmer climate before the British season.

Balanchine certainly encouraged their belief. She ran in the 1,000 Guineas of 1994 without a prep race, and at 20-1 finished only a short head behind the Irish-trained Las Meninas, who set a course record.

Balanchine ran next in the Oaks at Epsom, for which she was made the 6-1 third favourite. The conditions were atrocious. The race was run in driving rain on soft ground, but Balanchine stayed on strongly under Frankie Dettori to give Godolphin their first Classic winner by two and a half lengths. Insofar as his disciplined style permits, Sheikh Mohammed was exultant: 'This experiment has obviously worked. We will now have to think about campaigning horses from Dubai all over the world.'

The Godolphin team then took a bold step. They deviated from the usual fillies' targets to let Balanchine take on the colts in the Irish Derby at the Curragh. There, Frankie Dettori took her to the front half a mile out and she stayed on strongly to win by four and a half lengths from King's Theatre, the runner-up in the Epsom Derby. 'Unbelievable', said the not normally under-quoted Dettori.

The plan then was to send this outstanding filly to the Prix de l'Arc de Triomphe, but shortly after her race in Ireland she suffered a severe attack of colic, an affliction that can be a killer. Balanchine's life was saved by

Frankie Dettori is led in on Balanchine after winning the Oaks,
Epsom, June 1994.

an emergency operation, but there was no chance of her
racing again in her three-year-old season. It was almost a
year before she saw a racecourse again, in the Prince of
Wales Stakes at Ascot, but she could finish only fifth of six
after being eased down towards the end of the race. Next
time out, in the Prix Foy, she appeared to be nearly back
to her best, going down by only a short head to Carnegie,
who had won the Arc she had to miss.

After that, Balanchine did contest the Arc, but it was a disappointing performance: in the hands of Walter Swinburn, she never fired and finished well down the field behind Lammtarra, before being immediately retired to stud.

Career highlights:
1994: Oaks, Irish Derby

83. ALCIDE

My earliest racing memories are stuffed, as the Jockey Club was in those days, with double-barrelled grandee names, like those two dapper figures Sir Humphrey de Trafford and Captain Sir Cecil Boyd-Rochfort. The former owned and the latter trained a horse who might have occupied a much higher place in this list had he been able to run in the Derby of 1958, for which he had been favourite.

Alcide, though laid back on the track, was a high-mettled character in the yard and on the gallops, given to exuberant pirouetting and rearing. Some said that the swelling on his ribs that caused him to be scratched from the Derby resulted from his own boisterous prancing and bucking one morning. Bruce Hobbs, then Boyd-Rochfort's highly valued assistant and later a successful trainer in his own right, believed instead that the hot favourite for Epsom had been given a hefty disabling blow, probably breaking at least one rib. The horse was found in his box in agony at evening stables, scarcely able to move for pain. Almost certainly it was a particularly crude example of the nobblers who were then highly active in racing, to the benefit only of the bookmakers.

Alcide, ridden by Harry Carr, beats Gladness by two lengths
to win the King George VI and Queen Elizabeth Stakes at Ascot,
July 1959.

There had been a deluge of ante-post money for Alcide
in the Derby run-up.

Although beaten on his first outing at two, Alcide's
record in his remaining 11 races was eight victories and
three short-head defeats: he was never a lucky horse, but
he was certainly something special. As a two-year-old, he
had won the Horris Hill Stakes with a charge that took
him from last to first. At three, he was kept out of the
2,000 Guineas, which the stable won with the specialist
miler Pall Mall. He started his season instead in the one-
and-a-quarter-mile Royal Stakes at Sandown Park, but
went down by a short head when a typical Lester Piggott
ride on Noel Murless's Snow Cat caught Alcide and Harry
Carr on the line.

Although unsuited by the course, Alcide next won the
Chester Vase and then, before his injury, ran away with
the Lingfield Derby Trial by 12 lengths, with Snow Cat

this time well behind him. After that, money poured on him for the real thing at Epsom, an obvious temptation for the dirty end of the trade.

Alcide's eventual return after his injury came in the Great Voltigeur Stakes, which he won by 12 lengths, and he was just as dominant, eventually, in the St Leger. Lobbing along uninterestedly at first, he decided to take off in the straight and reached the line eight lengths ahead of the rest. In his memoirs, jockey Harry Carr noted: 'He was the best colt I had ever ridden but he, and he alone, decided when the time had come in a race to throw off his lethargy and get down to business in earnest.'

Luck came into it again when Alcide was four. His main target that year was the two-and-a-half-mile Gold Cup at Ascot. First time out, he was beaten narrowly in the Jockey Club Cup, and he then won the Victor Wild Stakes at Kempton by 20 lengths in a new course record. He also won the Winston Churchill Stakes at Hurst Park. But Alcide's luck was out once again for the Gold Cup. Two weeks before the race, he rapped a joint and missed a vital stage of his preparation, while his regular jockey Harry Carr had to go into hospital for the removal of kidney stones. In the Gold Cup, Alcide battled all the way down the straight with the French colt Wallaby II, but went down by another of those short heads.

Then came a truly bold move from his connections. A month later, for Alcide's final race, he was dropped back a mile in distance to contest the King George and Queen Elizabeth Stakes. He confirmed his quality at the more fashionable distance by coming from last to first in the straight to beat Gladness by two lengths and thus showed himself one of the best horses in Europe, with a range of 12 to 20 furlongs.

There was that year a further indication that it was the

nobblers and not any health problem that had kept Alcide at home in his box in his Derby year of 1958. Following that experience, stable security had been increased when the next year Boyd-Rochfort once again had the Derby favourite in his yard, in the shape of Parthia. The security man alerted Bruce Hobbs in the middle of the night to say that Alcide's box was empty. So it was. Alcide, whose box was three doors away from Parthia's, was found having a sniff around in the fillies' yard. It looked as though the nobblers had been in again before the security man's patrol, but had picked on the wrong box. There was no point nobbling Alcide again, because there was no ante-post market on the Gold Cup.

Career highlights:
1958: Chester Vase, Great Voltigeur Stakes, St Leger
1959: Gold Cup (Ascot)
1959: King George VI and Queen Elizabeth Stakes

82. YEATS

Big, strong and obviously masculine, Yeats was a racehorse with presence, one of those animals very much aware of his surroundings and seemingly aware that he was himself a focus of attention. He probably should have been a Derby winner: he was unbeaten in three races before Epsom, including the Derrinstown Stud Derby Trial, but as favourite for the race had to be pulled out with an injury the year North Light won, and then spent almost a year off the track.

At four, Yeats gave a taste of what might have been by leading all the way over the Derby course under Kieren Fallon to win the Coronation Cup of 2005, beating the

Johnny Murtagh celebrates Yeats's fourth consecutive
Gold Cup win at Ascot, June 2009.

future Japan Cup winner Alkaased and the dual previous
winner of the Coronation Cup, Warrsan. Failed attempts
at the Grand Prix de Saint-Cloud in France, the Irish
St Leger and the International Stakes at Woodbine in
Canada followed. But it was his remarkable record from
then on in staying races, particularly the Gold Cup at Ascot,

that turned him into one of the great favourites of the British racing public.

Yeats's first race as a five-year-old, 247 days after he had raced at Woodbine, was the gruelling two-and-a-half-mile Gold Cup at Ascot. Yeats took up the running four furlongs out under Fallon, and won by four lengths from the Prix du Cadran winner Reefscape. Achieving a rare double, he then won the Goodwood Cup by five lengths under Mick Kinane, and was sent to Australia for the Melbourne Cup where, better suited by a steady wind-up and a relentless grind, he failed to cope with the stop-start pace changes of that particularly challenging race.

In his six-year-old season, Yeats scored his second success in the Gold Cup at Ascot, and then nearer his Ballydoyle home and at his third attempt, he picked up the Irish St Leger, a first one for trainer Aidan O'Brien, who also ran Scorpion, the second horse home.

At Ascot in June the next year, 2008, Yeats became only the second horse in history, after Sagaro, to win a third Gold Cup, defeating his regular pursuer Geordieland, who must have been tired of the sight of Yeats's rump, by five lengths. After that, Yeats won another Goodwood Cup by seven lengths and in the autumn he won the Prix Royal Oak at Longchamp.

Many in the Ascot crowd were keener to see his run in the next Gold Cup, in 2009, than any other race on the prestigious Royal Ascot card, and when Aidan O'Brien's doughty warrior made history by winning by three and a half lengths, the welcoming scenes, with jockey Johnny Murtagh holding up four fingers for the cameras, were more like Cheltenham than the usually more decorous Ascot. No one could be in any doubt, this was a stayer with the aura of greatness about him, not a relentless plodder, but a class act with stamina to beat them all.

Yeats won 15 of his 26 races, all of them in the best of company. After the Ascot success, Aidan O'Brien, who has prepared so many Classic contenders, confessed that he had never felt under more pressure over a race: 'You dream and dream, we were in this position and we never would be again. We knew we had a wonderful horse, but fairytales never come true.' This time they did.

Career highlights:
2004: Ballysax Stakes
2005: Coronation Cup
2006: Gold Cup (Ascot), Goodwood Cup
2007: Gold Cup (Ascot), Irish St Leger
2008: Gold Cup (Ascot), Prix Royal Oak
2009: Gold Cup (Ascot)

81. MOSCOW FLYER

Barry Geraghty is as good a jump jockey as we have seen in decades. But Frankie Dettori he isn't. Geraghty's hugely successful association with Jessica Harrington's great two-mile chaser Moscow Flyer encouraged him occasionally to try Frankie's famous 'flying dismount', jumping from the saddle in the winners' enclosure. But Geraghty could never quite master it and at least once he ended up as a faller.

Part of Moscow Flyer's appeal was his fallibility. The racing public develops particular affection for the flawed genius and enjoys his or her successes all the more, and while Moscow Flyer was brilliant when he stood up, he had his unsteady moments as well as his electric ones. He was a character, a horse who disliked the wet (something of a handicap when you are trained in Ireland), and who flatly refused to move from the yard if it was snowing.

He first caught the public eye at the Cheltenham Festival of 2002, winning the Arkle Chase, the old Cotswold Chase which has become the two-mile championship for juniors destined to star in future runnings of the Queen Mother Champion Chase. Next year, he was back looking for the big one. The Queen Mother field in 2003 included stars like Edredon Bleu, Flagship Uberalles, Tiutchev and Florida Pearl. Moscow Flyer got a little close to the water and didn't quite meet the fourth last as his jockey wanted, but he was going best of all. With a sixth sense, Barry Geraghty pulled out from behind the leaders, Seebald and Latalomne, before the second last – and was glad he did so, since both clipped it and fell. With Irish punters heavily engaged, it was then over the last and away, with the crowd's cheers encouraging Moscow Flyer to prick his ears as he coasted to victory and inspiring Geraghty's first flying dismount. Said his trainer: 'He must have been watching too much Flat racing. While he did remain upright, he wouldn't have got more than four-point-five from a gymnastics judge.'

Moscow Flyer himself had fallen on his very first outing. He had another tumble at Punchestown at the end of his first Queen Mother season. Commentators started talking of a 'three-wins-and-a-fall' pattern emerging, since at one stage his record over fences read 111F111U111U111U111, but his trainer drily pointed out that 'Moscow', as he was known in the yard, couldn't count and he did break that statistical hoodoo in 2005.

When Moscow fell at the fourth in the Cheltenham Champion Chase in 2004, his trainer explained why it had happened. Having suffered from a runny nose, he hadn't been given the prep race she had wanted, and he was too fresh, a condition that made Moscow more prone to jumping errors.

Moscow Flyer, ridden by Barry Geraghty, on his way to winning
his second Melling Chase, Aintree, April 2005.

The confidence of trainer, jockey and maybe horse
was rapidly restored with victories over two and a half
miles at Aintree and then at Punchestown. But the Queen
Mother Champion Chase of 2005, when Moscow would
be 11, was what mattered.

Martin Pipe's Well Chief was the new kid on the block.
The Paul Nicholls team were happy with Azertyuiop,
who had won the title when Moscow fell in 2004. Would
Moscow Flyer still have the speed or was this the time to
try him, with a pedigree that would give hope of him lasting such a distance, over three miles instead? All three
top contenders went to Sandown for the Tingle Creek
Chase in December 2004, and Moscow, who had won it
the previous year too, simply crushed his rivals. As his
trainer said, he was telling the world that he was still the
best two-mile chaser around, so there would be no more
thoughts of the three-mile King George. Instead, there

was a winning pipe-opener in the Tied Cottage Chase at Punchestown, and he went on to Cheltenham.

Having already won an Arkle, a Queen Mother Champion Chase and two Tingle Creeks, Moscow Flyer didn't have a lot to prove in 2005 and, in the event, neither Azertyuiop nor Well Chief was able to mount a significant challenge. His faithful fans, some no doubt clutching their rabbits' feet or four-leaved clovers, cheered Moscow Flyer over the third last, the second last and the final obstacle before he led Well Chief by two lengths to the line. He was back as the champion. Not since Royal Relief in 1974 had any horse reclaimed the two-mile championship after losing it, but Moscow did. In celebration, Barry Geraghty tried the flying dismount again, and this time ended up on his backside. Said Jessica Harrington: 'You'd think he'd have perfected it by now. He needs lessons in elegance.'

Moscow Flyer did come back for one more run in the Queen Mother in 2006, the year that a promising young chaser called Kauto Star fell in the race, but he could only plug on into fifth and was immediately retired. In the specialism of the sprint chase, Moscow Flyer was as good as they get, when he stood up. His jumping record overall was 26 victories from 44 runs, and he was unbeaten in the 23 chases he had completed before Rathgar Beau beat him at Punchestown in April 2005.

A beloved character when he was racing, Moscow Flyer continued to do his bit for the sport. He was retired to the Irish National Stud to make regular public appearances for the Irish Horse Welfare Trust.

Career highlights:
1999: Punchestown Champion Novice Hurdle
2000: Punchestown Champion Hurdle

2002: Arkle Chase, Paddy Power Dial-a-Bet Chase
2003: Tingle Creek Chase, Tied Cottage Chase, Queen Mother
    Champion Chase, Paddy Power Dial-a-Bet Chase
2004: Melling Chase, Tingle Creek Chase
2005: Tied Cottage Chase, Queen Mother Champion Chase,
    Melling Chase, Punchestown Champion Chase

80. BLUE PETER

Asked once what were the biggest potential dangers in politics, Prime Minister Harold Macmillan drawled, 'Events, dear boy, events …', and the sixth Earl of Rosebery would surely have applied Macmillan's comment to racing. Without the arrival on the scene of one Adolf Hitler, Rosebery's Blue Peter would almost certainly have come to be included on the roll of British Triple Crown winners.

Rosebery was a man of many interests: among other distinctions he was Liberal MP for Edinburgh, President of the MCC and Senior Steward of the Jockey Club. But it was his racing life, it seemed, which he enjoyed the most.

Blue Peter was trained by Jack Jarvis at Newmarket but took time to develop. As a juvenile he was fifth of 19 to Heliopolis in the Imperial Produce Stakes at Kempton and second to Foxborough in the Middle Park. It was as a three-year-old in 1939 that he came good, first winning the Blue Riband Trial Stakes at Epsom and then, as the 5-1 favourite, triumphing in the 2,000 Guineas from Admiral's Walk and Fairstone.

His next race was the Derby in which he was ridden by Eph Smith. In a big field of 27, the pair went to the front early in the straight and Blue Peter kept on well to win by four lengths from Fox Cub and the ever-present Heliopolis. Jarvis noted in his memoirs that the crowd

Lord Rosebery's Blue Peter, ridden by Eph Smith, winner of
the Derby in May 1939.

gave Rosebery a terrific reception 'in the course of which
Lord Rosebery's allegedly stiff collar seemed to dissolve
altogether'. That is what racing does.

A huge crowd next turned up to see Blue Peter contest
the Eclipse at Sandown, in which he came home ahead of
Glen Loan and Challenge, who had made the early running before Blue Peter burst between the two race leaders
and went away.

After that Jack Jarvis began preparing Lord Rosebery's
colt for the St Leger, but on 3 September Neville
Chamberlain announced that Britain was at war with
Germany. The St Leger, along with many more racing
fixtures, was cancelled; so was a planned match against
the French Prix du Jockey Club winner Pharis, and

Blue Peter was immediately retired to his owner's Mentmore Stud.

On Blue Peter's death in 1957 Lord Rosebery declared: 'He was just like a human being. Although a placid animal he was particular about what he ate: give him something he didn't like and he would take one look at it and turn away. He was the best horse I ever had and he had only half a career.' Of all the horses produced by this prolific breeder Blue Peter was the one he loved the best.

Career highlights:
1939: 2,000 Guineas, Derby, Eclipse Stakes

79. WAYWARD LAD

He may have been in more scrapes than a potato peeler but for me Graham Bradley was one of the finest jump jockeys I ever saw ride. Of the good horses he rode over 23 years, Brad told me once, the one who had 'almost everything' was Wayward Lad. He wrote in the autobiography he neatly entitled *The Wayward Lad*: 'He had a very high cruising speed with the ability to quicken off it and inject pace that could settle a race very quickly. He was majestic over a fence.'

It was that quality which enabled Wayward Lad three times to win the King George VI Chase at Kempton, the flat track three-mile chasing championship, and Fred Winter called him the best natural jumper since Pendil. So what was Brad's 'almost'? Simply that Wayward Lad just didn't have quite enough stamina for the extra two furlongs and the uphill finish at Cheltenham, and so, despite figuring in some fine races there, he never won a Gold Cup.

Wayward Lad with Jonjo O'Neill at Cheltenham, March 1983,
year of the 'Famous Five'.

Wayward Lad was one of the 'Famous Five', finishing third when trainer Michael Dickinson was responsible for the first five home in 1983, and it was Wayward Lad too who ran second to the great mare Dawn Run in the 1986 Gold Cup. Had Cheltenham not introduced a mares' allowance of 5lb after she won the Champion Hurdle in 1984 then Wayward Lad probably would have been a Gold Cup winner. At his peak she was the only horse to have won more than Wayward Lad, who was Monica Dickinson's pet and whom the Yorkshire matriarch rode out every day.

By the end of his career in 1987 Wayward Lad had won 28 of his 55 races on 16 different racecourses, his victories including two in the Edward Hanmer Chase and two in the Charlie Hall. He had been very special in the lives of

Tony, Monica and then Michael Dickinson. Sadly, at the end of his racing days there was a dispute between his two owners, Mrs Shirley Thewlis, who owned 60 per cent, and farmer Les Abbott, who had the other 40 per cent. She wanted Wayward Lad to retire to the Dickinsons as a hack, he wanted the horse to go point-to-pointing, which would have been a bit like having a former Test cricketer whose knees had gone playing for village green teams. The only way it could be resolved was by sending the horse to the sales, which left a sour taste in many sporting mouths – but there was a happy ending.

With the aid of an American training family who were good friends, when the hammer went down at 42,000 guineas it was the Dickinsons who bought the horse back themselves. Auctioneer Harry Beeby announced to applause: 'Wayward Lad is sold to go back to Harewood – I hope he enjoys his retirement as much as we have enjoyed watching him race.' The supposedly tough Monica Dickinson couldn't hold back her tears. She marched into the ring and gave Wayward Lad a huge hug and a handful of Polo mints, declaring: 'We would have gone higher if we'd had to.'

Career highlights:
1982, 1983, 1985: King George VI Chase
1983, 1985: Charlie Hall Chase
1985, 1987: Martell Cup

78. PINZA

On the morning of her coronation in June 1953 an attendant asked the Queen how she was feeling. The response was that she was feeling fine – because she had just had a call from her trainer Captain Cecil Boyd-Rochfort telling her that her colt Aureole had successfully completed his preparation for the Derby.

Four days later Aureole finished second at Epsom to Pinza. But the Queen, like many in the crowd, was probably still delighted with the result because the race was won for the first and only time by jockey Sir Gordon Richards, just knighted in the Coronation Honours List, on Pinza. It was his 28th attempt to win the Blue Riband of the Turf. The new Queen, who had wished him well in the paddock beforehand, summoned the great sportsman afterwards for a private audience to congratulate him. In most racing folk's memories the fact that he carried the champion jockey to victory that day is what Pinza is remembered for, but it is not exactly fair to the horse's real achievements.

Pinza first caught the eye at Doncaster's St Leger meeting in 1952 when, still obviously green and inexperienced, he burst six lengths clear of his opponents within a furlong in the Tattersalls Sale Stakes. Though he was beaten in the Royal Lodge Stakes at Ascot when Neemah outspeeded him at the finish of a slowly-run race, Pinza made clear he was a Classics candidate for the next year when winning the Dewhurst Stakes impressively by six lengths.

Unfortunately, during the winter Pinza slipped on a road and injured an elbow joint. The injury did not mend properly and required further treatment, reopening the wound the next March. For a buzzy horse like Pinza who had to have a lad on his back even in the parade ring before races, the enforced inactivity was a particular handicap, not improving his behaviour.

Pinza had to miss the 2,000 Guineas and was not considered remotely ready when he finally reappeared over ten furlongs in the Newmarket Stakes only three weeks

Pinza, with newly-knighted Sir Gordon Richards aboard, passes
the post to win from Aureole in the Derby, June 1953.

before the Derby, for which at that stage he was a 33-1
shot. To the amazement of his connections Pinza took
the lead in the Newmarket race two furlongs out and ran
away from his field. Had Gordon Richards not eased him
before the finish he would have won by far more than his
four-length margin, and in no time Pinza had become the
joint favourite for the Derby with Premonition, despite
the question marks over whether such a heavy-topped
horse would be able to act on Epsom's gradients and
turns.

On the day, paddock observers were surprised to see a
joint favourite for the big race still bulky around his middle, but Pinza, it seems, was like one of those boxers who
performed best when not sweated down to his minimum.
He was no better than tenth at the top of the hill, where
Charlie Smirke sent Shikampur into a clear lead. It took

a big horse like Pinza time to wind up to his full speed in the straight but once he did so there was no question about the eventual result. He went past Shikampur in a few strides and was kept up to his work by Richards to win by four lengths from Aureole and Pink Horse.

The result was much the same in the King George VI and Queen Elizabeth Stakes at Ascot. Pinza had played up in the parade ring and sweated up badly but once let go in the straight by Gordon Richards he sailed past the Arc winner Nuccio. Aureole again chased him home but without any prospect of getting to him. Pinza was thus unbeaten in his three races as a three-year-old and had beaten the best of the older horses too in his Ascot race. He was being prepared for the St Leger when he injured a tendon in training and was retired.

Career highlights:
1952: Tattersalls Sales Stakes, Dewhurst Stakes
1953: Derby, King George VI and Queen Elizabeth Stakes

77. THE TETRARCH

A blotchy grey whose coat looked as though a decorator had walked paintpot in hand into a turbo-fan, The Tetrarch became known to the racing public as 'The Spotted Wonder'. But if his rivals saw spots before their eyes they were normally the blotches on this extraordinarily fast animal's backside. He was possibly the speediest horse ever seen in Britain.

Ridden regularly by 'Come on Steve' Steve Donoghue and trained by Atty Persse, the heavy-punting Irishman, at Stockbridge in Hampshire, the two-year-old started seven races in 1913 over five and six furlongs and won every

The Tetrarch, dubbed 'The Spotted Wonder', won all seven
of his 1913 starts. (May 1913)

one of them. In only one, the National Breeders Produce
Stakes, was he seriously tested and that was only because
he was left four or five lengths in a chaotic start. He still
won that contest by a neck.

His speed from the off was so incredible that he usually had his rivals gasping after a mere two furlongs. The
Tetrarch dominated in the Woodcote Stakes, spreadeagled
the Ascot field in the Chesham Stakes by ten lengths and
won by similar margins in races like Goodwood's Rous
Memorial Stakes and the Champagne Stakes. Nobody
could live with his sheer pace.

His phenomenal speed saw him hailed as a wonder. The Tetrarch was voted Horse of the Year and the
National Sporting Library's website in the USA labelled
him as 'possibly the best two-year-old of all time'. Steve
Donoghue said he never encountered another horse with

such power behind the saddle: 'To be on him was like riding a creature that combined the power of an elephant with the speed of a greyhound.'

The tragedy was that The Tetrarch's two-year-old career was curtailed by injury in October 1913. He then had further injury problems in training as a three-year-old and was retired without ever getting back on a racecourse. We will never know how good he might have been as an older horse or what his best distance would have been.

At stud The Tetrarch was the sire of the useful Tetratema, 12 of whose 13 victories were over sprint distances, and he also sired the original 'flying filly' Mumtaz Mahal. But he was not sprint-bred himself and he also sired three St Leger winners. What he achieved in his two-year career was exciting enough but The Tetrarch's story will remain one of racing's tantalising 'what might have been' speculations.

Career highlights:
1913: Woodcote Stakes, Chesham Stakes, Rous Memorial Stakes, Champagne Stakes

76. ROBERTO

Some horses are great on a consistent basis – Sea The Stars, Sea-Bird, Frankel. Others demonstrate their greatness on particular days and only just edge into a collection like this on the grounds of their very best performances, with others having to be forgotten. Roberto, named after the Pittsburgh Pirates baseball star Roberto Clemente by the team's American owner John K. Galbreath, owes his inclusion here to two brilliant jockeys, Lester Piggott and the Panamanian-born Braulio Baeza. They each managed to bring out his best on two days that really mattered. On one of them Roberto won the Derby in one of its most pulsating finishes ever, on the other he became the only horse ever to beat Brigadier Gerard.

Roberto, who was trained in Ireland by the inimitable Vincent O'Brien, did most of his juvenile racing at the Curragh, winning a maiden and the National and Anglesey Stakes. He also had a disappointing outing in France in the Grand Criterium. In 1972, having won on his seasonal debut at Phoenix Park, he then went to Newmarket and finished second to High Top in torrential rain in the 2,000 Guineas.

Then came controversy. Roberto had been ably ridden at Newmarket by Australian Bill Williamson, who had been told he was keeping the mount in the Derby. Lester Piggott was down to ride his stable companion Manitoulin. But Williamson then suffered minor injuries in a fall at Kempton on 27 May, a week before the Derby. Although Williamson had recovered, Roberto's owner-breeder John Galbreath used the injury as an excuse to switch Piggott on to Roberto, while promising the angry Australian that he would receive the same 'present' as Piggott should Lester win.

It turned out to be one of the most famous Derby finishes ever. Had the contest been staged on any other track, Rheingold, a 22-1 shot, would probably have won. Had any other jockey than Piggott been aboard Roberto, Rheingold would probably have won. As it was, Barry Hills' stable jockey Ernie Johnson rode a great race on a horse unsuited to the Epsom undulations, only to face a nightmare in the last furlong as his horse hung violently left with the inward-sloping camber of the course. He didn't want to use his whip and lose the race for interference

Derby winner Roberto, ridden by Braulio Baeza, wins
the Benson and Hedges Gold Cup at York by three lengths from
Brigadier Gerard, August 1972.

and could only try desperately to keep Rheingold straight
while Lester Piggott was driving Roberto remorselessly up
inside him with a battery of whip strokes that would lead
to the direst of penalties under modern rules. As Johnson
said after the race: 'The winning post came just a stride
too late.'

By a short head Roberto achieved his Derby victory.
Rheingold secured his consolation by winning the next
year's Arc, and Williamson, who later conceded he could
not have ridden the finish that Lester did, got his present.
Williamson was cheered in for the two winners he rode
that day. Lester, normally a Derby-day hero, was actually
booed by a section of the crowd who reckoned he had
'jocked off' the popular Australian.

Roberto went on to the Irish Derby, facing four colts
he had beaten at Epsom. But after his two-year-old days he
never again won two consecutive races and at the Curragh
he finished in twelfth place, behind all four of them.

The next day Rheingold won a big race in France and Lester Piggott talked his way into Rheingold's saddle to face Roberto in his next run in the Benson and Hedges Gold Cup at York. Williamson was committed elsewhere and so O'Brien and Galbreath hired Braulio Baeza, a star on the US circuit, for his very first ride in Britain. Since the great Brigadier Gerard, unbeaten in 15 races, was contesting the Benson and Hedges, it seemed a rather academic point anyway who was riding the rest.

Baeza gave Roberto a true American ride, blasting out from the gate and successfully running the others off their legs with a furious, unrelenting gallop. The Brigadier got within a length at one stage but Roberto won by three in a new course record. It was a classic front-running performance that reflected great credit not just on the jockey but on a horse who that day had the courage to match his rider's ambition.

Inconsistency soon reasserted itself, however, when Roberto was beaten by Hard To Beat in the Prix Niel and finished only seventh in the Arc.

Roberto went on to a four-year-old career of just three races. He won only one of them, but it was the same old story: when he was good he was very, very good. His victory came back at Epsom over the Derby distance in the Coronation Cup. There may only have been four rivals but he dominated. Never out of a canter, Roberto coasted home by an easy five lengths and in doing so he recorded the fastest time for the course and distance since Mahmoud had won the Derby 37 years earlier.

Career highlights:
1972: Derby, Benson and Hedges Gold Cup
1973: Coronation Cup

75. PENDIL

Fred Winter was the only man to have both ridden and trained winners of the Cheltenham Gold Cup, the Grand National and the Champion Hurdle. He won his Gold Cup as a trainer with Midnight Court in 1978, but Pendil, the horse who should have won Winter a brace of Gold Cups, never won the race once.

Pendil was probably the most talented of all the jumpers Winter trained, and those included Bula, Crisp, Killiney and Lanzarote. Pendil won 16 of his first 18 races over fences. In 1972 he took the Arkle Trophy at the Cheltenham Festival, the Welsh Champion Chase, the Black and White Whisky Gold Cup, the Benson and Hedges Chase and the King George VI Chase, which he won virtually in a canter.

A horse who brought reality to the expression 'spring-heeled', Pendil, who had an intuitive partnership with his regular jockey Richard Pitman, was a fast, fluent and sometimes spectacular jumper. Although his career was interrupted twice by tendon injuries, he won six hurdle races and 21 chases and was at one stage talked about as the 'next Arkle'. Between the autumn of 1971 and the end of the 1973–74 season he was beaten only twice. Sadly for Pendil, and for Fred Winter, both occasions were in the Gold Cup.

On Boxing Day 1972 Pendil had hammered The Dikler, trained over the wall from Winter's yard by Fulke Walwyn, in winning the King George VI Chase. The Dikler had been third in the last two Gold Cups and Pendil came to the 1973 Gold Cup as the odds-on favourite at 4-6. Charlie Potheen set a fearsome gallop but Pendil sailed past him down the hill to take the lead at the third last. He was being cheered home by his supporters when Ron

Pendil, ridden by Richard Pitman, sails over the last fence in
the Cheltenham Gold Cup, ahead of The Dikler (*left*), who went
on to win. (March 1973)

Barry conjured a great run out of The Dikler. Walwyn's
massive, eccentric but also powerful talented horse
caught Pendil on the run-in and beat him by a short head
in record time.

The next year Pendil and The Dikler clashed again in
the Gold Cup, which was also contested by Ireland's hope
Captain Christy. Pendil, on the strength of his many victories elsewhere, was favourite again. He was going easily at
the third last when disaster struck. He jumped the fence
perfectly but High Ken, just ahead of him, didn't and as
he fell he brought down the favourite. Captain Christy,
ridden by the recovered alcoholic Bobby Beasley, went on
to score a remarkable victory with The Dikler in second
place.

There was no better chaser in the country over two
and a half to three miles than Pendil, who won the King
George VI Chase, the flat track championship, twice. But
the question of whether he had enough stamina to win

over the 3m 2f of the Gold Cup was never really answered. A Cheltenham Gold Cup winner, it seems, he was destined not to be.

Career highlights:
1972: Arkle Trophy, Welsh Champion Chase, Black and White Whisky Gold Cup, Benson and Hedges Chase, King George VI Chase
1973: Massey Ferguson Gold Cup, King George VI Chase

74. NEVER SAY DIE

On a cold grey afternoon in the first week of June 1954 the lop-eared chestnut Never Say Die earned his place in history: a 33-1 shot in a field of 22, he became the first of the nine Epsom Derby winners to be ridden by the incomparable Lester Piggott. But it took some luck for the two to be united at Epsom.

Firstly Never Say Die, by Nasrullah out of Singing Grass, was nearly scratched from the race after a trial at another course, after which his jockey reported that he was hanging (i.e. pulling away from a straight course). The message got to Never Say Die's owner, the American breeder Robert Sterling Clark, that the horse had been hanging right. But in fact he was hanging left so it was not going to be a problem on the left-handed Epsom track.

Even when it was decided to run Never Say Die, two other jockeys were approached before Piggott. Manny Mercer was already committed and Charlie Smirke declined the opportunity.

The joint 5-1 favourites for the race that year were Rowston Manor, who had won the Lingfield Derby Trial, and the French colt Ferriol. The Guineas winner Darius,

Never Say Die comes home to give Lester Piggott the first of his nine Derby wins, June 1954.

ridden by Mercer, was at 7-1. At Tattenham Corner Rowston Manor led, closely attended by the Queen's Landau, Darius and Blue Sail, who was ridden by the American champion jockey Johnny Longden. Coming into the straight Darius took the lead and Never Say Die followed him. A furlong or so out, Never Say Die swept past Darius and won by two lengths, ahead of the fast-finishing Arabian Night.

Neither at the end of the race nor immediately afterwards did Lester Piggott indulge in any of the Mickael Barcelona-style antics so beloved of exultant modern sportsmen. He remained imperturbable. As he says: 'I could not and would not manufacture elation.' With the owner absent there was no party – instead Lester went home to Lambourn and mowed his parents' lawn! The satisfaction, he says, was simply that of a job well done – although he did make an arrangement with the manager of a Reading cinema for a private showing of the race recording a week later.

Never Say Die, who was trained at Newmarket by Joe Lawson, met Arabian Night again in the Henry VII Stakes at Ascot just a fortnight later, but in a very rough race neither finished in the money. Lester Piggott, who had pushed for the narrowest of gaps and whose fierce determination to win often had him in trouble with the stewards in those days, was suspended for the rest of the meeting and the Jockey Club harshly withdrew his licence for the rest of the season.

Never Say Die, the first American-bred horse to win the Derby since Iroquois in 1881, was presented to the English National Stud by his owner, but not before he had also triumphed in the St Leger, demolishing the field and winning in a canter by 12 lengths. His jockey that day though was Charlie Smirke, who did not this time turn down the opportunity occasioned by Lester's disciplinary difficulties.

Career highlights:
1954: Derby, St Leger

73. FIFINELLA

A South African winery manager in Franschoek told me
one day as we tasted his wares: 'The Chardonnay grape
is like a blonde with no brains – you can do what you
like with it. But with the Sauvignon grape you can only
do what the Sauvignon grape allows.' Had Fifinella been
a grape variety and not a racehorse she would have
been the Sauvignon to end them all. The contemporary
records agree: she was a hussy, a filly with a mind of her
own. Fifinella did what Fifinella pleased. But when she
was good she was very, very good.

In 1915 Fifinella, trained by Dick Dawson at
Newmarket, was the champion two-year-old. The chestnut
filly with a white blaze and two white socks, who was bred
by the publisher Sir Edward Hulton, won the Fulbourne
Stakes on her racecourse debut; and after finishing second in the Bibury Club Stakes she came home first in the
Cheveley Park Stakes by eight lengths, leading all the way
at 1-10 in the hands of Steve Donoghue.

Her three-year-old career was eagerly awaited. But
when the 1,000 Guineas came round Fifinella was having
a bad hair day. She was in a sulk. Her playing up at the
start earned her a smack from jockey Joe Childs and she
was then reluctant to take hold of her bit. The result of
her playing around was that she allowed Canyon to beat
her in the first Classic by three-quarters of a length.

Connections then ran Fifinella in the Derby, which,
thanks to the war, was being run at Newmarket as the
'New Derby Stakes'. For much of the race it looked as
though temperament was again going to compromise
her ability. At the rear of the field she was moody and
un-cooperative but then suddenly, in the straight and not
far from home, she decided to respond to her jockey's

The headstrong filly Fifinella, who won the 1916 Derby by a neck, and then the Oaks two days later.

entreaties as others began falling back. Hampered on her way to catch the leaders, she ran on strongly in the final furlong for a rider famous for his 'late rushes' and won by a neck from Kwang-Su and Nassovian.

Two days later Fifinella ran in the 1916 Oaks and this time it was a different story. Said Joe Childs, whose four brothers Albert, Arthur, Henry and Charles were all jockeys too: 'She was almost a different animal. No nervousness, no fretfulness and she appeared as though she was looking forward to the event.' On her best behaviour, Fifinella won smoothly by five lengths. She thus joined Signorinetta (1908) and Tagalie (1912) as one of the select band to have won the two races. No filly has won the Derby since. For her owner 1916 was a good sporting year – as well as his two Classics with Fifinella he won the

Waterloo Cup coursing with his greyhound Harmonicon. Fifinella's jockey too had his canine interests: in retirement he maintained a controlling interest in Portsmouth Greyhound Stadium.

Career highlights:
1915: Cheveley Park Stakes
1916: Derby, Oaks

72. MTOTO

Many horses who earn the adjective 'great' have completed their racecourse careers by the end of their three-year-old season. Had Mtoto's achievements been measured at that point he would never have been heard of again: in his first seven contests the only race he won was an insignificant maiden at Haydock Park. Foot problems – only cured by spending a winter in the moisture-full meadows of an Irish stud – had limited his early progress in the hands of Newmarket trainer Alec Stewart and it was only as a four- and five-year-old that Mtoto's career took off.

A son of Busted out of the French mare Amazer, Mtoto was himself to become a leading sire, but his talent took time to show on the racecourse. He had two great qualities that don't often come together in a horse: a huge stride and quite extraordinary finishing kick. The downside was that like his sire Busted he was a nervy sort who would panic if there were horses behind him and who pulled too hard in his early races.

The first signs that he had improved significantly from three to four appeared when he beat the talented Allez Milord by two and a half lengths in the 1987 Brigadier Gerard Stakes. Mtoto then went on to Ascot and won the

Mtoto (*right*), ridden by Michael Roberts, comes in to win
the Eclipse by a neck from Shady Heights (*left*), with Triptych
in the background, Sandown, July 1988.

Prince of Wales Stakes by a similar margin. After that it
was decided he was good enough to take on the best in
the Eclipse Stakes, that year being contested by the Derby
winner Reference Point and the mare Triptych, winner of
that year's Coronation Cup.

Riding Reference Point Steve Cauthen set out to test
his rivals with a stiff pace. Coming round the final bend,
South African champion Michael Roberts gave Mtoto an
extra inch of rein and a tap on the shoulder to test how
he was going. When his mount stepped up a gear effort-
lessly at that pace he simply couldn't believe it and knew
he could join Reference Point when he chose. Two out he
did so and from then on the two gave the crowd a treat
with a tremendous tussle. Mtoto edged ahead and then
Reference Point came back at him, but it was Roberts'
horse who held on to win by three-quarters of a length in
a new record time for the Eclipse. Triptych was a length
and half away, the nearest pursuer after that was ten
lengths behind her.

Having had to miss the King George because of unsuitable ground and having been a sick horse for a while, Mtoto was then prepared for his first venture abroad in the Prix de l'Arc de Triomphe. He wasn't fully fit but still finished fourth, with Triptych this time just ahead of him as Trempolino and Tony Bin occupied the first two places.

The next year, 1988, was to be Mtoto's best. His opening contest against five other contenders for Goodwood's Festival Stakes was an unusual experience: Mtoto was first past the post but course markers had been incorrectly placed and the race was declared void. In his next race, the Prince of Wales Stakes at Royal Ascot, he only narrowly beat the Lockinge Stakes winner Broken Hearted but that did not stop the bookmakers making him the 6-4 favourite when he went back to Sandown for that year's Eclipse. Once again Triptych, who had collected another Coronation Cup at Epsom in the meantime, was in the field, as were Indian Skimmer, winner of the previous year's Prix de Diane, and Shady Heights.

Shady Heights led into the straight and Mtoto, who had missed the break, was last turning for home. He passed Triptych and Indian Skimmer a furlong out but this time it was Shady Heights with whom he had to battle all the way to the line. Using hands and heels rather than the whip, Roberts got him home by a neck. Mtoto's second victory in the Eclipse was a rare milestone, last achieved by Polyphontes in 1924 and 1925. Only two other horses had ever scored back-to-back Eclipses.

Mtoto then reverted to a mile and a half in the King George at Ascot where the good to soft going was responsible for his price being pushed out to 4-1 while Unfuwain, a 15-length winner of the Princess of Wales Stakes, was cut to 2-1. In the race Mtoto was held up at the rear until entering the straight. His speed took him past Unfuwain at the furlong marker and he held on well to win by two lengths, with Tony Bin in third.

There were some familiar opponents then lined up against him for Mtoto's final appearance in that year's Arc after he had warmed up with a victory in the Select Stakes at Goodwood. In Paris Michael Roberts had only six of the two dozen runners behind him as they turned into the straight. As Tony Bin carved his way through the field he tracked him on Mtoto and then, showing phenomenal acceleration, tried to overhaul him. They failed only by a fast-narrowing neck with Boyatino and Unfuwain third and fourth and that year's Derby winner Kahyasi sixth.

At stud Mtoto proved to be a good sire of middle-distance horses and stayers, including Shaamit, who won the Derby, Celeric, who won the Gold Cup at Ascot, and Presenting, who became the leading National Hunt sire. Mtoto was grandsire both to Cheltenham Gold Cup and Hennessy winner Denman and Grand National winner Ballabriggs.

Career highlights:
1987: Eclipse Stakes, Prince of Wales Stakes
1988: Eclipse Stakes, Prince of Wales Stakes, Select Stakes, King George VI and Queen Elizabeth Stakes

71. MUMTAZ MAHAL

How highly in Hall of Fame terms do you rate a horse that has not performed over the Classic distances and that has shown its best at two years old, when racehorses are still babies with their bones not fully formed? It is a constant argument, but if we are to give a high ranking to any such horse then Mumtaz Mahal must be one. So long as we

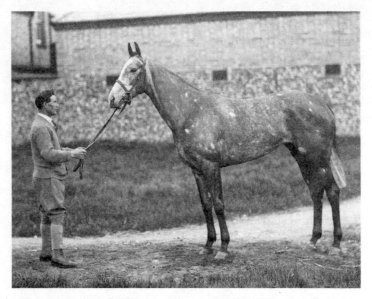

Mumtaz Mahal, the fastest two-year-old filly of the 20th century
and later a prolific broodmare.

take horses to the track at two, then records like hers
cannot be ignored.

The National Horseracing Museum argues: 'Mumtaz
Mahal was just about the best two-year-old filly seen in the
20th century.' Certainly she was the fastest. Mumtaz Mahal
was champion two-year-old, champion sprinter and Horse
of the Year in her time. She went on to have a formidable
record as a broodmare, with her grandsons Mahmoud,
Nasrullah and Abernant all of the highest class.

A blotchy grey daughter of The Tetrarch, Mumtaz
Mahal, like him, was all about speed. In six outings as a
two-year-old in 1922 she was beaten once, but that was in
the mud at Kempton Park when she was conceding 7lb
to the winner. Trained at Whatcombe by Dick Dawson,
she won her other five starts that season by ten lengths
or more, including Ascot's Queen Mary Stakes and the
Molecomb Stakes.

At three Mumtaz Mahal was runner-up in the 1,000 Guineas over a distance that was patently too far for her. She was lengths ahead at the top of the hill but did not last out. One more attempt at longer distances failed before she reverted to sprinting and dazzled as the fastest filly ever. Rider George Archibald toyed with the opposition at Goodwood in the King George V Stakes although she won by only a length. In the Nunthorpe Stakes at York he let her go and she pelted home by six lengths.

'Mumpty', for whom Aga Khan III paid 9,100 guineas – the highest price for a filly at auction since Sceptre's 10,000 – was, by all accounts, a feisty filly. If any bullock was turned out in a field with her she made its life a misery.

Career highlights:
1922: Molecomb Stakes, Queen Mary Stakes
1923: King George V Stakes, Nunthorpe Stakes

70. THE MINSTREL

Walking under a ladder doesn't bother me, nor does spilling salt, though I am careful to say 'Good morning Mr Magpie' to the first black and white bird I see in a day. Superstition is a funny thing and I have never quite understood why some racing folk still believe that you cannot trust a chestnut with four white socks. Even Vincent O'Brien was said to have shared that superstition. The Minstrel was born looking that way: it did not stop him being a decent Derby winner, although he was lucky to have found himself in the race at all.

Lester Piggott in his prime talked his way into the saddle of several leading candidates for the Derby, not always to the pleasure of his fellow jockeys. With The Minstrel he was responsible for talking the horse into the race too.

A three-parts brother to Nijinsky trained by Vincent O'Brien, The Minstrel had won three out of three as a two-year-old, including a four-length victory in the Dewhurst, but because he was small (O'Brien's brother Phonsie commented at the Keeneland sales when he was bought for $200,000 that he had a labrador nearly as big), connections had assumed his chance was in the 2,000 Guineas of 1977 rather than the Derby.

In the event The Minstrel, a 6-5 favourite at Newmarket, never looked the part in the Guineas. Lester Piggott had to work on him from early on and even when he got him racing they could not catch Nebbiolo and Tachypous.

Given another chance in the Irish 2,000 Guineas, The Minstrel this time beat Nebbiolo, but was again worsted himself, this time by Pampapaul. Two Classic attempts, two failures for a horse always thought of as a miler, and O'Brien's main Derby hope Valinsky had disappointed too. What to do? 'Run The Minstrel in the Derby and I'll ride him', said Piggott, and they did, against the much-lauded French favourite Blushing Groom.

Blushing Groom did not stay the last two furlongs at Epsom. Hot Grove had made his bid under Willie Carson and at that point The Minstrel had three lengths to find. Surely an uncertain stayer could not do that, but under the same rat-tat-tat relentless driving that Piggott had given Roberto against Rheingold, he did. With his ears flat back, The Minstrel grabbed his race in the last 50 yards. No horse he rode, said Piggott, showed greater courage.

Piggott was gloriously justified and though some feared that such a hard race would have left its mark on The Minstrel's mind he was no single tune singer. The

The Minstrel, with Lester Piggott aboard, at the King George VI
and Queen Elizabeth Stakes, Ascot, July 1977.

tough little colt went on to win that year's Irish Derby in
some comfort, surviving an objection from Frankie Durr
on the runner-up before returning to England to take on
all-comers in the King George VI and Queen Elizabeth
Stakes.

His ten rivals that day included seven Classic winners
and perhaps surprisingly it was Peter Walwyn's Orange
Bay, a former Italian Derby winner, who provided the
sternest opposition. Pat Eddery sent Orange Bay clear
in the straight, only to see The Minstrel move smoothly
upsides a furlong out. Game over? Not a bit of it. With the
first-time blinkers on Orange Bay boosting his concentration and stiffening his resolve, Eddery fought Piggott
every inch to the line, where The Minstrel prevailed only
by a head in what proved to be his final race. It was a gutsy

performance from both horses, much like the famous contest between Grundy and Bustino. I bet Lester never worried after that, if he ever had before, about how many white socks a chestnut displayed.

Career highlights:
1976: Dewhurst Stakes
1977: Derby, Irish Derby, King George VI and Queen Elizabeth
*   Stakes*

69. ARD PATRICK

Considering all the fuss that is made, quite rightly, about the remarkable filly Sceptre, it is hard that Ard Patrick only seems to make the footnotes of racing history. He did, after all, twice defeat the filly who won four Classics.

Trained by Sam Darling, Ard Patrick was a top-class juvenile and the winner of six of his 11 races. Campaigning at the highest level, he was only once out of the first three. In 1902 he began by running third in the 2,000 Guineas. Ard Patrick then scored an easy victory in that year's Derby, in which Sceptre was fourth. Ridden by Skeets Martin, he was returned at the unusual price of 100-14. He went on that year to win the Prince of Wales Stakes on a disqualification.

Ard Patrick had only two races as a four-year-old and he won them both. One was the Princess of Wales Stakes but the one that is remembered is the 1903 renewal of the Eclipse at Sandown in which he faced Sceptre and Rock Sand. Sceptre had won four Classics the previous year, Rock Sand, the 5-4 favourite, had already won the 2,000 Guineas and the Derby and was to go on to collect his Triple Crown in the St Leger.

Ard Patrick, winner of the 1902 Derby, was sold to the German
government for 20,000 guineas. (June 1902)

Ard Patrick had by then been bought by the German
government but still ran in the colours of his previous
owner John Gubbins. He was ridden by that year's champion jockey Otto Madden, Sceptre by the comparatively
inexperienced Fred Hardy. Ard Patrick led turning for
home with the two other Classic winners in behind, both
sitting on his shoulder seemingly poised to strike. Soon
though there were cries from the crowd of 'the favourite's
beat' as Rock Sand cracked and fell away.

Sceptre went by Rock Sand and seemed to have the
measure of Ard Patrick. With the crowd apparently silent
in the intensity of the struggle rather than shouting their
fancy home, the *Sporting Life* next day reported: 'The
struggle between the pair was of the most enthralling
character, as every stride the mare looked like getting

there, but she couldn't. Hardy rode her with one hand in the other tickling her quarters with the whip, while Madden shoved Ard Patrick along, trusting to his hands and amidst a tumult of cheers landed Mr Gubbins' black/ brown [horse] a gallant winner by a neck.'

It is clearly a race that lived on in the annals of the sport. When the *Racing Post* asked its readers a few years ago to vote on the greatest race of all time, the 1903 Eclipse made no. 23 in the list, although virtually nobody voting would have seen it. Clearly it is a strong folk memory still.

Career highlights:
1902: Derby, Prince of Wales Stakes
1903: Prince of Wales Stakes, Eclipse Stakes

68. GODIVA

The late Lambourn trainer Doug Marks had a twinkle in his eye and was a wonderful story-teller of tales true and false. The best yarn I ever heard him tell, though, was of how as an unknown apprentice he won two Classics – and though it was hard to believe it was perfectly true.

Having arrived in Newmarket to work for William Jarvis after his father had written to the Prince of Wales asking for help in getting him stable employment, young Douglas weighed around four stone 'and that was mostly head'. Unable to ride when he arrived, he was 18 months on the stable pony but begged as a lad to 'do' a Hyperion filly whom he loved to distraction.

Godiva was an awkward cuss, playing up at every oppor-tunity, but he somehow found the secret to her. When the stable jockey was killed in an air crash Doug was given the

Godiva, who won two Classics in 1940 – the 1,000 Guineas and
the Oaks – while ridden by apprentice jockey Doug Marks.

chance to ride her in races and won a Classic trial on her
at 16-1. After that when visiting jockeys came to ride work,
he used to regard every one who got on Godiva as a jeal-
ous father treats his daughter's suitors, none of them good
enough, and eventually Willie Jarvis, who trained her for
Esmond Harmsworth, took the risk of letting the inexperienced apprentice partner Godiva in the 1,000 Guineas.
His instructions were 'Don't do anything stupid', because
if the young rider had it would have reflected not on him
but on the trainer.

She was behind early on but Marks got such a tune
out of Godiva that she cruised to the front full of running. The cheeky lad thereupon turned to the senior
jockeys toiling behind him and urged the likes of Gordon
Richards to 'Come on!'. She won by five lengths.

In the Oaks, for which Godiva was favourite, Doug

had heard through the racing grapevine that the resentful senior jockeys had determined to ruin his chances by forcing him to make the pace. Undeterred, he dropped Godiva out at the start. 'I was well last at the first turn', he told me, 'but when you're in a Rolls Royce you don't worry about cyclists on the road ahead'. Trainer Jarvis, told that his favourite was well behind, started heading down from the stands wondering how he was going to face the derision and explain away his blunder in using an apprentice on such a tricky course. At the bottom of the steps he heard the crowd around him cheering his horse home. Doug Marks had threaded her through the field to win.

Sadly, Godiva never went to stud to breed others with her brilliance and perhaps her eccentricities. She died in the summer of 1940. Although he later had a successful and colourful training career, Doug Marks' riding opportunities disappeared when he contracted TB and spent much of the war years in an iron lung. Typical of the man, he used to describe it as a stroke of luck. Having enlisted in the RAF, he said, he would otherwise have been a rear gunner, and almost certainly I would have been talking to his ghost, not him!

Career highlights:
1940: 1,000 Guineas, Oaks

67. BAYARDO

Bayardo was a thinker, a horse who would sometimes stand still as a statue and look off into the distance for minutes at a time. He would refuse to go into his box until he chose. He knew what he wanted: until he was fed he used to bang his chin on the manger, making a noise that became known in his yard as 'Bayardo's drum'. But while some equine thinkers become truly quirky and used to getting their own way, for example refusing to start, Bayardo was a willing partner for his regular jockey Danny Maher early in the last century and won most of his races by coming from off the pace with a significant burst of speed at the end of the contest, which was how Maher insisted he should be ridden. But perhaps his most glorious success was in the Gold Cup at Ascot when the evidence is that it was Bayardo, not his jockey, who opted

Bayardo, ridden by Danny Maher, is led into the winners' enclosure after winning the Gold Cup at Royal Ascot by four lengths, June 1910.

to storm off into the lead seven furlongs from the finish. Bayardo dominated British racing for three seasons and won 22 of his 25 races over distances from five furlongs to two and a half miles.

His biggest problem was his fleshy, sensitive feet that made him detest firm ground. The only thing he couldn't bear was having his ears covered: they were unusually large 'lop' ears, which he would flick back and forth in time with his stride while racing.

Bayardo was a genuine and consistent horse of the highest class but an unlucky one. Perhaps his colourful owner Alfred Cox had used up his ration in other areas. Cox was a jute merchant from Liverpool who won a run-down sheep farm in a poker game en route to Australia. His new property turned out to have lurking beneath it what became the Broken Hill silver mine.

When Cox, who raced under the name of Mr Fairie, returned home he turned to breeding and Bayardo was his most successful acquisition. Trained by Alec Taylor at Manton, he was unbeaten as a two-year-old, including the New Stakes (nowadays the Norfolk), the Dewhurst, the Middle Park and Richmond Stakes among his seven victories. That made Bayardo favourite for the 2,000 Guineas but unluckily he was injured while preparing for the first Classic. Alec Taylor wanted to scratch him but Cox insisted on him rushing a short preparation and running the colt, who could only finish fourth to Minoru.

Bayardo's next major target was the 1909 Derby, but again the fates were not with him. During that year's Epsom Blue Riband the favourite Sir Martin fell and Bayardo was one of those badly impeded. Rather than giving him a hard race in pursuit of a place his jockey let him coast home in fifth, again behind Minoru. It was a wise move: Bayardo won his next 15 races off the reel and was only ever once beaten again, in the final contest of his 25-race career.

Taking on older horses, he won both that year's Eclipse Stakes at Sandown and the Champion Stakes at Newmarket while in the St Leger he beat Minoru into fourth. Bayardo was so little affected by that race that he turned out two days later to win the Doncaster Stakes. Minoru's trainer Richard Marsh commented: 'When once Alec Taylor got Bayardo right as a three-year-old his excellence was undeniable. Fortunately for us this did not happen until after Minoru had won the Derby.'

As was often the way then with the breeding emphasis more on stamina, Bayardo was for the next season aimed at the Gold Cup at Ascot in which he tangled with Sea Sick II, the winner of the 1909 French Derby, the Prix du Jockey Club. More than half a mile out Bayardo simply took off, leaving the rest of the field in his wake and winning by a comfortable four lengths. His final appearance was in the Goodwood Cup when his jockey Danny Maher allowed his younger rival Magic, who was carrying 36lb less than Bayardo, to establish a lead of nearly a furlong. Eventually he set off after him at a furious pace but Maher had judged it wrong: he lost by a neck.

At stud Bayardo was a notable success, particularly as the sire of Triple Crown winner Gainsborough. But yet again he was unlucky. He died at only 11 of a thrombosis that paralysed his back legs.

Career highlights:
1908: New Stakes (Ascot), National Breeders Produce Stakes, Richmond Stakes, Middle Park Stakes, Dewhurst Stakes
1909: Prince of Wales Stakes, Eclipse Stakes, St Leger, Doncaster Stakes, Champion Stakes
1910: Chester Vase, Gold Cup (Ascot)

66. PARK TOP

Patience is a virtue. For owners and trainers it is a necessity, and with the talented mare Park Top plenty of patience was required by her owner the Duke of Devonshire and her trainer Bernard van Cutsem.

Park Top was by Kalydon, a sire whom van Cutsem had bred, owned and trained, out of Nellie Park. She was a cheap buy at only 500 guineas but the Duke probably took some convincing that she was a bargain. He had owned Nellie Park himself and she had done little on the racecourse. Minor injuries and the cough kept Park Top off the track as a two-year-old, but when she did come out in 1967 as a three-year-old there was an encouraging start: she won a maiden at Windsor, a better race at Newbury and then the Ribblesdale Stakes at Royal Ascot. She was on her way. But then after a win in the Brighton Cup, a handicap, Park Top went to France and ran a poor race in the Prix Vermeille and they shut down for the season.

Coming out again at four, Park Top proved something of a disappointment. True, she won another Brighton Cup and a race in France, but otherwise it was a story of worthy placed efforts in reasonably good races. Was it worth persevering? It certainly proved to be: like Daylami, Park Top truly blossomed at five.

She began with victory in a mares' race in France and then ran in the Coronation Cup, taking on the second, third and fourth in the previous year's Derby. She did not just beat them. With Lester Piggott sitting motionless until the final furlong while Connaught and Mount Athos scrapped all-out, Park Top simply sauntered by them when asked. Next came an easy victory in the Hardwicke Stakes at Royal Ascot.

Park Top, who had by then fully engaged the public's

Park Top comes home to win the Brighton Cup handicap,
August 1967.

affection, should have become the first filly to win the
Eclipse but Geoff Lewis rode a rare bad race on her at
Sandown, getting her into every kind of trouble, and to
the trainer's fury the clear favourite was beaten by Wolver
Hollow. Three weeks later for the King George VI and
Queen Elizabeth Stakes, with Lester Piggott back on
board, she was made joint favourite with the Grand Prix
de Saint-Cloud winner Felicio. She quickened impressively in the straight, took charge and won convincingly
by a length and a half.

Then it was back to France. Park Top next won the
Prix Foy and then at Longchamp she contested the Arc.
Sensibly playing to the stamina of a winner of the Gold
Cup at Ascot, Bill Williamson kicked Levmoss into a clear
lead early in the straight. Park Top set out after him but
as so often in the Arc there were traffic problems along

the way and she still had three-quarters of a length to find at the line.

The season ended, unfortunately with a whimper. The Champion Stakes back at Newmarket proved one race too many. Park Top's usual finishing kick was missing and she was beaten by the unconsidered French filly Flossy. She had done enough though to earn the Horse of the Year title and the racing public was delighted to hear the Duke announce that she would stay in training as a six-year-old.

Her owner was serious. He spent 30,000 guineas acquiring Shaft at the December Sales to be Park Top's pacemaker in 1970. Unfortunately Shaft was then injured and 1970 did not prove as fulfilling as Park Top's glory year. She won La Coupe at Longchamp but in the Coronation Cup in the absence of Shaft there was no pace early on. Lester seemed to overdo the waiting tactics and Park Top's finishing run failed to catch Caliban by three-quarters of a length. A tendon injury kept her out of a much-anticipated clash with Nijinsky in the King George. She came back and won the Cumberland Lodge Stakes at Ascot with ease, though finishing lame, and her final race, wearing bandages on both front legs, was the Prix Royalieu at Longchamp. Coming from the back as usual, the odds-on Park Top never reached the leaders and could only dead-heat for third. Holes in their pockets, the Parisians jeered her off the course. It was just as well her band of loyal fans in Britain were not there in strength to see such a disappointing swan-song or there might have been a nationalistic fracas or two. It wasn't such a bad career though, overall, for a 500-guinea filly!

Career highlights:
1967: Ribblesdale Stakes
1968: Prix d'Hedouville

*1969: Coronation Cup, Hardwicke Stakes, King George VI and
       Queen Elizabeth Stakes, Prix Foy*
1970: La Coupe, Cumberland Lodge Stakes

65. DAYLAMI

Just how many horses have passed through Sheikh
Mohammed's Godolphin empire over the years is impossible to calculate. Many are homebreds but Godolphin has
never hesitated to open the cheque book and acquire
horses that have shown talent in other hands. There was
remarkable evidence of that in 1998. When Daylami,
handled by Godolphin's no. 1 trainer Saeed bin Suroor,
won the Coral Eclipse Stakes at Sandown that year the
other two horses in the frame were his stable companions Faithful Son and Central Park – all three of them
acquired from other yards.

The well-travelled Daylami was one of the most successful examples of the buying-in policy: the older he got
the better he seemed to run, and his 11 victories included
seven Group Ones, culminating in a smashing success in
the Breeders' Cup Turf at Gulfstream Park Miami.

A handsome grey colt by Doyoun out of Daltawa
who was bred by the Aga Khan, Daylami was originally
trained in France by Alain Royer-Dupré. As a juvenile he
won at Longchamp and Evry and was second to Shaka in
the Grand Criterium. In his three-year-old career, during
which he raced only over a mile, Daylami won the Prix
de Fontainebleau and the Poule d'Essai des Poulains,
in which he swept from last to first despite the bog-like
conditions. Before being purchased by Godolphin he
was placed also in the St James's Palace Stakes, the Prix
Jacques Le Marois and the Prix du Moulin.

Daylami (*left*), ridden by Frankie Dettori, wins the Coronation Cup from Royal Anthem, Epsom, June 1999.

There were thus no Classics in Daylami's trophy cupboard but at four he truly began to realise his potential, reappearing at the Curragh to take the ten-furlong Tattersall's Gold Cup, a Group Two race. He then ran third to his stablemate Faithful Son in the Prince of Wales Stakes at Ascot, although there were valid excuses as Frankie Dettori encountered traffic problems when trying to make his run.

Daylami comfortably turned the tables on Faithful Son in the Eclipse, coming home half a length ahead of him with the pair six lengths clear of Central Park. It was the first European Group One race in which all the first three horses had come from the same stable.

On his next outing Daylami moved up to a mile and a half for the first time in the King George, in which he came fourth behind Swain. He then crossed the Atlantic to contest the Man o' War Stakes at Belmont Park. On that occasion he raced closely behind the leaders and then produced a strong run in the straight to catch Buck's Boy in the closing stages and win by one and a quarter lengths. He concluded that season by dropping back to ten furlongs in Newmarket's Champion Stakes but disappointed in only finishing third to Alborada.

Daylami, whose original iron-grey colour had by now become almost white, was kept in training by the Maktoum family, who believed that the horse had 'more to give and more to prove'. It was a wise decision because at five years old Daylami produced the best form of his life.

He began the year in Dubai. Contesting the World Cup there, he ran on well after being hampered, but only well enough to finish fifth. Daylami then crossed to Ireland again for the Tattersall's Gold Cup, now a Group One race, but after taking the lead in the straight he was passed and beaten by the filly Shiva. The best, however, was to come: in June Daylami produced a sustained run through the last two furlongs to beat quality horses in the Coronation Cup, his first victory over a mile and a half, even though he had to work hard to wear down Royal Anthem.

He missed the Eclipse because trainer Saeed bin Suroor felt he needed more time and then in July won the King George VI and Queen Elizabeth Stakes by five lengths. Pundits noted that it wasn't the strongest of fields for the race but he certainly thrashed those who did turn up on the day, with Godolphin's second string Nedawi in second place. It was during that race that Frankie Dettori realised just how much of a turbo there was under Daylami's grey coat. He also came to realise that it took time to stoke him up and that he needed a furlong to find top gear. 'You'd be scrubbing away on his back for a couple of hundred yards and then, whoosh, he'd take off and fly by the others as if they were standing still.'

Daylami, who was possibly at his best over ten furlongs, was even more devastating in his next race, the Irish Champion Stakes at Leopardstown. He was only second favourite in what the bookies treated as a match between him and Royal Anthem, the eight-length winner of the Group One International Stakes at York. Having shadowed the leaders through the early stages, Daylami moved through easily on the inside and once in the straight he drew right away to win by nine lengths from the filly Dazzling Park with Royal Anthem only fifth.

Naturally then he was aimed at the Prix de l'Arc de Triomphe. Frankie believed he would win it but the ground there in 1999 was desperately heavy and the Godolphin team thought hard about withdrawing him. When it became clear in the race that Daylami was struggling to reach the leaders, he was eased by Dettori to save him for his next assignment as Montjeu motored on to win.

That next assignment proved to be the grey's best performance of his career, in the Breeders' Cup Turf. No European-trained horse had ever won a Breeders' Cup race round the tight seven-furlong track at Gulfstream Park in Florida, but that did not stop Daylami starting as the 16-10 favourite in the field of 14.

There was another factor in play. Frankie Dettori, normally so much a man for the big occasion, had been much criticised for an eccentric ride on Swain in the previous year's Breeders' Cup Classic. US Turf writers were suggesting he couldn't handle American tracks. In 1999 both Daylami and Frankie met the challenge superbly.

Daylami's old rival Buck's Boy stoked up the pressure with a fast time for the first six furlongs but Frankie had him covered. He moved Daylami up to third behind Buck's Boy and Royal Anthem entering the straight and was travelling so well that from that point the only real question was how big his winning margin would be. His powerful finishing kick in fact took him two and a half lengths clear at the line with Royal Anthem second and Buck's Boy third.

As he rode back into the winners' enclosure a pumped-up Dettori shouted 'What about Swain now!' As for Daylami, the question was: was he unlucky not to have been a two-time Breeders' Cup winner? He had been sent over for the previous year's race at Churchill Downs but was withdrawn on the day with an illness. The winner in 1998 was Buck's Boy, the horse he had now beaten both at Gulfstream Park and at Belmont Park in the Man o' War Stakes.

In the International Classification that year Daylami was rated as the best horse in the world, equal with Montjeu on 135. He was named American Champion Male Horse in the prestigious Eclipse Awards and as a bonus won his connections a $1 million prize as the winner of the inaugural World Series racing championship, a competition with points awarded for nine major international middle-distance races. He also won the Cartier Horse of the Year award.

Career highlights:
1997: Prix Fontainebleau, Poule d'Essai des Poulains
1998: Tattersall's Gold Cup, Eclipse Stakes, Man o' War Stakes, Belmont
1999: Coronation Cup, King George VI and Queen Elizabeth Stakes, Irish Champion Stakes, Breeders' Cup Turf

64. USER FRIENDLY

One night in Newmarket in 1985 jockey Steve Cauthen, owner Bill Gredley and trainer Clive Brittain, three men who know more about racing than most, decided after a good bottle or three that they could 'design' a Derby winner. What you needed for starters, they determined, was a sire and a dam who had both demonstrated emphatically the capacity to handle under pressure the twists and turns and gradients of the highly individual Epsom Downs track.

Bill Gredley's mare Rostova, trained by Clive Brittain, had comfortably won the Great Metropolitan Handicap that year. Slip Anchor, ridden by Cauthen, had been a runaway winner of the Derby. 'I'm bound to get a nomination to Slip Anchor', said Steve. 'Do you want it?' 'Yes please', said Bill. For her part Rostova descended from one of the Classic lines in the Stud Book, the Picture Play family of Mr Jim Joel. Close relatives of hers had won the Guineas, the Derby and the St Leger and so off she was sent to mate with her Derby winner.

The result was not exactly what the three doctors had ordered, being a filly. But User Friendly, as Bill Gredley named her on sending her to Clive to be trained, did indeed prove her ability over the Epsom track, and over most other tracks that mattered, as she ran up a string of victories including three Oaks, started favourite for the Prix de l'Arc de Triomphe and became Europe's Filly of the Year in 1992. Not surprisingly she walked away with Britain's 'Racehorse of the Year' award.

But back to the beginning. User Friendly failed to reach her reserve (reputedly 25,000 guineas) at the Newmarket October Sales in 1990 and didn't see a racecourse as a two-year-old. She was so backward and showed

George Duffield and User Friendly gain a comfortable victory
in the St Leger at Doncaster, September 1992.

so little initially when put into training that she was sent
home to Gredley's Stetchworth Stud. When she came back
she began to improve faster than any filly Clive had seen.

User Friendly started her racecourse career as a 25-1
shot in a Sandown maiden at the end of April. Despite
running green she took the eye in the paddock and drew
clear, ridden out to win in clear-cut fashion despite being
slowly away. The lucky man on board was George Duffield,
because Michael Roberts, who then rode most of Clive's
horses, had taken another mount as a favour to a friend.
Duffield then kept the ride for her remarkable career.

User Friendly next faced four opponents in the Oaks
Trial. The others came off the fence turning into the
straight and she hugged the inside and won with her ears
pricked.

When I was writing Clive's biography George told me:

'I started riding work on her between the Oaks Trial and the Oaks and she improved phenomenally. Not just two or three pounds. Each work morning she was improving six, seven or eight pounds. The piece of work she did just before the Oaks was absolutely incredible. It was level weights with Terimon (a Coronation Cup entry) and she finished upsides. Come the Oaks I knew the way she wanted riding. It needed to be a test of stamina. Even though she'd got lots of quality, lots of class, she was bred to get two miles standing on her head.'

User Friendly slipped round Tattenham Corner under her 45-year-old jockey and set sail for home, defying the others to come and catch her. They couldn't and she won by three and a half lengths from the favourite All At Sea, ridden by Pat Eddery.

The Irish Oaks followed, although that proved a tougher test because User Friendly had had a little setback in training after Epsom. She won again, though, and then it was on to the Yorkshire Oaks on ground firmer than she liked. There it was all about class, quality and guts. Feeling her joints, User Friendly didn't look like winning for a fair way. She lugged left and her jockey was tugging at the right rein to keep her on a straight course, but in the end she reeled in the others and forged clear to beat Bineyah by two and a half lengths.

After the Yorkshire success Bill Gredley paid £25,000 to supplement his filly and take on the colts in the St Leger, although the real aim for the autumn was the Prix de l'Arc de Triomphe. Connections were worried about getting her jarred up by running on unsuitably firm ground and played a game of chicken with the Doncaster authorities, threatening to pull the race's main attraction out of the final British Classic unless the course was watered – as, in the end, it was.

Six colts took on the unbeaten filly in the St Leger but the race proved tailor-made for User Friendly. Lester Piggott made the pace on Mack the Knife. In the straight User Friendly moved up. One kick in the belly and it was all over. George Duffield says: 'I lobbed along in mid div getting a nice tow then I appeared half way up the straight. I looked over both shoulders and saw everybody was beaten and I thought "You're home and dry boy, away we go". She won well.'

After that three and a half length victory User Friendly went on to the Arc with a record of six wins from six races, including three Classics. She was only the third filly to land the Oaks, Irish Oaks and Yorkshire Oaks treble and only the seventh Oaks winner of the century to go on and win the St Leger. (Dunfermline, Sun Princess and Oh So Sharp were among those to have completed that double.) It was hard to make a case for any rival as the best filly in Europe, and although not even Nijinsky had managed to win both the Leger and the Arc she was made favourite to do so.

The field of 18 runners for the Arc that year included the winners of the English, Irish and French Derbies as well as the Oaks – 12 Group One winners in all. But there was no obvious pacemaker in the field and early on they dawdled. As a result there is controversy to this day about the tactics of User Friendly's veteran jockey. George Duffield and Bill Gredley, two men of strong opinion, differ on the precise instructions her jockey was given, even on whether he was formally instructed at all. All they agree on is that he employed the wrong tactics and should have forced the pace sooner on a filly whose ability to stay was proven.

Says George Duffield: 'On the winner Subotica he'd followed me all the way. I'd towed him through and he just had enough pace to get past and beat me a neck. If I could have set a more testing gallop from much further out I don't think I would have got beat. I think I would have won a neck instead of him winning a neck.' In his book he insists: 'I'd love to have gone on but my hands were tied. I had explicit instructions.'

Bill Gredley still insists that he didn't tell George Duffield not to make the pace: 'It's just not true.' But they still speak about each other with mutual respect.

User Friendly was taken to the well once too often that autumn, running disappointingly in the Japan Cup, and she was never the same force as a four-year-old, even though she did win the Grand Prix de Saint-Cloud. But it was a rare feat to win four Group Ones in a season, and User Friendly didn't forget her big-race rider. When George Duffield saw her at stud at Coolmore several years later he went into the paddock and she followed him everywhere he went.

Career highlights:
1992: Epsom Oaks, Irish Oaks, Yorkshire Oaks, St Leger
1993: Grand Prix de Saint-Cloud

63. MONKSFIELD

The tussles over several years between Night Nurse, Sea Pigeon and Monksfield for the Champion Hurdle gave Cheltenham Festival-goers some of their best fare ever. Night Nurse's all-round record may make him supreme but there was no gutsier horse than little Monksfield. He managed both to dethrone the mighty Night Nurse, who liked to dominate from the front, and twice to defy the speedy Sea Pigeon, who liked to come from behind. What

Monksfield (*left*) and Night Nurse clear the last fence before
going on to finish in a dead heat in the Templegate Hurdle,
Aintree, April 1977.

his opponents, especially Sea Pigeon and his riders, came
to learn was that you should never tackle Monksfield too
early because he was a fighter who would always respond
to a challenge.

The tough little 'Monkey', a character who kept the
other horses in his yard awake with his snoring and who
had a taste for Granny Smith apples, was unusual for a
jumper in that he was an entire horse, not a gelding. He
was trained in Ireland by Des McDonogh, who didn't
believe in shielding his horses from competition. By the
time he came to the 1978 Champion Hurdle Monksfield
had already participated in 52 races over four years.

That season, however, he had been two months off
the course in the autumn with a leg infection. Maybe the
unaccustomed rest had done him good but when it came

to the race that year Monksfield was really on song. That year Night Nurse, who had won for the previous two years, was in trouble, not skating over his hurdles with the usual facility. Monksfield's rider Tommy Kinane knew that he had to draw the finish from speedsters like Sea Pigeon and he set sail for home two hurdles out. Approaching the last, Frank Berry, who was deputising on Sea Pigeon for the injured Jonjo O'Neill, brought his mount up to challenge. It was too soon and Monksfield responded by sticking his neck out and drawing away again up the hill to win by two lengths, with Night Nurse back in third. At 44 it made Kinane the oldest man ever to win a Champion Hurdle.

The same two dominated the finish the next year. This time Jonjo O'Neill was back on Sea Pigeon and Dessie Hughes had taken over on Monksfield. But Jonjo too, on his own admission, got it wrong. He attacked Monksfield on the final bend and jumped the last in the lead, confident that he was going to win. Both took the last obstacle perfectly, but halfway up the run-in Sea Pigeon began to 'empty' on the sticky going. Brave little Monksfield, who never admitted defeat, clawed his way back, inch by inch. Sea Pigeon's stride shortened and in clinging mud that had probably blunted his rival's speed Monksfield re-passed him 50 yards out to win by three-quarters of a length. Cheltenham veteran Mick O'Toole described it as 'one of the greatest races I have seen at this course', while Sea Pigeon's trainer Peter Easterby observed laconically: 'It's a pity pigeons can't swim.'

If the struggles with Sea Pigeon were legendary, Monksfield's battle with Night Nurse in the Templegate Hurdle at Aintree, when they dead-heated after going head to head for the last three flights, should have been the subject of an epic poem. Monksfield, probably better suited by the Liverpool course, won that race on two more occasions. He also won the Welsh Champion Hurdle. After his long and strenuous career Monksfield was probably past his best by the time Sea Pigeon finally beat him in the 1980 Champion Hurdle.

Career highlights:
1977: Templegate Hurdle (dead heat with Night Nurse)
1978: Champion Hurdle, Templegate Hurdle
1979: Champion Hurdle, Welsh Champion Hurdle

62. SWAIN

Swain will be remembered by most of us for the races he won; Frankie Dettori, who shared many of those victories, will probably remember him to his grave for one he lost.

Swain was a battler, a fighter and a horse who seemed to go on improving throughout his career. He achieved the rare distinction in 1997 and 1998 of winning the all-age King George VI and Queen Elizabeth Stakes two years running, the only colt ever to do so (although the feat had been performed in 1973 and 1974 by the mare Dahlia).

His victory in 1998 made him the oldest horse ever to win the race: no six-year-old has won it before or since. But it was not just occasional brilliance that made Swain one of the top international horses of his generation, it was his sheer consistency: he was one of those horses by whom we judged the rest, a dependable yardstick and a true professional who was placed in 19 of his 21 starts and won ten of them.

The well-named Swain, by Nashwan out of Love Smitten, began his career in France where as a

Swain, ridden by Frankie Dettori, comes in to win
the King George VI and Queen Elizabeth Stakes, Ascot, July 1998.

three-year-old in 1995 he won the Group Two Grand Prix
de Deauville and the Group Three Prix du Lys in Sheikh
Mohammed's colours when trained by André Fabre. He
won three more races and was well-fancied for that year's
Prix de l'Arc de Triomphe in which he finished third to
the outstanding Lammtarra.

Swain ran five times in 1996, achieving his first
Group One by winning the Coronation Cup at Epsom.
Campaigned only at the highest level, he was fourth that
year in the Arc and third in the Breeders' Cup Turf.

In 1997 Swain transferred to Godolphin and to the
Newmarket yard of Saeed bin Suroor. That year he took
the first of his two King Georges in a terrific battle with
Pilsudski but was seemingly below par at Longchamp, finishing only seventh in the Arc.

In 1998 the globe-trotter's season began in Dubai where on the artificial surface he finished second to Silver Charm in the World Cup. He was defeated in the Coronation Cup and in Ascot's Hardwicke Stakes that year but Frankie Dettori still backed Swain's experience and chose him in preference to Daylami for the King George, in which he beat the Derby-winner High Rise and Royal Anthem. Just as impressively, Swain then dropped back to ten furlongs and won the Irish Champion Stakes.

Sheikh Mohammed and the Godolphin team had planned that Swain would end his career in a blaze of glory by winning the Breeders' Cup Classic at Churchill Downs that year. They were pleased with Swain's preparation and in Frankie Dettori he had an outstanding big-race jockey. But even great sportsmen have their off days and something went wrong for Frankie that night. For some reason as they swung into the straight and prepared for the expected battle with Silver Charm the head-down Dettori went for his whip and delivered a barrage of blows that resulted in Swain ducking across the track and losing his chance. His mount straightened up only when the whipping stopped, and the outsider Awesome Again won with Silver Charm second and Swain a neck away in third. Frankie agrees he hit Swain too often and threw away a winning chance, but he still claims that the horse was affected by a battery of lights and ducked away unpredictably towards the grandstand.

He felt victimised by the media onslaught on his ride and it nearly destroyed both his confidence and his relationship with the Godolphin team. Saeed bin Suroor said: 'Swain has won two King Georges, a Coronation Cup, an Irish Champion Stakes, second in the World Cup. He can handle any ground and any surface. He was a brilliant horse. I am not upset and I understand we can't win all the

time but I wish we had done something better.' He added:
'Frankie is our jockey. We like him. We love him. We need
him to stay at the top all the time. All of the people watching the race there and on TV all over the world know he
made a mistake – but that happens in a race.'

Frankie wept in his wife's lap on the plane back and
was depressed when the new season began in Dubai. It
took a heart-to-heart with Sheikh Mohammed and Sheikh
Mo's reminder that he was the man who had ridden seven
winners in a day at Ascot to restore his equilibrium, but
fortunately for racing fans worldwide that did the trick.

Though he tangled throughout his career with horses
of the quality of Helissio and Pilsudski, Swain finished it
having amassed nearly $4 million in prize money. For me,
any time he ran he was worth the admission money on
his own.

Career highlights:
1996: Coronation Cup
1997: King George VI and Queen Elizabeth Stakes
*1998: King George VI and Queen Elizabeth Stakes, Irish
Champion Stakes*

61. ABERNANT

Noel Murless and his patron Sir Reginald Macdonald
Buchanan went to look at some yearlings together in 1947
as Murless prepared to take over at Beckhampton from
the retiring Fred Darling. Murless's eye was caught by a
grey. 'You don't want him', said Darling, 'He's just a little
rat'. But Murless persisted and having seen the horse's
action Darling relented. That was how Murless came to
train one of the fastest horses of the last century.

Abernant, ridden by Gordon Richards, at Bath, April 1949.

Sheer speed is an essential part of the mix that rocks racing people's socks and Abernant, sired by Derby winner Owen Tudor out of a daughter of the speedy Mumtaz Mahal, was a true pigeon-catcher who thrilled racegoers with his electric acceleration. Stretching the legs and lungs of his opponents with his searing early pace, Abernant often had most of his opponents demoralised by halfway. He was also an astonishingly consistent achiever in fast-run races where one tiny miscalculation by horse or jockey can ensure defeat.

The dark grey Abernant dominated in his two-year-old year in 1948, his five victories over five and six furlongs with Gordon Richards in the saddle including the

Chesham Stakes, National Breeders Produce Stakes, the Champagne Stakes and the Middle Park Stakes.

With a record like that, owner Reginald Macdonald Buchanan and trainer Noel Murless, encouraged by Gordon Richards, were bound to experiment with the 2,000 Guineas and their gamble nearly came off. Abernant's scorching speed had plenty of his rivals in trouble and with Richards sitting mouse-like desperately trying to nurse him home he succumbed only in the final stride to Nimbus (whom he had beaten six lengths in the Champagne Stakes).

After that brief foray, the head took over from the heart and they planned a race programme reverting to sprints. It brought spectacular success. Abernant won all the top four speed races: the King's Stand Stakes at Ascot, the July Cup at Newmarket, the King George V Stakes at Goodwood and the Nunthorpe Stakes at York, most by a comfortable margin.

Although he ran like a bullet, Abernant, a great favourite of Gordon Richards, was surprisingly relaxed. Before the Nunthorpe, Richards recalled, Abernant was looking round at everything. He saw four children playing marbles and started playing with them like a dog. Then the starter said 'Come on jockeys, line up'. In a moment Abernant was focused and went off like a machine.

The next year, 1950, he won the July Cup, the King George V Stakes and the Nunthorpe all over again, ending his career with 14 victories from the 17 races in which he ran (he was second in the other three). As a measure of his achievement in his specialist field, the 142 handicap rating accorded to Abernant by Timeform was the same as that given to the unbeaten Prix de l'Arc de Triomphe winner Ribot, who won all his 17 starts. Their joint mark was the fourth-highest ever awarded.

Career highlights:

1948: Chesham Stakes, National Breeders Produce Stakes, Champagne Stakes, Middle Park Stakes

1949: King's Stand Stakes, July Cup, King George V Stakes, Nunthorpe Stakes

1950: July Cup, King George V Stakes, Nunthorpe Stakes

60. CAPTAIN CHRISTY

Former jockey Bobby Beasley could be a morose fellow, but he must have had a sense of humour. A reformed alcoholic, when he left racing he took the bold step of running a pub. Friends said that he used to come downstairs of a morning, survey the spirits measures behind the bar and jeer: 'You thought you were going to get me, you little bastards, but you didn't.'

Beasley was associated with plenty of fine horses but his outstanding victory, most of the Irish nation will agree, was the one he scored in the 1974 Gold Cup on that brave, talented but chancy little chaser Captain Christy, on the day that the *Times* sports page headlined 'The Greatest Comeback Since Lazarus'.

As a glamour boy youngster Beasley had won the 1959 Gold Cup on Roddy Owen. The next year he took the Champion Hurdle on Another Flash and in 1961 he won the Grand National on the grey Nicolaus Silver. There were top rides for Paddy Sleator, Fred Rimell and Fred Winter but then came some bad falls, weight problems and a losing struggle with the bottle. Beasley quit the saddle and his weight rose to over 15 stone.

With the aid of friends and Alcoholics Anonymous, Beasley fought his way back to fitness and started looking around for rides at about the time his old friend

Captain Christy, ridden by Bobby Beasley, crashes through the last fence ahead of The Dikler before going on to win the Cheltenham Gold Cup, March 1974.

Pat Taaffe began training. Captain Christy was a talented but headstrong young hurdler who crashed as many obstacles as he jumped, and a mutual friend suggested to Taaffe that the experienced old hand Bobby Beasley might be just the man to screw Captain Christy's head on for him.

So it proved. The comeback veteran rider and the fizzy young jumper hit it off, rapidly winning a string of races together. Captain Christy beat the Champion Hurdler Bula in the 1972 Irish Sweeps Hurdle. Beasley and Captain Christy were only third in the 1973 Champion Hurdle but won the Scottish equivalent despite knocking a few timber frames out of the ground. Coming into the 1974 Cheltenham Festival, owner Pat Samuel scorned the novice events and ran Captain Christy against his seniors in the Gold Cup – a win or bust philosophy that the horse himself seemed to typify, either winning or capsizing in most of the races he ran.

Calming his erratic partner into playing a waiting game, Beasley shrewdly avoided trouble during the race when High Ken fell and brought down the luckless Pendil. With only The Dikler, the previous year's winner, left in front of him Captain Christy crashed through the final fence but Beasley gave him time to sort himself out and they smoothly passed The Dikler on the run to the line and went on to win by five lengths.

Beasley retired not long after that and it was Bobby Coonan who rode Captain Christy when he led all the way to beat Pendil, winner for the two years previously, in the 1974 King George VI Chase at Kempton. Captain Christy was pulled up on bottomless ground in the 1975 Gold Cup but after finishing second both in the Whitbread Gold Cup and the Grand Steeplechase de Paris he put up an amazing performance in the 1975 King George. With Gerry Newman in the saddle he again led all the way, galloping his rivals into submission and beating the mighty Bula by no less than 30 lengths.

Captain Christy even had a foray to the USA where he finished fourth in the Colonial Cup.

Career highlights:
1972: Irish Sweeps Hurdle
1973: Scottish Champion Hurdle, Irish Champion Hurdle
1974: Power Gold Cup, Cheltenham Gold Cup, King George VI
Chase
1975: King George VI Chase

59. CREPELLO

Blink twice and you would have missed most of Crepello's career. But those who were associated with him never doubted the brilliance of a colt whose racecourse appearances were a rarity thanks to his fragile legs. His regular pilot Lester Piggott placed him firmly among the five best horses he ever rode.

Leading trainer Clive Brittain came up the hard way as a long-time stable lad with Sir Noel Murless, who also managed Sir Victor Sassoon's stud. Clive was so impressed with the big heavy-topped chestnut he saw in the care of a lad at the Sassoon stud one day that he offered to buy him. 'Unfortunately he refused to sell him to me. But I did get to ride the horse at Murless's. I never sat on anything so explosive. He was a tremendous colt, really powerful behind the saddle. He had an unbelievable blend of speed and stamina which meant that he was never extended at home. I couldn't name a horse today that might have beaten him.' That horse was Crepello.

By Donatella out of Crepuscule, on breeding Crepello looked like being suited to extreme distance races like the Gold Cup at Ascot. But his racing career never reached that stage. It began with a narrow defeat by Fulfer in the Windsor Castle Stakes. Lester Piggott could have made more of a race of it but was under strict orders from Murless not to risk straining Crepello's legs. Running on each occasion with bandaged forelegs Crepello then ran fourth to Pipe of Peace in the Middle Park Stakes and concluded his juvenile career by winning the 1956 Dewhurst from the Queen's Doutelle by three-quarters of a length. Said Lester: 'He was always a bit lazy. Once he got to the front he never did more than he had to.'

Crepello was then trained painstakingly for the 1957

Classics, his mettle tested before the 2,000 Guineas and Derby by being galloped with top-class four-year-olds like the Eclipse winner Arctic Explorer. With those fragile fore-legs in mind and knowing that he was never going to be able to put too many miles on this particular racing clock, Murless didn't risk Crepello in a warm-up race before the 2,000 Guineas but sent him straight to Newmarket for the first Classic.

It was a superb training performance. For the Guineas speed is essential. Crepello looked like a stayer, moved like a stayer and was bred to stay, although Murless reck-oned he could have won over five furlongs. The firm ground on Guineas day was all against him. They drew the worst position of all, furthest from the rails. Piggott tucked him in behind the field until the Bushes and when he then unleashed Crepello's power the acceleration was truly impressive, although once he reached the front the still inexperienced colt idled somewhat and only held

Derby winner Crepello and jockey Lester Piggott in the winners' enclosure, June 1957.

off Quorum by half a length, with Pipe of Peace another short head behind.

After that performance Crepello was all the rage for the Derby, a distance much more likely to suit him. Again Piggott tucked him in behind the field in seventh or eighth place and was content to remain there until two furlongs from the finish. At that point he pressed the button and Crepello motored past the rest of the field to win by a length and a half in a time only just outside Mahmoud's record. What put his effort in true perspective was that the horse in second place whom he had beaten so effort-lessly was Ballymoss, who went on to win the Irish Derby, the Eclipse, the King George VI and Queen Elizabeth Stakes and the Prix de l'Arc de Triomphe.

Crepello continued in training but missed the King George because the ground was heavy and would have been too much of a risk for his tendons. Murless still hoped to win a Triple Crown with him, but while Crepello was being prepared for the St Leger he went lame and was retired rather than risk further damage to an ominously bowed tendon. He was thus undefeated in his last three races, all of them Group Ones and two of them Classics.

Career highlights:
1956: Dewhurst Stakes
1957: 2,000 Guineas, Derby

58. PILSUDSKI

Asked if she was worried about getting older, Gypsy Rose Lee declared: 'Honey, I've still got everything I used to have … though it's all just a little bit lower.' Some horses go on improving as they age, and Flat racers that are kept in training as four-, five- or even six-year-olds are often truly popular figures, giving Flat racing some of the loyalty and continuity that is the secret of jump racing's popularity. No one is better at fine-tuning the older boys and girls in the Flat racing class than Newmarket trainer Sir Michael Stoute, and Pilsudski was a prime example of his art.

Owned by Arnold Weinstock and his son Simon, Pilsudski was unplaced in his two runs as a two-year-old. In his five starts as a three-year-old he won a couple of valuable handicaps, including the Tote Gold Trophy at Goodwood. But it was really only when he came out again as a four-year-old in 1996 that the racing world found out what he was made of. He began by finishing second to his stable companion Singspiel, another in the same bracket of middle-aged racing stars, in the Gordon Richards Stakes and was then only eighth of 12 to First Island in the Prince of Wales Stakes at Ascot. But then after a couple of months off, things really started to click for Pilsudski.

He won the Brigadier Gerard Stakes and the Royal Whip Stakes at the Curragh and then travelled to Germany to take the Group One Grosser Preis von Baden, beating the 1995 winner, himself called Germany, and Sunshack. With Walter Swinburn in the saddle Pilsudski then went to Longchamp for the Prix de l'Arc de Triomphe in which he battled on to be second to Helissio. As Walter Swinburn said, he was no oil painting, but he was tough.

The glorious finale to Pilsudski's year, however, came in the Breeders' Cup Turf race at Woodbine in Canada, where he came between the race leaders to beat Swain and Shantou in a European 1-2-3 and to give Sir Michael Stoute his first Breeders' Cup success after 15 attempts.

Pilsudski, with Mick Kinane now taking over as his regular jockey, met the Arc winner Helissio again in

Mick Kinane on Pilsudski wins the Champion Stakes at
Newmarket, October 1997.

his opening race of the next campaign in 1997 and with
Stoute having left plenty to work on, he was third. He was
then expected to win the Hardwicke Stakes at Royal Ascot
but got caught in the dying strides by the fast-finishing
Predappio.

Pilsudski looked truly imposing in the paddock before
the Coral Eclipse at Sandown that year. With Kinane
on board again he was second favourite to the brilliant
filly Bosra Sham, then being described by Henry Cecil
as the best horse he had trained. Pilsudski was, though,
at a shorter price than that year's Derby winner Benny
The Dip.

In the race, Benny The Dip under Willie Ryan set a
slow pace and then effectively blocked off Bosra Sham
(on whom Kieren Fallon had a truly bad day) as Kinane

challenged on Pilsudski. By the time Fallon had switched Bosra Sham out, Pilsudski had gone and it was Benny The Dip who rallied to take second.

In one of the best-ever fields for the King George that year Pilsudski was second to Swain, ahead of Helissio, Singspiel, Shantou and Predappio. Often at his best in the autumn, he then went clear in the Irish Champion Stakes to trounce Desert King in what locals rated an 'awesome' performance.

Pilsudski was once again second in that year's Prix de l'Arc de Triomphe, this time behind Peintre Célèbre, and he turned in one of his best performances to win the Champion Stakes at Newmarket, with Kinane declaring of the old warrior: 'Not only is he the toughest I've ridden, he is one of the best.' That rounded off his European career but there was one more hurrah to come as the battle-hardened Pilsudski travelled East to take the Japan Cup by a neck before taking up stud duties there. That final year he won four Group Ones from eight starts, and in his career, after that slow start, he won 11 races in five different countries, a true ambassador.

Career highlights:
1996: Brigadier Gerard Stakes, Royal Whip Stakes, Grosser Preis von Baden, Breeders' Cup Turf
1997: Eclipse Stakes, Irish Champion Stakes, Champion Stakes, Japan Cup

57. SIR KEN

Several horses have won Cheltenham's Champion Hurdle three times. So far as I know Sir Ken, who took his first title in 1952, was the only one among them who was a killer (although it was not for want of trying in See You Then's case).

Sir Ken was trained by Willie Stephenson, who had spotted him at Auteuil when taking Mrs Stephenson to France for a weekend and snapped him up for £1,000. The shrewd Royston handler clearly knew what he had in his yard. Making his British debut, Sir Ken was backed down from 50-1 to 7-1 before winning the Lancashire Hurdle at Aintree on Grand National Day in 1951 and was then bought by Manchester businessman Maurice Kingsley.

Sir Ken, who hadn't scored over obstacles in France, won the Champion in 1952 at his first attempt. At the last he was upsides with Noholme and Approval but neither of them could match his finishing speed and he kicked away up the hill.

Sir Ken was not the nicest of characters: it was when he was out at grass that summer that he fought and killed a paddock companion, which sounds like taking the competitive urge a touch too far. But he was certainly consistent. Few of his contemporaries could touch him and he won 20 of the 29 races he ran over hurdles, as well as one on the Flat and four over fences. When he secured his second championship it was his 16th consecutive victory and this time the race was not run to suit. Sir Ken liked to come from behind but nobody had been prepared to make the pace and jockey Tim Molony was forced to go on from two furlongs out before holding Galatian by two lengths.

Sir Ken had perhaps lost a little of his zest when he went for his third title in 1954 as a 9-4 on favourite. He was a full three lengths behind Impney at the last. But then the champion showed he had courage too. Tim Molony drove him furiously into the last obstacle and then won a slogging match up the hill.

Sir Ken, winner of three Champion Hurdles,
training by the sea in February 1955.

Sir Ken ran in one more Champion Hurdle, finish-ing fourth in 1955. In 1956 he won what is now the Arkle Chase (the Cotswold) and the Mildmay Chase and he was fancied for the Cheltenham Gold Cup the follow-ing year when he fell. His record of 16 consecutive wins, finally ended at Uttoxeter in October 1953, stood until April 2012 when it was surpassed by the mighty Big Buck's at Aintree.

Career highlights:
1952, 1953, 1954: Champion Hurdle
1956: Cotswold Chase, Mildmay Chase

56. SILVER BUCK

The Yorkshire-based Dickinson family, Tony and Monica and their perfectionist son Michael, were a racing phenomenon who had huge success with their jumpers. Michael, the former champion amateur and then a top jockey before he took over the training licence from his father, was champion trainer three times in the four seasons he trained hurdlers and chasers in Britain. On Boxing Day 1982 he set a world record by sending out 12 winners on one day. He was then hired by Robert Sangster to train Flat horses at Manton in an experiment that failed, before resurrecting his Flat-training career in the States where he trained Da Hoss to win two Breeders' Cups. Then he switched his attention to developing the Tapeta racing surface.

One US racing journalist wrote: 'A fine line separates genius and eccentricity and nobody in horse-racing straddles that line quite like Michael Dickinson.' Perhaps the most appropriate horse Michael Dickinson trained therefore was Silver Buck, the nervy but brilliant jumper sired by the classy Flat-racer Silver Cloud. Though perhaps a little lacking in stamina Silver Buck was among the best of his time, winning a Cheltenham Gold Cup and two King George VI Chases and amassing a then-record amount for a jumper of £177,000 in first prize money.

Like a number of the Dickinson horses Silver Buck, who was known in the yard rather less grandly as 'Bucket', was originally obtained from Ireland for them by the gambler/trainer Barney Curley. He won four hurdles in his first season but finished only fourth in the Sun Alliance novice hurdle at Cheltenham. In his first season over fences Silver Buck again won four races on the trot. His successes included beating Alverton, a future Gold Cup

Race winner Silver Buck, ridden by Robert Earnshaw, in
the Cheltenham Gold Cup, March 1982.

winner, by six lengths and a memorable struggle with the
former Champion Hurdler Night Nurse in the Embassy
Chase Final, which Silver Buck eventually won by two and
a half lengths. His seven straight wins in the 1979–80 season included another epic struggle against Night Nurse
in the Edward Hanmer Chase.

Silver Buck, then in Tony Dickinson's charge, won
the King George both in 1979 and in 1980, on the first
occasion beating Jack of Trumps and on the second coming home ahead of the classy mare Anaglog's Daughter.
Questions were raised about his stamina after he could
finish only third in Little Owl's Gold Cup in 1981, ten
lengths behind the second-placed Night Nurse who
was the favourite to win Cheltenham's Blue Riband
in 1982.

Things did not seem to have worked in Silver Buck's interest when the ground turned heavy for that year's Gold Cup, suiting Ireland's Royal Bond, and when the 14-year-old Tied Cottage set a furious pace for the field of 22. But in an exciting contest he was among a group of five who broke clear at the top of the hill. The others were Tied Cottage, Sunset Cristo, the Whitbread winner Diamond Edge and his stable companion Bregawn.

Bregawn was ridden by Graham Bradley, Silver Buck by Robert Earnshaw, both of them riding in the Gold Cup for the first time, and Bregawn was the only one able to stay in contention when the dark brown (he was almost black) Silver Buck quickened before the second last. Silver Buck held him off up the finishing hill by two lengths and Michael Dickinson, a trainer for less than two years, had the first two home in the Gold Cup. It was all the more impressive since a lame Silver Buck had been con-fined to his box for a month in the New Year. Dickinson showed that he could have made it as a diplomat too: when the Queen Mother presented him with the trophy she declared, 'You can't have any ambition left now', to which his response was: 'I have ma'am. When you win the Gold Cup I would like to make the presentation to you.'

The next year, of course, was the one in which Dickinson performed the amazing feat of training the first five home in the Gold Cup. That time it was the still progressive Bregawn, again with Bradley aboard, who led them home, with Silver Buck, now an 11-year-old, finish-ing in fourth place. Though he had been beaten by sta-blemate Wayward Lad in that season's King George, Silver Buck had still scored another four victories, including a triumph over Burrough Hill Lad in the Edward Hanmer Chase at Haydock. In all, the prolific Silver Buck won 34 of his 48 races over jumps. Tragically he died when still in training as a 12-year-old, being spooked by something he saw and running riderless full tilt into a wall.

Career highlights:
1979: Embassy Chase Final
1979, 1980: King George VI Chase
1979, 1980, 1981, 1982: Edward Hanmer Memorial Chase
1980: Sean Graham Chase
1982: Cheltenham Gold Cup

55. SEE YOU THEN

Some horses are sublime on the track and stinkers in the stable. Such a one was See You Then, probably one of the smoothest jumpers of hurdles there has ever been. Oozing class, the son of Derby winner Royal Palace won the Champion Hurdle three years running from 1985 to 1987 – but he was definitely not the kind of character you would want to have to dinner.

Bought from Ireland by Italian owners to race in their home country, See You Then lodged temporarily with Nicky Henderson in Lambourn, thanks to local vet Frank Mahon, and ran second in the Triumph Hurdle. After one run over obstacles in Italy it was felt that his constant leg problems would be better looked after back in England, and Henderson and Mahon persuaded the owners to keep him in Lambourn for his remarkable career.

Nobody has trained more Cheltenham Festival winners than Nicky Henderson, and See You Then was the very first of them. But while it would be fair to say that this remarkable horse put his trainer on the map, it is a wonder he did not turn him grey in the process. See You Then had legs of glass and just getting him to the racetrack was an achievement. The other horses who won the Champion Hurdle three times (Hatton's Grace, Sir Ken, Persian War and Istabraq) became public favourites. It was never quite that way with See You Then because his racecourse appearances were so few that he was dubbed 'See You When?' in the media.

John Francome would have ridden him in the Champion in 1985 but was injured in the race before. Stable jockey Steve Smith-Eccles took over and rode him to all three big-race victories. In 1985 See You Then's task was made easier when favourite Browne's Gazette ducked round at the start and lost 15 lengths under Dermot

See You Then is congratulated by stable lad Glyn Foster (*left*) and trainer Nicky Henderson after winning the Champion Hurdle for the second year in succession, Cheltenham, March 1986.

Browne, later known as 'The Needle Man' and warned off for doping horses. As a 16-1 shot, See You Then hurdled slickly and quickened past the previous year's winner Gaye Brief after the last to win by seven lengths.

It was a similar story in 1986, although this time See You Then started as an odds-on favourite. He and Gaye Brief came to the last together, but See You Then sped away up the hill to win by a similar margin. In 1987 he had to struggle harder. This time it was Cheltenham favourite Barnbrook Again who was with him over the last hurdle. They tussled and then the American steeplechase Triple Crown winner Flatterer came after them. See You Then only beat him by a length and a half, with Barnbrook Again third.

When See You Then died in 2011 his rider recalled: 'I never rode any horse like him. He was foot perfect and never made a mistake.' Said trainer Nicky Henderson: 'He was the most sensational jumper of hurdles I've ever seen. I only schooled him once a year and he only jumped four hurdles – I've never seen a hurdler cross them so quickly. No one was as fast as him.'

To have won two Champion Hurdles with See You Then was a feat, to win three was a near-miracle. The horse was barely fit in 1986 after much of the winter's programme had been frosted off. Henderson drove a tractor all night to keep his all-weather gallops open and get him to the races. When based at Windsor House, Henderson had a swimming pool and See You Then probably swam more than he galloped. He would be taken to the beach as well, anything to spare the strain on his fragile legs.

You would have thought the horse might have appreciated all the special attention but far from it. He was a brute who loved to get his teeth into people. If he couldn't do that he would kick them. Says Henderson:

'Glyn Foster looked after him all his life and got bitten and kicked to ribbons over the years. Head Lad Corky Browne and I couldn't go in the box without him. Nor could Frank Mahon. We put a Yorkshire boot on him one day because we thought he was knocking a leg. It took us four days to get it off him.'

In the final year that See You Then won the Champion, he had just one prep race at Haydock. After a sleepless night wondering how See You Then's bandaged legs might have stood up to the strain, his trainer went down to the yard at 4.00am. 'His box door was open and there was Frank Mahon sat on the manger. I said, "What are you doing?" and he said, "I couldn't sleep. I thought I'd come and take those bandages off and see how he was." "So what are you doing up there?" He said, "He won't let me out." "But how are his legs?" "I don't know because he won't let me near him to take the bandages off."' By now Henderson too was penned in and trainer and vet had to stay there until the lad Glyn Foster finally came in to work.

Career highlights:
1985, 1986, 1987: Champion Hurdle

54. LOCHSONG

The mare Lochsong, the most popular sprinter of the 1990s, really only had two speeds: full stop and flat out. She was a jockey's nightmare, a horse with such a mind of her own that she could make riders as good as Willie Carson and Frankie Dettori look a genius one moment and a fool the next. But when she was in the mood she was breathtakingly fast.

Her legs were too dodgy to train her at all as a juvenile and the next season she fractured a shin. The mission entrusted to trainer Ian Balding by owner Jeff Smith, whose familiar purple colours with a paler lavender V were carried also by Persian Punch, was to win a race with her so Jeff could take her back to his Littleton Stud and breed from her. Having amazingly got Lochsong to win a poor maiden over six furlongs at Redcar, her trainer asked if he could run her just once more to give her lad Francis Arrowsmith, known as 'Scully', a ride.

Lochsong won a short head, this time over seven furlongs, and went off to Littleton, but in mid-winter her owner suggested that two out of three wasn't a bad record, why not try her again next season? If he had been brutally frank, said Balding later, she would never have had a three-year-old or subsequent career. Luckily he wasn't and Lochsong stayed in training in 1992 to win

Lochsong, ridden by Frankie Dettori, wins her second King George V Stakes at Goodwood, July 1994.

the unprecedented treble of the Stewards Cup, Portland Handicap and Ayr Gold Cup, thanks largely to Willie Carson discovering that she loved to dominate from the front and was best over the minimum trip of five furlongs. The next winter it was trainer asking owner for at least one more season.

In 1993 Lochsong started by running placed without winning in four Group races. She went home to the stud for a break and came back refreshed with Frankie Dettori hired to partner her because of Willie's other commitments. She won a Listed race at Sandown and then took the Group Three King George V Stakes at Goodwood. Frankie then bounced her out in the Nunthorpe at York, let her do her own thing, and she won that Group One. She did the same in the Prix de l'Abbaye at Longchamp, winning by six lengths. Her feats won her not just the Sprinter of the Year category in the Cartier Awards (a title she won twice) but the Horse of the Year title too.

Lochsong, who hated pre-race parades, was becoming more and more of a prima donna and Balding thought she should be retired after Longchamp, but Jeff Smith said it had taken them three seasons to find her best distance and she should have one more. He was gloriously justified when in explosive style she won the Palace House and Temple Stakes and then delighted the crowd with a front-running victory in the King's Stand Stakes at Royal Ascot.

Re-enter Willie when Frankie could not ride her as they tried six furlongs again in the July Stakes, but Lochsong had one of her mulish days, ran away with him on the way to the start and burned up all her energy before the race. With Frankie back on board and with no parade Lochsong won the King George V Stakes again. But then in the Nunthorpe at York she gave Frankie no chance of holding her, tore down to the start in record time and threw away another race. It was, he says, the only time he talked to her in Italian afterwards and it probably wasn't a conversation for the genteel.

After that it was a risk but connections determined on one more crack at the Abbaye in France. There the flying mare, allowed to go down early to the start, was cheered home by a huge British contingent as she dominated from the start and passed the post five lengths to the good with her ears pricked. That was to have been the finale but they were tempted to go for the Breeders' Cup in America too. There Lochsong probably left her race on the training track. In one unscheduled gallop she covered the last three furlongs in 33.1 seconds. No horse had ever clocked fractions that fast but in the race itself she was never going and Frankie wisely let her come home in her own time.

She was, he says, the people's favourite and his too, the ultimate sprinter. 'Five furlongs was plenty far enough while six furlongs was like a trip to Scotland for her.' The secret with Lochsong, he learned, was to let her do her own thing. Once he did that she learned herself to relax a little in the middle of a race and save something for the finish. She wasn't, says Frankie, the prettiest filly in the world and she could pull like a run-away train, but she was in her time the fastest thing on earth. 'If she wanted to run she was gone before the others could react.'

Career highlights:
1992: Stewards Cup, Portland Handicap, Ayr Gold Cup
1993: King George V Stakes, Nunthorpe Stakes, Prix de l'Abbaye
1994: King George V Stakes, Palace House Stakes, Temple Stakes, King's Stand Stakes, Prix de l'Abbaye

53. ONE MAN

His Cumbrian trainer Gordon Richards used to call One Man his 'little bouncing ball' which summed up the horse's zestful style. Like Desert Orchid, One Man was an eye-catching grey who jumped spectacularly and who loved to dominate. But One Man also had a flaw that served only to endear him to his faithful public. He just could not win at Cheltenham, the Olympics of jump racing.

Best at two and a half miles, One Man won 20 of his 35 races. He won all kinds of races at other tracks but he just did not seem to deliver at the Festival in Gloucestershire. After winning his first five races as a novice chaser he was made favourite there for the 1994 Sun Alliance Chase but finished back among the also-rans. One Man was favourite for the Gold Cup itself in 1996 and second favourite the next year. In those two years he had won the three-mile King George VI Chase at Kempton Park by a dozen lengths or more and he had won the Hennessy Cognac Gold Cup at Newbury over a similar distance to the Cheltenham race (although over a flatter track) in 1994, but at Cheltenham in the Gold Cup over 3m 2f he just could not manage the final hill. In the Sun Alliance and those two Gold Cups he was beaten 49, 34 and 35 lengths.

After the last of them, trainer Richards reflected: 'I have seen One Man come down the hill [the hill before the turn and climb to the winning post] in the last two Gold Cups and I have said to myself "Yes, Gordon, you've got a Gold Cup", but from the second last it was sad to see him.' In a moment One Man would empty. It was like watching a searchlight being turned off. In a moment the fluid galloper who had been flicking over his fences would be transformed into a wooden horse running through treacle.

One Man, ridden by Richard Dunwoody, leads the field over
the last fence to claim victory in the King George VI Chase
at Kempton, December 1996.

Some racing writers accused One Man of lacking courage when facing a real challenge. He was condemned as a
flat track bully. But in 1998 the frustrated Richards took a
bold gamble. Determined that his star chaser should have
a success to his name at the headquarters of jump racing,
he entered One Man not in a race over the three miles
or so he was accustomed to, but in the Queen Mother
Champion Chase, the helter-skelter two-mile 'sprint
chase'. He had not run over such a short distance in his
previous 33 contests, not since October 1992.

It proved a master-stroke. Champion trainer Paul
Nicholls told me once that the essence of the Champion
Chase is not so much having blinding pace at the end of
the race as being able to maintain a high cruising speed
for every yard of the two miles. That is just the ability

One Man had. He simply ground his rivals into the turf, setting and keeping up a pace they simply could not match, and over only two miles he had enough stamina left to get up the hill. This time the tank didn't empty and he was roared home by the Cheltenham crowd for one of the most popular victories the course has ever seen. Had he been differently campaigned, that could have been not his first but his third Cheltenham Festival victory.

Owner John Hales, who was to see another of his popular greys, Neptune Collonges, triumph in the Grand National in 2012, has always worn his racing heart on his sleeve and he wept tears of joy in the unsaddling enclosure. Tragically, just 16 days later an inconsolable Hales was weeping tears of a different kind at Aintree. In the Mumm Melling Chase, One Man had been giving the excited crowd a master class in jumping, arching over the first eight obstacles with enormous brio. Then he came to the ninth fence and for some reason, possibly even a heart attack, scarcely took off at all. He crashed chest-first into the fence, broke a leg and had to be put down on the spot. So swiftly in sport, especially in jump racing, can triumph turn into tragedy.

One Man, known as 'Solo' in the Greystoke yard, didn't have the power or the range of the other famous grey so often mentioned in the same breath, Desert Orchid, but he was an extraordinarily clever and agile jumper who won a special place in the hearts of the racing public.

Career highlights:
1994: Reynoldstown Chase, Hennessy Gold Cup
1995: King George VI Chase
1996: Charlie Hall Chase, King George VI Chase
1997: Pillar Chase, Charlie Hall Chase, Peterborough Chase
1998: Queen Mother Champion Chase

52. ARDROSS

Who is racing conducted *for*? Not, one sometimes fears, the paying public. Few races used to be more popular than the Gold Cup at Ascot, the two and a half mile contest for the true stayers' championship. From the end of the 19th century to the Second World War it was a main target for championship horses kept in training after their Classic year, won by Derby winners like Gainsborough and Solario. But gradually it went out of commercial fashion – breeders turned their backs on true stayers who instead were sent to contest middle-distance races like the King George VI and Queen Elizabeth Stakes, where the prize money was better and there was no risk of future stud fees being affected because a horse had won over more than a mile and a half.

Racegoers, though, used to love the true stayers' championships and the robust heroes who competed for races in their own Triple Crown: the Gold Cup, Goodwood Cup and Doncaster Cup. Ardross was one of those heroes who figured in the last golden age of the Gold Cup at Ascot in the late seventies and early eighties. In all truth his name should be bracketed with that of his long-time rival Le Moss, but Ardross added an extra ingredient.

Trained originally by Darkie Prendergast and then his son Kevin in Ireland, Ardross, who did not race as a two-year-old, first came to notice winning the Group Two Gallinule Stakes at the Curragh at 50-1 in 1979. It was the next year that saw the first of his epic Ascot confrontations with Le Moss. With the rest of the Gold Cup field burned off, the two slugged it out, no quarter given or taken, through the final two furlongs, Le Moss finally triumphing by three-quarters of a length. A 2lb turnaround in the weights saw Ardross reduce that gap to a neck in

Le Moss (Joe Mercer) beats Ardross (Christy Roche) by a neck
in the Goodwood Cup, August 1980.

that year's Goodwood Cup, a margin that was repeated
when the two turned the Doncaster Cup into another
two-horse duel. It was Le Moss's second Stayers' Triple
Crown but Ardross had been beaten by little more than
an aggregate total of one length in the three contests
totalling 7m 3f of distance run! Ardross, who was his worthy rival but who never quite succeeded in chasing down
Le Moss in their head-to-heads, had to be content with a
victory in the Jockey Club Cup as compensation.

Le Moss's career ended in 1980 with a narrow defeat
in the Prix Gladiateur: Ardross's was just beginning a new
phase as he was bought by Charles St George and sent to
Le Moss's trainer Henry Cecil.

Ardross's new connections had more comprehensive
plans for him. Although he started by winning them the

1m 6f Yorkshire Cup, quickening impressively at the finish, life was to be about more than galloping his rivals into
shreds over extreme distances. Long odds-on at Ascot,
Ardross won the 1981 Gold Cup there in complete comfort. Landed with a penalty for Goodwood, he still took
command two furlongs out to beat Donegal Prince. He
could have had the Stayers' Triple Crown but was then
routed not to Doncaster but to Paris for the Prix de l'Arc
de Triomphe, having shown he could win over shorter
distances by taking the 1m 5f Geoffrey Freer Stakes at
Newbury (with that year's Leger winner in third).

Mingling with the true bluebloods at Longchamp,
Ardross came home a respectable fifth. In his next outing
he beat the Arc winner Gold River, but that was over the
extra distance of the Prix Royal Oak.

As a six-year-old in 1982 Ardross opened with a victory
over 1m 4f in the Jockey Club Stakes. Before heading for
the Gold Cup at Ascot he also won a second Yorkshire
Cup and the Henry II Stakes at Sandown. At Ascot, faced
with only four rivals, he left them to conduct their own
race, coming home an easy three lengths ahead. After
that it was back to Longchamp for the big one in the Arc.

Ardross so nearly did it. They went too fast for him
early on but the determination he shared with his partner
Lester Piggott, underlined by the vigorous application of
Piggott's whip, took them past rival after rival. Sadly, when
they got to the winning post there was just one still left
to catch, the filly Akiyda, who scrambled home by a fast-
diminishing head. It was Ardross's glory hour, a defeat
so close, said Henry Cecil, that it was heartbreaking. He
believed his great stayer had only been beaten because
the filly Harbour had lost ground so rapidly that Lester
Piggott had to come round her. 'Had he been able to use
his long, raking stride in a clear run up the straight he

might have won.' Said Cecil of Ardross: 'There was only one thought in his mind during a race and that was to finish in front.'

Career highlights:
1979: Gallinule Stakes
1980: Jockey Club Cup
1981: Yorkshire Cup, Gold Cup (Ascot), Goodwood Cup, Geoffrey
    Freer Stakes, Prix Royal-Oak
1982: Jockey Club Stakes, Gold Cup (Ascot), Geoffrey Freer
    Stakes, Doncaster Cup

51. ORMONDE

When Ormonde, trained at Kingsclere by the great John Porter, ran in the 2,000 Guineas of 1886 the competition could scarcely have been tougher. The Bard had contested 16 races as a juvenile and won them all. Saraband had won a Kempton race with contemptuous ease and Minting was described by his famous trainer Mat Dawson as one of the finest horses he had ever known. Dawson boasted: 'When John Porter says he has a good horse you may be certain he has a damned good one, but he does not know what I have got. When it comes to a matter of talking Ormonde wins the 2,000 but when it comes to a matter of racing Minting will win.'

Ormonde won the Guineas in a canter, sending Dawson back to his hotel room in a sulk from which he took days to recover. The Guineas winner beat The Bard again to win the Derby by one and a half lengths and at Royal Ascot Ormonde won the St James's Palace Stakes and Hardwicke Stakes on successive days. He duly collected the Triple Crown by winning the St Leger in a

Top jockey Fred Archer on the unbeaten Ormonde,
the Triple Crown winner of 1886.

stroll as a 1-7 chance. When he won the Champion Stakes Ormonde's odds were a prohibitive 1-100.

There were reports from the touts in the winter that Ormonde had 'gone in his wind' and they proved to be accurate: he was from then on a 'roarer', but he was still good enough to win twice again at Royal Ascot in 1887, beating his old rival Minting once more in the Hardwicke by a neck and being cheered home as a popular hero after the near-silent crowd had heard him fighting for breath on his way around the course.

Ormonde was owned by the richest man in England, the first Duke of Westminster, and it was suggested that the Duke might ride Ormonde in the Royal Procession for Queen Victoria's Diamond Jubilee. That plan was scotched but the Triple Crown winner did come to London for a garden party at the Duke's Grosvenor House residence. He was unloaded at Waterloo and walked across Westminster Bridge and, with royal permission, through Green Park.

By all accounts Ormonde behaved impeccably at the party and was much admired by a cluster of royals and the cream of the aristocracy. He did, though, have a penchant for flowers, often nipping gentlemen's buttonhole blooms from their jackets on stable visits, and at the Grosvenor House bash Ormonde's one faux pas was to consume the carnations presented by the Queen of Belgium.

Ormonde had one other distinction: he was said to have been the model for the fictional horse Silver Blaze in Sir Arthur Conan Doyle's short story of that name. Sadly Ormonde, almost certainly the best horse of his century, did not spend the rest of his days in the land of his birth: after just two years at stud he was sold to Argentina.

Career highlights:
1886: 2,000 Guineas, Derby, St James's Palace Stakes, Hardwicke
Stakes, St Leger, Champion Stakes
1887: Hardwicke Stakes, Rous Memorial Stakes, Imperial Gold
Cup

50. BIG BUCK'S

There are good horses, champions, and there are horses that totally rewrite the record books: early in 2012 Big Buck's powered into the third category. First he won the Ladbroke World Hurdle, the three-mile hurdlers' championship at the Cheltenham Festival, for the fourth consecutive time. That made him the first hurdler ever to win four Grade Ones at the Festival. Then he went on to Aintree to complete a quartet of victories too in the BGC Liverpool Hurdle. That was his 17th consecutive victory, surpassing the record of 16 wins amassed by the three-times Champion Hurdle winner Sir Ken back in the 1950s.

Although he too was an outstanding hurdler, some of Sir Ken's successes in a less competitive age were achieved against lesser opposition: 11 of Big Buck's first places were achieved in Grade One contests. The new record was an extraordinary achievement that reflected great credit not just on an astonishingly tough and consistent horse but on trainer Paul Nicholls and his team at Ditcheat in Somerset. People forget how hard it can be simply getting a jumper to the racecourse ready to run.

With Big Buck's the irony was that he was bought for a very hefty sum by Andy Stewart as a potential chaser and he might never have had a long-distance hurdles career had not jockey Sam Thomas come off him at the last fence in the Hennessy Gold Cup in 2008. Nicholls was furious with his stable no. 2 at the time for not riding to orders, but in the end Sam Thomas's unseating did Big Buck's and his connections a favour in turning their minds towards a hurdling career for a horse who had never seemed in love with jumping the bigger obstacles. The other factor, Paul Nicholls told me at Aintree just before he won the Grand National with Neptune Collonges, was that if Kauto Star hadn't been in the yard at the time he might have persevered with trying to turn Big Buck's into a chaser.

When I asked him what made Big Buck's such a phenomenon he did not hesitate: 'Pure class', coupled with the horse's remarkable soundness. He could not recall an occasion, he said, when he had not been able to get Big Buck's ready for a targeted race.

Ironically Big Buck's was beaten in his first nine races over hurdles, all of them in France, before he joined the Nicholls yard. His life-changing moment and the start of an incredible new career came in the Cheltenham Handicap Hurdle on 1 January 2009 when he won his first three-mile event, chased home by the future Grand National winner Don't Push It. There followed a Cheltenham success story over the smaller obstacles that was to outdo those formidable Festival characters Baracouda and Inglis Drever. But he wasn't just a Festival specialist peaking once a year: en route to his record Big Buck's won a brace of Cleeve Hurdles, three Long Walk Hurdles at Ascot, three Sportingbet Long Distance Hurdles and of course those four Liverpool Hurdles too.

Year after year new challengers emerged: Time For Rupert, Punchestowns, Oscar Whisky, Grands Crus, Voler La Vedette ... but when it came to a confrontation Big Buck's always saw them off. His third World Hurdle victory was typical: Ruby Walsh had dropped his whip and

Big Buck's, ridden by Ruby Walsh (*centre*), jumps the last on their way to victory in the Cleeve Hurdle at Cheltenham, January 2009.

Grands Crus actually touched down first after the last, but Ruby manoeuvred his mount over to eyeball his opponent and away he went with a surge of power. 'This horse knows where the line is', exulted Nicholls, while Ruby commented: 'Big Buck's always gets me out of trouble. He's different gravy.' At first Big Buck's liked to come from behind, taking time to wind up and sometimes hitting a flat spot during his races. As he matured the flat spots disappeared and they could let him dictate the pace in front as well if it suited: whether he was the arrow or the target became immaterial.

On the racecourse it would be hard to find a tougher horse, but at home Big Buck's is a bit of a fussy old crackpot. He is an inveterate box-walker who constantly paces around his stable. Put him on the horse-walker alone and he cries like a baby. He doesn't like travel, so has never been sent, for example, to Punchestown to add to his winning tally and has only raced at five UK tracks. He even has funny food habits: he's the only horse in the Nicholls yard with a haynet, otherwise he would trample his food into the ground. A bit of an oddball perhaps, but on the racecourse we have rarely seen such a professional. As Tony McCoy said once after riding him when regular pilot Ruby Walsh was injured: 'You don't have to say anything about a horse like him, just look at his form.'

Career highlights:
2009: Cleeve Hurdle, Ladbrokes World Hurdle, Liverpool Hurdle, Long Distance Hurdle, Long Walk Hurdle
2010: Ladbrokes World Hurdle, Liverpool Hurdle, Long Distance Hurdle, Long Walk Hurdle
2011: Ladbrokes World Hurdle, Liverpool Hurdle, Long Distance Hurdle, Long Walk Hurdle
2012: Cleeve Hurdle, Ladbrokes World Hurdle, Liverpool Hurdle

49. PETITE ETOILE

Prince Aly Khan's grey filly, sired by Petition, trained by Noel Murless, hardly excited attention with her first run in 1958. She was beaten by eight lengths – and that was in a two-horse race. She went on, however, to become a public favourite, winning the first two legs of the Fillies' Triple Crown the next year and retiring as the winner of 14 races. In all her 19 contests she was never out of the first two, and if there is one horse indelibly associated in my mind's eye with Lester Piggott's bottom-up racing position and ability to ride a killer finish, then she is the one. She also had some endearing characteristics: the observant Murless noted that she worked most happily when led and followed by fellow greys.

Described by her trainer as 'quirky and unpredictable', the highly-strung Petite Etoile opened her three-year-old career in 1959 by winning the Free Handicap before going on to take the opening fillies' Classic, the 1,000 Guineas, at Newmarket. Lester Piggott had chosen to ride Collyria, Noel Murless's other runner in the race, and the lucky jockey was Doug Smith, who was staggered by Petite Etoile's acceleration into the Dip as she won the race in a time two seconds faster than the colts' equivalent, the 2,000 Guineas.

There was much speculation whether such a headstrong filly would last the distance of the Oaks but she did so comfortably, winning that by three lengths. She was undefeated in her six races that year, which included the Yorkshire Oaks, the Sussex Stakes and the Champion Stakes in the autumn.

In 1960 when she was Horse of the Year, Petite Etoile beat the 1959 Derby winner Parthia with ease in the Coronation Cup at Epsom. Lester Piggott held her up,

Petite Etoile (*right*) loses out to Aggressor in the King George VI
and Queen Elizabeth Stakes at Ascot, July 1960.

asked for an effort 100 yards out and won in a canter with
the filly still hard held. The pair repeated the victory a
year later, with Piggott again gliding up to the leaders
within the last furlong and winning on a tight rein. Both
victories were part of a remarkable bluff: both Murless
and Piggott were convinced the filly only truly got a
mile and a quarter and they were proved right when as
a five-year-old she ran in the Aly Khan Memorial Gold
Cup at Kempton. This time Duncan Keith on Sir Winston
Churchill's High Hat made it a searching test of stamina
at a fast pace. The filly got within a length of him in the
final furlong but could do no more. When the new young
Aga Khan inquired of Lester why he had not gone away
and won, he tilted his head and answered simply: 'He ran
me into the ground.'

Petite Etoile was first or second in every one of her races, she won two Classics and she regularly beat the colts. But what we remember her for most of all is that electrifying turn of foot that was so skilfully employed by Lester Piggott.

Career highlights:
1959: 1,000 Guineas, Oaks, Champion Stakes, Sussex Stakes,
      Yorkshire Oaks
1960: Coronation Cup
1961: Coronation Cup, Coronation Stakes, Rous Memorial
      Stakes

48. GIANT'S CAUSEWAY

When Michael Tabor and the Magniers purchased the mare Mariah's Storm, a winner of ten races in the USA, for the top price paid in America in 1996, she was in foal to Storm Cat. The resulting foal, a strong, well-muscled chestnut colt with two white stockings, was Giant's Causeway, one of the best racecourse battlers I have ever seen.

Newmarket trainer Sir Mark Prescott once told me of his former stable jockey George Duffield: 'The reason he was such a good jockey, day in day out, was that however menial the racecourse and the horse, he could crank himself up to give it the ride of its life. He could go to ride one with no chance at Carlisle and by the time he'd got to Carlisle he'd have convinced himself that if he got hold of it enough he might just win.' Duffield was a jockey with the ultimate will to win, and it is a measure of Giant's Causeway's determination that when George got off Giant's Causeway after winning the Eclipse on him in the year 2000 he declared: 'He wanted to win even more than I did, which took a lot of doing.'

Trained by Aidan O'Brien at Ballydoyle in Tipperary, Giant's Causeway won all three of the races he contested as a two-year-old, including the Prix de la Salamandre at Longchamp on desperate ground. Those he beat included Bachir, who was to become a dual Guineas winner.

Back at the Curragh to open his account as a three-year-old, Giant's Causeway beat Tarry Flynn by three-quarters of a length in the Gladness Stakes and on the strength of that was made 7-2 favourite for the 27-runner 2,000 Guineas at Newmarket. He took the lead going into the final furlong but was beaten for speed when King's Best then burst through and left him three and a half lengths behind. Three weeks later in the Irish 2,000 Guineas he again took on Bachir, who had won the equivalent race in France, but was beaten a neck after a fierce struggle.

Then in the St James's Palace Stakes at Ascot Giant's Causeway returned to winning ways, scoring by a head from Valentino, with Bachir this time back in sixth. After that came the Eclipse at Sandown with Duffield substituting for Giant's Causeway's usual rider Mick Kinane.

It was a hot field including the future Arc winner Sakhee, Henry Cecil's filly Shiva, Fantastic Light and the Aga Khan's Kalanisi, who had won the Queen Anne Stakes at Royal Ascot. Two furlongs out Sakhee dropped back and Giant's Causeway took the lead, pursued by Kalanisi and Shiva. Inside the last 200 yards Pat Eddery drove Kalanisi up and he and George Duffield on Giant's Causeway engaged in a furious eyeball-to-eyeball struggle. It was one of those duels that those of us who saw it will never forget. It was ding and dong, tit for tat, blow for blow, so much so that both jockeys were afterwards referred to the Jockey Club to receive ten-day bans for

Giant's Causeway and Mick Kinane win the Sussex Stakes by
three-quarters of a length from Dansili under Olivier Peslier,
August 2000.

excessive use of the whip. Shiva was to some extent a suf-
ferer, being squeezed for room as the two colts responded
to every urging from their jockeys, but it was Giant's
Causeway who in the end prevailed by a head and the
stewards allowed the result to stand.

It was a case of two tough iron horses ridden by two
tough men, and those who suspected that both animals
might have suffered from giving their all in such a do-
or-die contest were soon proved wrong. Dropping back
to a mile Giant's Causeway, who never did anything the
easy way, won the Sussex Stakes at Goodwood by three-
quarters of a length from Dansili. A few weeks later he and
Kalanisi locked horns once again when they contested
the Juddmonte International at York. Kalanisi looked
likely to win when he swooped late, his rider wisely keeping him out on the track away from Giant's Causeway.
But Kalanisi began to hang in towards his rival, igniting
Giant's Causeway's fighting spirit, and after another thrilling duel Giant's Causeway surged ahead again to win by
a head.

'The Iron Horse', as some in the media christened him, was out again 19 days later to win the Irish Champion Stakes from Greek Dance. That was his fifth Group One victory off the reel but the Juddmonte had shown the way Giant's Causeway could be beaten. In the Queen Elizabeth II Stakes at Ascot for his last race in Britain, John Gosden's Observatory challenged him wide and late, giving Giant's Causeway no time to see the danger and fight back, and he went down by half a length.

In his final race – and his first one on dirt – Giant's Causeway took on the mighty Tiznow in the Breeders' Cup Classic at Churchill Downs, USA. Forced to run wide for much of the race after a slow start, he was two lengths down entering the straight yet briefly drew alongside Tiznow on the charge before the American champion reasserted to deprive him of a final victory.

None of Giant's Causeway's five successive Group One victories was secured by more than three-quarters of a length, another factor that made him exciting to watch, but his career demonstrated that you don't need to win races by wide margins to be a champion, and he lost nothing in reputation by that defeat.

Career highlights:
1999: Prix de la Salamandre
2000: Gladness Stakes, St James's Palace Stakes, Eclipse Stakes,
Sussex Stakes, Juddmonte International, Irish Champion
Stakes

47. BROWN JACK

Allocating relative positions in the top 100 to horses who have made their careers respectively over jumps or on the

Flat is about as far from an exact science as you can get, and as a schoolboy who ran his alkali and acid supplies together in his O level chemistry exam, science was never my forte anyway. At least in the case of Brown Jack we have a horse who could have made it into the top 100 either way if this volume had been restricted to Flat or jumping horses.

Spotted by Irish trainer and bloodstock agent Charlie Rogers grazing on a lawn when his then owner gave him a lift, Brown Jack was bought by trainer Aubrey Hastings, who knew that one of his owners, Sir Harold Wernher, was looking for a future Champion Hurdle winner.

Brown Jack soon proved himself a wise buy and though only four horses lined up when the Champion Hurdle was run for only the second time at Cheltenham in 1928, the *Sporting Life* had little doubt that the previous year's winner Blaris, Brown Jack, Zeno and Peace River were the four best timber-toppers in the land.

Zeno made the running until Brown Jack took him on at the second last. Blaris could not go with him and it was Peace River who joined him in the air at the last. Once on the flat, however, Brown Jack had the better speed and won by one and a half lengths in a time eight seconds faster than the previous year. Another star had placed himself in the racing firmament.

Thanks partly to Brown Jack's participation, another big Cheltenham championship was up and running. But Brown Jack was not to be one of those who figured more than once on the Champion Hurdle honours board. His future lay elsewhere. Before sending him out on the track, Aubrey Hastings had asked champion jockey Steve Donoghue to watch his running and advise if Brown Jack might be worth running on the Flat. After Brown Jack's victory, Hastings came up to Donoghue and said 'Well?'

The jockey replied: 'Yes, he will win on the Flat – and I will ride him.'

How right he was. Brown Jack, who it is no exaggeration to say was one of the most popular horses of the last century, became a public institution, taking racing off the sports pages and into the news. He won at Royal Ascot for seven consecutive years and took the Queen Alexandra Stakes, at 2m 5f the longest Flat race in the calendar, on six consecutive occasions. Brown Jack also won an Ascot Stakes, a Goodwood Cup, a Doncaster Cup, an Ebor Handicap (under 9st 5lb) and a Chester Cup, proving himself one of the greatest stayers of all time. Steve Donoghue found him one of the most co-operative

People's champion Brown Jack with Steve Donoghue on board, circa 1928.

partners he ever had: 'I've only had to talk to him during a race for him to do exactly as I want.'

Why wasn't he a Gold Cup winner at Ascot too? The answer to that is that it is not only dress that determines where you may go and what you may do at Royal Ascot. Because he was a gelding, lacking the key elements required for a later life at stud, Brown Jack was barred from participation in the Gold Cup at Ascot.

Brown Jack, trained by Ivor Anthony after the death of Aubrey Hastings, was retired at the age of ten immediately after he had won the Queen Alexandra Stakes for the sixth and final time in 1934. The result and the announcement prompted some of the most emotional scenes ever witnessed on a British racecourse. Exclusive Royal Ascot may have been Brown Jack's most accustomed backcloth but he was truly the people's champion.

Career highlights:
1928: Champion Hurdle, Ascot Stakes
1929–1934: Queen Alexandra Stakes
1930: Goodwood Cup, Doncaster Cup
1931: Chester Cup, Ebor Handicap

46. SIR IVOR

Raymond Guest, an accomplished all-round sportsman and former US Navy commander and Senator, was an admirer of all things Irish who eventually became Ambassador to Dublin. Vincent O'Brien was a great admirer of US-bred horses and so the two were a natural pairing. They won their first Derby together with Larkspur in 1962, the year seven horses fell in the race, and in 1968 they repeated the feat with Sir Ivor.

Guest was a highly successful owner who saw his choc-
olate colours with pale blue hoops carried to victory in the
Cheltenham Gold Cup and Grand National by L'Escargot.
Like his trainer he was also a man who enjoyed a gamble, and after Sir Ivor had won the second race of his life
at the Curragh in 1967 Guest and the breeding expert
Abe Hewitt persuaded William Hill to let them have a
bet of £500 each way on the big colt at 100-1 to win the
next year's Derby. As Sir Ivor went on to win the National
Stakes in Ireland and then to hammer the best France
had to offer in the Grand Criterium at Longchamp, Hill
came bitterly to regret the price he had given them.

O'Brien that winter sent a group of young horses to
over-winter near Pisa in Italy. At one stage Sir Ivor developed an abscess in his foot and had to be put on the easy
list. Full of bounce when he started exercising again, he
got rid of his rider and was in danger of falling into a
deep dyke before he was recovered. Back at Ballydoyle he
proved an intelligent horse who started pulling up in his
gallops at the point where he had done so as a two-year-
old. O'Brien out-smarted him by extending the start of
the gallop to a point a couple of furlongs earlier.

Sir Ivor won his Guineas trial, though only narrowly,
in poor ground at Ascot and then beat the much-fancied
Petingo in the 2,000 Guineas, catching him in the Dip
and going away. After that William Hill tried everything
to get Guest to cancel his bet, even threatening to pub-
licise the details. But the bet remained in place and the
horse made it to Epsom even if his owner could not: he
was deputed that day as Ambassador to open the Kennedy
Arboretum in County Wexford. There the ceremony was
neglected for a while as the participants clustered around
a portable TV with the visibly trembling Ambassador to
watch the broadcast of the race. Amid the congratulations

afterwards he was asked about the wager and noted: 'Don't forget that Uncle Sam will take 77 per cent of the money.'

It was a relatively straightforward Derby that year and yet an electrifying spectacle. In a small field Sandy Barclay took Connaught ahead early in the straight trying to exploit his stamina and to expose any chink in Sir Ivor's stamina. He went five lengths clear and was still four lengths up a furlong out. The crowd thought it was all over. But Lester Piggott was confident in his mount's powers of acceleration: in a sustained burst he caught the St Paddy colt and went clear to win by a comfortable one and a half lengths. He called it the most exciting of all his nine Derbies and the Press were ecstatic about the quality of his and the horse's performance. An amazed Sandy Barclay said that the winner had gone past him as if he had just jumped into the race.

Sir Ivor, ridden by Lester Piggott, comes home to win the Derby, May 1968.

Surprisingly, Sir Ivor failed to win in his first four races after the Derby. Under Vincent O'Brien's agreement with Piggott it was Liam Ward who rode his horses in Ireland, and it was Piggott on Ribero (beaten 12 lengths by Connaught in his previous race) who beat Sir Ivor at the Curragh on a more galloping track that exposed his difficulty in truly getting a mile and a half.

Then came the Eclipse at Sandown. There Lester Piggott, back in Sir Ivor's saddle, reported that the horse had been jarred up by the firm ground in the Irish Derby and did not let himself go as he was beaten into third place by Barclay on Royal Palace.

O'Brien then went easy on Sir Ivor for his prep race in France for the Arc, with the result that he was beaten in the Prix Henry Delamarre. In the big race he simply did not have the stamina to make a fight of it with Vaguely Noble, an outstanding horse at the distance, and he was beaten three lengths.

Sir Ivor did confirm his quality, though, by winning the Champion Stakes at Newmarket and by taking the Washington D.C. International at Laurel Park from Czar Alexander and Fort Marcy – the first time a Derby winner had raced in America since 1923. Lester Piggott rated him the best of all his nine Derby winners, not just because of his remarkable acceleration but because of his professionalism: 'More than any horse I ever rode, Sir Ivor knew what he was supposed to do and always did his best to do it. In short, Sir Ivor knew how to race.'

Career highlights:
1967: Grand Criterium
1968: 2,000 Guineas, Derby, Champion Stakes, Washington
*   D.C. International*

45. COTTAGE RAKE

Cottage Rake has a double place in racing history. He makes the list with ease because he won three successive Cheltenham Gold Cups but he would deserve to be there anyway because it was his exploits that first alerted the wider racing world to the talents of Vincent O'Brien.

Vincent O'Brien's father Dan had been canny enough to win the Irish Cambridgeshire with Solford and Astrometer from a tiny yard at Churchtown, County Cork. But when he died in 1943 he left his son little more than the equine management skills he had implanted. Vincent rented the stable and gallops from his stepfather, one of those rare Irishmen not interested in racing, and took out a licence. That very first year his Dry Bob dead-heated for the Irish Cambridgeshire and his Good Days won the Cesarewitch.

Vincent's first top jumper was Cottage Rake, a son of the jumping sire Cottage who had the speed to win four Flat races. Cottage Rake's Cheltenham achievements would put O'Brien on the map, but it took a fair measure of good fortune before he got the chance to train him. Twice Cottage Rake was sold to would-be English owners and twice the deal was aborted because the vets who checked him out found fault with his wind.

O'Brien too was warned of a technical infirmity but his vet advised that at Cottage Rake's age he didn't think he would be affected by it. O'Brien called the only man he knew with any money, Frank Vickerman, and urged him to buy Cottage Rake. Vickerman did so, although he too was on the point of backing out until he discovered his deposit was non-recoverable. That autumn his young trainer won the Irish Cesarewitch with Cottage Rake and entered him for the Gold Cup.

Come March 1948 and there was the comparatively unknown Irish contender, a 10-1 shot ridden by Aubrey Brabazon, lining up for the big race alongside the 7-2 favourite Cool Customer, owned by Major 'Cuddy' Stirling Stuart (the first would-be buyer of Cottage Rake) and Dorothy Paget's Happy Home, ridden by Martin Molony.

Cool Customer fell at the first, the only fall of his career. Second time round Cottage Rake and Happy Home raced down from the top of the hill and over the last two fences in a thrilling duel. Martin Molony knew his inexperienced rival had speed from the last so he hurled his mount into the final fence in search of a massive jump that might hustle Cottage Rake into a mistake or leave him flat-footed. Aubrey Brabazon, confident of his mount's finishing speed, needed to play his

Cottage Rake, ridden by Aubrey Brabazon, at the Cheltenham Gold Cup, March 1948.

card late, although that could be a risky proposition on Cheltenham's rising run-in. Both employed the right tactics, but although Cottage Rake did not land particularly smoothly his rider simply gave him a few strides to collect himself and then pressed the pedal. Never touched with the whip, he sprinted up the hill past Happy Home to win by a length and a half.

Brabazon said later: 'The Rake had such speed that I could afford to ease him up at the last three fences and still pass Miss Paget's good horse halfway up the final hill.' Asked later in his career about the best race he had ridden, Molony did not point to a victory. Instead he instanced that Gold Cup duel with Cottage Rake and the huge, courageous jump he inspired from Happy Home at the last, gaining about a length and a half in the air.

There were no big viewing screens in those days and Vincent O'Brien, standing down at the last fence, had no idea which horse had won until he saw Aubrey Brabazon touching his cap to acknowledge the cheers of the crowd as they came back to the winners' enclosure.

It was a remarkably similar story in the 1949 Gold Cup, delayed until April after racing was frosted off in March. That was a lucky break for Cottage Rake who had been coughing and who thus gained extra recovery time. This time it was Cool Customer who took on Ireland's hope and who led him down from the top of the hill and over the last. It was a real battle but again 'the Brab' was only waiting to play the speed card and went past his rival on the run-in to win by two lengths.

The next winter Lord Bicester's Finnure, receiving 11lb, beat Cottage Rake in the King George VI Chase at Kempton Park, raising English hopes of defeating him at Cheltenham. But in March 1950 it was the same old story, summed up in the Irish jingle:

Aubrey's up, the money's down
The frightened bookies quake
Come on, my lads, and give a cheer
Begod, 'tis Cottage Rake

Only three other English chasers joined Finnure in taking on the two-time champion and this time the result was clear a long way out. Aubrey Brabazon gave Cottage Rake a slap and caught his fellow riders napping with a tactical burst of speed coming down the hill the second time. In no time he was half a dozen lengths clear and the others never looked like making up the deficit. In the end he won what was to be his last Gold Cup by ten lengths.

Career highlights:
1947: Irish Cesarewitch
1948, 1949, 1950: Cheltenham Gold Cup

44. EASTER HERO

Truly great politicians are those who 'change the weather', who force parties other than their own to alter their policies. Easter Hero was a horse who in the 1920s began to change people's notions about what made a good steeplechaser. Until his arrival chasers had mostly been burly, large-framed animals built for endurance rather than speed. Easter Hero was the first of a new kind of steeplechaser – lighter-framed, agile and athletic.

An elegant chestnut gelding by the well-known jumping sire My Prince, Easter Hero had class stamped all over him. His style was impetuous, his jumping was spectacularly bold, he had character and he never seemed to be far from a drama. He was what journalists call 'good copy'.

At the age of seven after an indifferent early career that included a win at Manchester, Easter Hero, bred near Dublin, was sold for £500 by his English owner, a Mr Bartholomew, to Frank Barbour, a businessman and trainer who was Master of the West Meath Foxhounds in Ireland. Barbour moved the next year to Wiltshire and during the 1927–28 season he transformed the former erratic jumper. Although Easter Hero was still seen by some traditionally-minded pundits as 'lacking in substance', Barbour won five chases with him, including two at Aintree.

Those looking forward to his appearance at the 1928 Gold Cup were disappointed. Before the meeting opened Easter Hero was purchased by a mystery buyer, who wanted him trained for the Grand National and had him pulled out of the Cheltenham Festival. The new owner was a millionaire Belgian financier called Captain 'Low' Lowenstein, who paid Barbour £7,000 for the horse with a contingency of £3,000 should he win a Grand National.

In that year's Grand National Easter Hero, carrying a massive 12st 7lb, was leading the field in imperious style when he reached the open ditch at the Canal Turn. Taking off much too soon, he landed on top of the fence, straddling it and, in his struggles to free himself, baulking many of the other runners. It caused a massive pile-up like that in 1967 when the outsider Foinavon won. Only nine horses escaped the 1928 melee, only two reached the last fence and when Billy Barton fell there the race was left at the mercy of the 100-1 outsider Tipperary Tim.

A few months later Lowenstein disappeared from his private plane over the North Sea, with no trace ever found. Easter Hero was bought by the American millionaire Mr J.H. 'Jock' Whitney, who transferred him to Jack

Anthony's yard at Letcombe Regis to be prepared for the next year's Gold Cup.

Whitney, once listed as one of the ten richest men in the world, had been an outstanding polo player and he and his sister ran his mother's Greentree Stables.

The 1928–29 winter was a terrible one in Britain. Continued frost and snow saw the 1929 Festival delayed for a week. Partly thanks to the weather, Easter Hero's run-up to the Gold Cup consisted of victories in four hurdle races in each of which he was partnered by George Duller. In that year's race, ridden by Dick Rees, Easter Hero dominated his field with his high cruising speed and swift fencing. The 7-4 chance was well clear after the first circuit and when most in the stands expected him

Easter Hero, ridden by Tommy Cullinan, after winning the Cheltenham Gold Cup, March 1930.

to stop after showing such pace he simply flew again and won on the bridle 20 lengths clear of Lloydie.

Just ten days later Easter Hero ran for a second time in the Grand National. In what was acknowledged as one of the bravest efforts ever seen in the race, he finished second of the 66 runners. With the shoe on his near fore twisted, broken and hanging loose all the way from Valentines, Easter Hero was in no condition to resist the late surge by Gregalach who passed him to win by six lengths.

Easter Hero won his second Cheltenham Gold Cup in 1930, again as the favourite. Because his regular partner Dick Rees had been claimed for Gib, Easter Hero was ridden by Tommy Cullinan. Easter Hero gave the crowds a shock by diving at the first fence and then making a severe blunder at the second. Cullinan managed to steady him and by the end of the first circuit he led by ten lengths. Gib seemed to struggle to keep up with Easter Hero's cruising speed down the back but then drew level at the top of the hill. They came to the second last fence together but Gib, perhaps feeling the pressure by then, hit it and toppled over, leaving Easter Hero to stroll home once again by 20 lengths.

Easter Hero had injured himself and could not run at Aintree in 1930. He then developed tendon trouble and missed most of the rest of the year. The 1931 Cheltenham Festival was lost to the weather. In his preparations for that year's Grand National Easter Hero won three races and was made favourite for the Aintree spectacular but he was knocked over at Becher's second time around. He was then pulled out the very next day to contest the two-mile Champion Chase. By modern standards that is incredible. It is a bit like asking a human athlete to compete in the 1,500 metres and the 400 metres on successive days, but Easter Hero still managed a dead heat with Coup de Chateau. His sporting owner took that as a sign of declining powers and let him end on that winning note. He was shipped over to the USA and spent the rest of his days hunting with his owner over the Virginia countryside.

Career highlights:
1929: Cheltenham Gold Cup
1930: Cheltenham Gold Cup
1931: Aintree Champion Chase

43. OUIJA BOARD

If Steve Cauthen was known as the Six Million Dollar Kid after a lucrative teenage season on the US tracks, Ouija Board was the six million dollar filly – that was the sum she amassed in her four-season international career during which she won ten of her 22 races, seven of them Group Ones.

Racing in the distinctive colours of Edward Stanley, the 19th Earl of Derby – black, white cap and a single 'lucky' white button below the collar – Ouija Board was trained at Newmarket by Ed Dunlop but she raced in seven countries and was as popular in the USA as she was with the crowds at home. Blessed with searing powers of acceleration and nurtured by a popular, approachable team who wore their hearts on their racing sleeves, she gave the whole British racing scene a lift.

Winning once in her three outings as a juvenile in 2003, the Cape Cross filly – remarkably, given the record of his forebears, the only horse the Earl of Derby had in training – really came good at three. She won the Pretty Polly Stakes by six lengths and then went straight to

Epsom for the Oaks where she proved all too good for Aidan O'Brien's All Too Beautiful, winning the Classic by seven lengths in the hands of Kieren Fallon. Surprisingly, it was the first Classic winner for the Derby family since Watling Street's wartime Derby in 1942. So easily was Ouija Board going during the race that Fallon checked her forward momentum and tucked her in again three furlongs out before going clear. He never had to make use of his whip.

Supplemented for the race for 40,000 euros, Ouija Board then won the Irish Oaks. It looked as though Kieren Fallon had had to work harder for that victory by a lesser distance but he reported that the filly was incredible. She just went to sleep then woke up and accelerated when asked.

There was no point aiming any lower than the Arc with such a classy filly, possessed of a real turn of foot, but Ouija Board wasn't always an easy ride with her tendency to drop herself out in the early stages, and at Longchamp, ridden for the first time by Johnny Murtagh, she got boxed in. By the time he had extricated her it was too late and although Ouija Board was flying at the finish she was third behind Bago and Cherry Mix.

Ouija Board ended her magnificent season by travelling to Lone Star Park in Texas for the Filly and Mare Turf, a trip finally determined when her doubting owner, on crutches after a tennis injury, had them removed by his wife Cazzy who refused to give them back until he agreed to go to the Breeders' Cup!

She had pushed in the right direction. In the Breeders' Cup race Ouija Board, reunited with Kieren Fallon, was always in touch, moved fourth at halfway and took the lead a furlong out to win smoothly. It prompted the Americans to accord her the prestigious Eclipse Award

Ouija Board, ridden by Kieren Fallon, wins the Oaks at Epsom,
June 2004.

for Outstanding Female Turf Horse, an honour that she
was to repeat in 2006.

Ouija Board's reappearance in 2005 was delayed until
Royal Ascot in June, that year held at York. She lost a shoe
and finished tailed off behind Azamour in the Prince of
Wales Stakes and had a summer of problems with shin
splints, a stress fracture, a sore throat and coughing, but
they finally managed to get a prep race into her before
another Breeders' Cup, when she won the Princess Royal
Stakes at Newmarket in September. From there she was
US-bound once more for the Breeders' Cup, this time
ridden by the American ace Jerry Bailey, who got off
Intercontinental to ride her at Belmont Park.

The story of the race was a simple one. Intercontinental
set off in front and stayed there. By the time the other
jockeys tried to close the gap it was too late. Ouija Board,
on softer ground than was ideal for her and with a difficult

outside draw, moved into third and then into second up the straight but was beaten one and a quarter lengths.

Because the long list of injury niggles had resulted in a comparatively light season she then contested both the Japan Cup and the Hong Kong Vase. In Japan Ouija Board was a close up fifth after being bumped in the final stages, but with Fallon back on board she won the Hong Kong Vase by two and a half lengths in extraordinary style. Watchers including her owner gasped in amazement as he had her at the back of the field in a slow-run race with a wall of horses ahead. But his concern had been to settle her. Having done so, Fallon then found a gap and scorched through with Ouija Board going clear to win by two and three quarter lengths. It was, said Lord Derby, a ride of pure genius.

That was not how he and her trainer felt about Fallon's riding of Ouija Board in the Sheema Classic in Dubai where she started her 2006 season. When she failed to figure in the shake-up, Fallon, riding his first race for three months and having arrived too late for an earlier mount, blamed the fireworks preceding the race, but trainer and owner reported that she hadn't turned a hair at those.

Back at Sha Tin in Hong Kong for the Queen Elizabeth II Cup in April it was Frankie Dettori who was riding. Ouija Board was beaten a head and a short head in a tight finish after traffic problems down the back straight. At Epsom in June she was beaten in the 2005 Coronation Cup by Shirocco and then won a really hot race for the Prince of Wales Stakes at Ascot contested by Electrocutionist, David Junior, Notnowcato, Ace and Manduro. With Olivier Peslier riding Ouija Board won by half a length from Electrocutionist and went on to the Eclipse at Sandown, where she had another Continental rider in the shape of Christophe Soumillon, the eighth pilot she encountered in her career.

On a tricky course for those without regular experience Soumillon rode a rare stinker, never putting the mare in the right place to challenge. She finished with cuts and bruises and only fifth place. But Ouija Board then showed her toughness as well as her class in one of the best races I have ever seen. In the Nassau Stakes at Goodwood she and Alexander Goldrun, each of them with five Group One victories on their CVs, battled nose-to-nose for the last two furlongs, before Ouija Board and Frankie Dettori got the verdict in the tightest of photo-finishes.

The amazing mare battled fiercely again on her next outing in the Irish Champion Stakes at Leopardstown. This time with Jamie Spencer up she passed Dylan Thomas, ridden for Coolmore by Kieren Fallon, a furlong out but Fallon forced the colt past her again to win by a neck. After that came a third and final Breeders' Cup trip to America, this time to Churchill Downs in Kentucky. Frankie Dettori was back on board Ouija Board for the Filly and Mare Turf. She was a hot favourite and though they appeared boxed in three furlongs out, Frankie extricated her and she sprinted clear of the field to win both the race and another Eclipse award. Ouija Board was the first British horse ever to win a Breeders' Cup twice.

She went on from there to Japan to finish third in the Japan Cup behind Deep Impact and was to have concluded her career with one more effort in the Hong Kong Vase. Victory would have seen her draw level with Allez France as the winner of eight Group Ones, and even second place would have made her the highest stakes winner in British racing history, but Ouija Board suffered a slight soft tissue injury on the eve of the race and her retirement was announced. To give a glimpse of what is involved in the life of a modern superstar racehorse, she had travelled 74,000 miles by air in 26 different flights.

Career highlights:
2004: Epsom Oaks, Irish Oaks, Breeders' Cup Filly and Mare Turf
2005: Princess Royal Stakes, Hong Kong Vase
2006: Prince of Wales Stakes, Nassau Stakes, Breeders' Cup Filly and Mare Turf

42. BURROUGH HILL LAD

It would be unthinkable amid a list of the 100 greatest horses not to include one of Jenny Pitman's chasers – not least because Jenny, with whom I sometimes find myself sharing racing platforms, would never let me forget it. The first woman to win either big race, Jenny trained two Grand National winners in Corbiere and Royal Athlete and two Cheltenham Gold Cup winners in Burrough Hill Lad and Garrison Savannah. But it is Burrough Hill Lad, whose career was sadly curtailed by injury, who stands out in terms of sheer quality.

Known in the yard as 'Buzby', Burrough Hill Lad won at Liverpool as a novice and in the 1983–84 season came home first in all five races he contested. They included the Welsh Grand National at Chepstow and the Gainsborough Chase. Come Gold Cup day in 1984 he was second favourite to the talented and experienced Wayward Lad.

John Francome, a regular partner of Burrough Hill Lad, was riding Brown Chamberlin out of loyalty to Fred Winter and he set a sharp gallop in the early stages of a truly run race. Wayward Lad failed to show his usual sparkle and three out Brown Chamberlin, Burrough Hill Lad

Burrough Hill Lad, ridden by John Francome, being led into
the winners' enclosure at the Hennessy Gold Cup, Newbury,
November 1984.

and Drumlargan drew clear of the rest. Brown Chamberlin
had looked to be coming down the hill best but northern jockey Phil Tuck on Burrough Hill Lad had plenty
of horse under him. As he surged up to the leader at the
second last Brown Chamberlin showed the strain by diving right. Burrough Hill Lad flew the last and roared up

the finishing slope to win by three lengths. Within a year of becoming the first woman to train a Grand National winner Jenny Pitman had repeated the feat with the Gold Cup.

A relentless galloper and a strong individual, the near-black Burrough Hill Lad will probably be remembered as much for his victory that autumn in the Hennessy Gold Cup in which he carried the top weight of 12 stone. Among those he was giving significant weight concessions to were the Irish-trained Drumlargan, the previous year's runner-up Gaye Chance, Canny Danny whom Jimmy Fitzgerald had trained to win the Sun Alliance Chase at Cheltenham, and Everett, representing Fulke Walwyn, who had trained seven Hennessy winners. Everett's jumping didn't stand the test, Drumlargan never really showed and by the third last the chief contenders, all in line, were Canny Danny, Gaye Chance and Phil The Fluter. It was time for Burrough Hill Lad to assert and at that point Francome unleashed his power. He landed full of momentum and drove clear in a few strides. The big, bold chaser increased his margin at the second last and flew the final fence in style to be applauded all the way to the line. Canny Danny made a bit back on the run-in but was vanquished by four lengths with Gaye Chance another 20 in arrears. It was a measure of Burrough Hill Lad's stature that the only other Gold Cup winners to have taken the Hennessy were Mill House and Arkle.

But if you need stamina in abundance to win the Welsh National and courage to fight off a field of top handicappers in the Hennessy you certainly don't win the King George VI Chase at Kempton without a touch of real class, and that is where Burrough Hill Lad followed up. He took the winter classic in 1984 beating Combs Ditch and Wayward Lad. He missed the 1985 Gold Cup with an injury but was out again in 1985–86 to win the Gainsborough Chase at Sandown for the third time in a row. His leg problems, however, forced Burrough Hill Lad also to miss the 1986 Gold Cup in which many reckoned he would have had the beating of the victorious Dawn Run and Wayward Lad.

In the end the horse's catalogue of injuries – Jenny Pitman once declared: 'He's had as many operations as Joan Collins and as many men working on him' – prevented her star chaser from realising his full potential. Nevertheless, John Randall and Tony Morris asserted in their *A Century of Champions*, covering racing up to 2000, that the three greatest steeplechasers since Arkle were Captain Christy, Desert Orchid and Burrough Hill Lad.

Career highlights:
1984: Welsh Grand National, Cheltenham Gold Cup, Hennessy Gold Cup, King George VI Chase

41. GRUNDY

Peter Walwyn and his wife Bonk have been much-loved figures in the life of the racing village of Lambourn, vital contributors to its facilities and esprit de corps. There was much joy therefore when in 1975 Peter became one of the surprisingly few Lambourn trainers to win a Derby in modern times with the handsome Grundy.

A dark chestnut with a flaxen mane and tail whose natural swagger as a yearling at the Overbury Stud had impressed his trainer before owner Carlo Vittadini acquired him at the sales, Grundy soon acquired a CV to match his looks. In 1974 he proved himself the best two-year-old in England. First time out he won the

Granville Stakes at Ascot the day Dahlia won her second King George: he was to tangle with her later. He then 'came home bouncing' after winning the Sirenia Stakes at Kempton. Grundy won the seven-furlong Champagne Stakes at Doncaster and demolished his competitors in the Dewhurst Stakes, coming six lengths clear of the Middle Park winner Steel Heart despite the soft going, which would not have suited such a classic mover. He went into the winter as the favourite for the next year's Classics.

In March 1975, however, there was a scary moment for his trainer. Grundy was led out of the covered ride at Seven Barrows with blood streaming down his face. Another horse, Corby, had lashed out with his hind legs and caught Grundy with a clear imprint of his shoe just two inches from his eye. Grundy recovered quickly (as a foal he had shown his robust nature by recovering swiftly from the 100 stiches needed in his stomach after he straddled a barbed wire fence) but it held up his work. Probably because of that interruption Grundy was beaten on his seasonal debut in dire conditions in the Greenham.

Hopes were still high for the 2,000 Guineas but over the winter Henry Cecil had acquired the leading Italian two-year-old Bolkonski and at Newmarket his 33-1 shot finished faster than Grundy to push him into second place in the first Classic by half a length. Walwyn believed it had not helped Grundy that to circumvent the actions of striking stable lads the Guineas was started by flag that year from a point that shortened the course by 70 yards.

A consolation prize was swiftly collected in the shape of the Irish 2,000 Guineas a fortnight later over a stiffer course and then it was on to Epsom. Some had questioned Grundy's staying ability but in the Derby he settled well behind a fast pace and rounding the turn was looking all over the winner behind Anne's Pretender. A furlong and a half out he quickly went clear, erasing all fears about his ability to stay, and he finished three lengths clear of Nobiliary with Hunza Dancer another seven lengths away in third.

On the Sunday after the Derby Walwyn got a shock. Carlo Vittadini's agent told him on a plane back from Paris, where Patch had finished a head second in the French Derby and Corby (the colt who might have ended Grundy's career) had won the Prix du Lys, that Grundy had been sold to the National Stud for a million dollars, with Vittadini keeping 25 per cent. It had been agreed, he said, that the colt would run no more than four more races and these would not include the Prix de l'Arc de Triomphe.

Grundy (*right*), ridden by Pat Eddery, wins the King George VI and Queen Elizabeth Stakes ahead of Bustino in 'the race of the century', Ascot, July 1975.

A disgruntled Walwyn secured Vittadini's agreement to run him in the Irish Derby and Grundy scored an easy success at the Curragh, quickening up at the distance to win by two and a half lengths from the unbeaten King Pellinore. His next race of course was the wonderful King George VI and Queen Elizabeth Stakes that year, often dubbed 'the race of the century'. The Ascot showpiece has since 1951 provided Europe's top horses with a crucial midsummer championship event for all ages and many memorable races, but Grundy's clash with the year-older Bustino in 1975 remains the Big One, the race that everybody kicks themselves for missing if they didn't see it.

When Sean Magee asked 30 top jockeys to describe 'The Race of my Life' for his book of that title it is significant that Joe Mercer, who rode Bustino into second, chose the same race as Pat Eddery, who won it on Grundy. If not *the* race of the century it was certainly one of the races of them.

Owned by Lady Beaverbrook and trained by Dick Hern, the stoutly-bred Bustino had won the St Leger in 1974, having been somewhat run off his legs early on in the Derby. But he was no slouch over 12 furlongs. On his return to action in 1975 Bustino smashed the course record for a mile and a half at Epsom.

Grundy, the horse with the film star looks and the CV to match, was the horse to beat at Ascot and if there was a way to beat him, Hern had reckoned, then it was to test Grundy's stamina to the limit: Bustino was therefore provided with not just one but two pacemakers, Highest and Kinglet.

Bustino broke so well that he was momentarily in front, but the pacemakers in the green and brown colours soon settled into their role. So fast was the pace they set that both of them bowed out before the straight, forcing

Joe Mercer on Bustino to go to the front himself before he had wanted to.

One part of the plan had worked. Grundy had had no chance to snatch a breather and he was still four lengths adrift of Bustino. Star Appeal had been dropped and the race was already between the two of them. With Bustino seemingly beginning to feel the strain out in front, Eddery asked for more and moved Grundy up to him. But there was no capitulation, only a renewed surge from Mercer and Bustino. Eddery and Grundy matched it. At the furlong pole Grundy's nose inched in front for the first time, but Bustino came back to edge it by a nostril again.

Grundy pushed back once more and this time inch by inch he gained the advantage. It was neck-and-neck, eyeball-to-eyeball, every sinew striving with the crowd on their feet.

As Mercer gave Bustino a smack his mount's tongue came out and he changed his legs but he kept on battling. Grundy edged ahead. Bustino responded and closed a few inches but then in the last 50 yards it was over and Grundy was clear by half a length. Grundy had not only won, he had been pushed by Bustino to break the course record by a full two and a half seconds. It was a measure of their intense contest that even the third horse home, the great racemare Dahlia, had broken the old record five lengths behind Bustino.

For a minute the two principals seemed almost too shattered to walk to the winners' enclosure. The two brave horses had fought each other almost literally to a standstill. Both had played their part in an enthralling spectacle. Perhaps, though, they had played it too well. Grundy produced nothing in his next race and Bustino broke down without getting to the racecourse again.

They always knew how to celebrate at Seven Barrows,

and the poolside party went on until the early hours. Perhaps Grundy had joined in: unusually he stood still long enough on the Monday for the artist Peter Biegel to paint his portrait.

Grundy came out of most of his races very well but the titanic struggle at Ascot had obviously taken more out of him than was appreciated at the time. He ran next in the Benson and Hedges at York but could finish only fourth and after that the decision was taken to retire him there and then.

Career highlights:
1974: Champagne Stakes, Dewhurst Stakes
1975: Irish 2,000 Guineas, Derby, Irish Derby, King George VI
*   and Queen Elizabeth Stakes*

40. FANTASTIC LIGHT

It is not just what you win but whom you compete with that matters, and Fantastic Light owes his position in racing history partly to the fact that in his two exciting duels with the impeccably-bred Galileo the score came out at 1-1. Trained first by Sir Michael Stoute for Maktoum al-Maktoum and then by Saeed bin Suroor for Godolphin, Fantastic Light won Group One or Grade One races in five of the six countries where he raced. Twice he won the Emirates World Series and in 2001 he was named both United States Champion Male Turf Horse and European Horse of the Year.

A bay horse with a white blaze and three white feet, Fantastic Light never bothered with a maiden, starting his career by taking a couple of minor stakes races at Sandown Park in August and September 1998. He then finished last of three in a Listed race at Goodwood.

At three in 1999 he won the Sandown Classic Trial but then failed in the Lingfield Derby Trial over a mile and a half. He ran second at Ascot in the ten-furlong Prince of Wales Stakes and was third in the Eclipse back at Sandown behind Compton Admiral. Later in the summer things improved as he won the Group Two Great Voltigeur Stakes at York and the Arc trial at Newbury. However, he appeared to be flying too high when only 11th of the 12 who finished behind Montjeu in that year's Prix de l'Arc de Triomphe.

We had, though, only enjoyed the hors d'oeuvre. Fantastic Light was continuing to improve, as was demonstrated by his first run as a four-year-old in March 2000. On his last appearance trained by Michael Stoute and ridden by Kieren Fallon he won the Dubai Sheema Classic on World Cup night. His summer campaign in Britain

Fantastic Light and Frankie Dettori win the Prince of Wales Stakes from Kalanisi and Kieren Fallon at Royal Ascot, June 2001.

that year had its frustrations. Fantastic Light was second to Daliapour in the Coronation Cup and though he beat her in the King George he was no match for Montjeu and finished second again.

But Fantastic Light, who had also finished fifth behind Giant's Causeway in the Eclipse, enjoyed greater success when winning the Man o' War Stakes at Belmont Park in the USA, his first Grade one. In the Breeders' Cup he was only fifth behind Kalanisi but there were excuses: Frankie Dettori was twice baulked when trying to find room to challenge. Fantastic Light was then switched to the Eastern circuit, finishing third in the Japan Cup and running out a convincing winner of the Hong Kong Cup.

All that too could be called a prelude. The year 2001, when Fantastic Light was a five-year-old, was his best season. In March he was beaten just a nose in the Dubai Sheema Classic and from there he went to Ireland to win the Tattersalls Gold Cup, beating Kalanisi by a neck with Golden Snake third. He beat Kalanisi again by a comfortable two and a half lengths in the Prince of Wales Stakes at Ascot after a decisive injection of speed.

Suddenly connections were saying they had no fears about taking on the impressive Derby winner Galileo. The pair met in the King George with the crowd seeing it as an intriguing clash between the two racing superpowers of Ballydoyle/Coolmore (Galileo) and Godolphin (Fantastic Light).

Galileo took the lead in the straight then Dettori moved out to challenge Mick Kinane. The pair raced side by side for 50 yards but then Galileo pulled ahead to win by two lengths. Another highly anticipated clash between the two took place in the Irish Champion Stakes at Leopardstown over two furlongs less. This time Fantastic Light went past a Ballydoyle pacemaker to lead two furlongs out. Mick Kinane immediately brought Galileo to challenge and the two raced together all the way to the line. At one point Galileo edged ahead but then Fantastic Light fought back and held his advantage to win by a head. The racing world hoped for a third clash, a decider, in that year's Breeders' Cup at Belmont Park, but in the end, sadly, they went for different races.

Fantastic Light ran in the Breeders' Cup Turf. He made his challenge in the straight and ran on well to beat off the St Leger winner Milan in a new course record, the rest of the field five lengths behind them. It was a fine end to his career. He had won four of his six races that season: the Tattersalls Gold Cup, the Prince of Wales Stakes, the Irish Champion Stakes and the Breeders' Cup Turf and, crucially, the score stayed at evens with the younger Galileo.

Career highlights:
2000: Dubai Sheema Classic, Man o' War Stakes, Hong Kong
Cup
2001: Tattersalls Gold Cup, Prince of Wales Stakes, Irish
Champion Stakes, Breeders' Cup Turf

39. MILL HOUSE

Mill House was 'The Big Horse' who became the underdog and who was loved just as much in the shadow of the great Arkle as he was for his own early triumphs. Had Mill House not been born in the same year as Arkle he too would have racked up a series of Cheltenham Gold Cups. As it was, he was demoralisingly beaten time and time again by the Irish champion and yet he came back for one glorious crowd-rousing finale at Sandown Park.

Trainer Fulke Walwyn's dream that the great big bay might be another Golden Miller began well. He went to the start for the 1963 Gold Cup as a magnificent specimen, nearly 17 hands and yet in no way ungainly or obviously overgrown. Mill House had the muscle to go with his powerful frame, an economical jumping style that saw him flick over his fences as if they were made of matchsticks and a sympathetic pilot in Willie Robinson.

That year, with the likes of Fortria in his wake, Mill House powered down the hill, cleared the last imperiously and was applauded up to the finish as he won by 12 lengths. Cheltenham was his and looked like being so for years. But at that same meeting Arkle had won the Broadway Chase and life was never to be quite the same again for Mill House.

The key clash came in the Cheltenham Gold Cup of 1964. Back in November the giant champion had given Arkle 5lb and beaten him by eight lengths in the Hennessy Gold Cup, although on that occasion Arkle had slipped badly after one fence. Since then Mill House had won a King George VI Chase at Kempton and as they paraded for the Gold Cup after a brief snow flurry it was 'The Big Horse', as Fulke Walwyn liked to call him, who loped around the parade ring as the 13-8 on favourite. His leaner Irish rival was at 7-4 and the rest were at 20-1 or more.

Willie Robinson, full of confidence, took Mill House straight into the lead, powering over his fences, ready to test Ireland's hope all the way. At first Arkle seemed to have a little trouble staying with him, but then he too settled into a rhythm, fencing economically. Mill House had set a good gallop, but as they went out on the second circuit English binoculars were lowered for nervous exchanges about why their fellow hadn't shaken him off yet.

Mill House, ridden by Willie Robinson, heads to victory in
the Hennessy Gold Cup at Newbury, November 1963.

Up the hill, round the turn and down the hill they
came, and as they jumped the second last and rounded
the bend into the straight Arkle moved upsides, challenging Mill House to show what he was made of. Willie
Robinson went for his whip and dropped it, but it
wouldn't have made any difference if he'd had a golden
wand. To ecstatic Irish cheers Arkle and Pat Taaffe were
off and away, over the last and up to the finishing line five
lengths clear. He had not just beaten Mill House, he had
crushed him. Fulke Walwyn declared: 'I can still hardly
believe that any horse living could have done what Arkle
did to Mill House.'

Mill House, who suffered from back problems, never
beat his Irish rival again. In the 1964 Hennessy Arkle gave
him 3lb and beat him 28 lengths into fourth. In their final

head-to-head in the Gallaher Gold Cup at Sandown Arkle gave Mill House 16lb and beat him by 24 lengths. But that didn't mean his career came to nothing. In those days champions like Arkle and Mill House ran in the big handicaps too. After Arkle's first Cheltenham Gold Cup victory over his rival in 1964 Mill House was beaten only three lengths in the Whitbread Gold Cup at Sandown by the useful chaser Dormant, to whom he was giving 32lb. That wasn't the performance of a horse whose spirit had been crushed, but Arkle was something else.

In 1965 Mill House took him on once more in the Gold Cup at Cheltenham but this time the Irish horse almost played with him, moving away in the later stages and winning by 20 lengths. A fall or two and an injury or two dotted Mill House's career after that, but he did win 15 of his 30 races over fences and there was a glorious-heart-warming finale for all his fans in the 1967 Whitbread Gold Cup at Sandown Park.

David Nicholson, who rode him that day, was worried about Mill House lasting a trip that was beyond his best distance but found the old horse in imperious long-striding mood, measuring his fences beautifully: 'I let him have his way and settled down to enjoy the most exhilarating ride of my life.' At the business end of the race Mill House pinged the Pond fence and took the second last well enough. But then suddenly at the last the old champion faltered and his weariness began to show. Kapeno was making up ground fast behind him but with tremendous courage The Big Horse dug to the very depths to hang on and win by a length and a half. They pulled up with the horse out on his feet, but as David Nicholson recorded, the applause as they headed back up the Rhododendron Walk to the winners' enclosure somehow drained the tiredness from Mill House's huge frame:

'By the time he entered the winners' enclosure he was the king being greeted by his adoring public. The reception that day was fantastic – certainly the best I've ever known as a jockey – and made it the most emotional moment of my riding life.'

Many a stiff upper lip wobbled that day and Sandown has heard few greater ovations for anything on four legs.

Career highlights:
1963: Cheltenham Gold Cup, Hennessy Gold Cup,
* King George VI Chase*
1967: Whitbread Gold Cup

38. RHEINGOLD

The greatest triumph of Barry Hills's remarkable career was winning the Prix de l'Arc de Triomphe with Rheingold. The only ambition Barry never realised was winning the Derby, and of the four horses he trained to be second in the big race Rheingold was the one who brought him closest to achieving that ambition. Rheingold went down by the width of a nostril to the Lester Piggott-ridden Roberto in the closest finish to the race since the 1884 dead-heat.

Arguments will rage for ever as to whether Rheingold's jockey Ernie Johnson should have gone for his whip, risking a disqualification if his hanging mount had veered further, or whether he was right to have invested everything in keeping straight and praying for the winning post to come before Lester got to him.

When I was writing his biography Barry told me: 'Piggott always said Ernie Johnson should have given Rheingold a couple of good smacks rather than try to keep straight and won the race and then argue it out in the Stewards' Room. In other words he should have made sure of winning the race first and argued about it afterwards.' But might he not have lost it then in the Stewards' Room? 'Of course. Especially in those days. They don't sling them out as easy these days.'

Ernie Johnson says of Rheingold: 'He was basically a horse that was never made for Epsom. He was a big, leggy type of horse, he wasn't an Epsom horse.'

Rheingold was owned first by Henry Zeisel, a former leader of the Vienna Philharmonic Orchestra. Then a nightclub owner operating a cash economy, he would arrive at the Hills yard to pay his bills with carrier bags stuffed full of fivers. Just before the Derby he sold 80 per cent of the colt to a syndicate.

Rheingold had made a winning racecourse debut at Newcastle in August 1971, landing a stable coup. He was

Rheingold (*left*), ridden by Ernie Johnson, is pipped to the post by Lester Piggott on Roberto in the Derby, June 1972.

second to Crowned Prince both in the Champagne Stakes and the Dewhurst but ran down the field in the Observer Gold Cup (now the Racing Post Trophy). As a three-year-old he ran poorly in the Blue Riband Trial at Epsom but then began improving by leaps and bounds, winning the Dante.

After the Derby, with French rider Yves Saint Martin substituted for the luckless Johnson, Rheingold hacked up next time out in the Grand Prix de Saint-Cloud. 'He was a much better horse that day', says his trainer. Rheingold was also a horse with a sense of his own importance. He was fed first in the yard because if he wasn't he would flick the door with his foot, making a noise until his grub arrived.

After the Paris success Rheingold ran in eight more races and won five of them. His only bogey was the Benson and Hedges at York, for which he twice started favourite and in which he was twice beaten. Before the end of his three-year-old season he was injured and it was a huge relief to his owners when he came out as a four-year-old in the John Porter Stakes at Newbury and won in emphatic style. Rheingold then won the Prix Ganay in France and the Hardwicke Stakes before returning to France to collect a second Grand Prix de Saint-Cloud.

He seemed to have lost his sparkle when beaten by Arc rival Dahlia in the 1973 King George VI and Queen Elizabeth Stakes at Ascot, and he looked a Longchamp no-hoper when struggling home in third place at York in August. But Hills took the horse back to Lambourn and rekindled Rheingold's enthusiasm with a meticulous Arc preparation.

Ten days before Rheingold's big race, when Lester Piggott came down to partner the horse in a gallop, his trainer was content his work programme and psychology had succeeded. 'Rheingold showed me then that not only was he as good as ever, he was actually better. It was then that I knew we could win the Arc.' He had another £1,000 on at 12-1.

At Longchamp Rheingold was in the first half dozen throughout the Arc. Lester took him to the front soon after rounding the home turn to lay down his challenge. Allez France went with him as the pair left the rest of the 25-strong field for dead, and in the end Lester drove home two and a half lengths clear of Yves Saint Martin on the classy local favourite with the previous year's French Derby winner Hard to Beat third. Says Barry: 'Rheingold beat Allez France nearly three lengths and Allez France won the race the next year. On that particular day I don't think much would have beaten him, not in my lifetime. I think he would have been up to the great Sea-Bird that day – he wouldn't have been far behind him anyway.'

Career highlights:
1972: Dante Stakes, Grand Prix de Saint-Cloud
1973: John Porter Stakes, Prix Ganay, Hardwicke Stakes, Grand
Prix de Saint-Cloud, Prix de l'Arc de Triomphe

37. DENMAN

Was there ever a jumper who pulled more potently on the jumping public's heartstrings in the past decade than Kauto Star? If there was, it came in the huge shape of the horse who occupied the next box to Kauto in Paul Nicholls' Ditcheat yard, the mighty Denman.

Denman didn't win as many Gold Cups as Kauto Star. He never won a King George VI Chase. But 'The Tank' , as he was affectionately labelled by his one-time part-owner

Harry Findlay, did win a Gold Cup and he won it by remorselessly destroying a top-class field including Kauto Star. He twice carried massive weights to startling success in the Hennessy Gold Cup Handicap. He won 13 of his first 14 races, he earned well over a million pounds in prize money, and in six races at the Cheltenham Festival including four Gold Cups Denman was never out of the first two.

If Kauto Star was an athlete, Denman was a power-house. Those who watched him knew that he was a true competitor who gave his all. There was talent, bags of it, but there was nothing fancy, nothing flashy, nothing aris-tocratic about his bearing – just inherent power and all-out effort. It was Coe and Ovett on four legs. You might have been nervous inviting the charming Kauto Star for a drink for fear that his choice of venue could have involved putting on a tie to visit a classy but traditional club. With the slightly more grumpy, down-to-earth Denman you knew you would have been OK for a pint in the pub. But either way the appearance on the scene together of these two wonderful stable companions has given us the most glorious jump-racing for decades. There will never be another double act like it.

Denman started life with former top jump jockey Adrian Maguire in Ireland. He was bought by Paul Nicholls' landlord and chief patron, the prosperous and decorously polite dairy farmer Paul Barber, who later sold a half share to the fast-talking professional gambler Harry Findlay, a man whom Nicholls described as 'an open mouth in search of a microphone', and the odd couple partnership gave an extra dimension to the story.

Denman himself arrived on the scene when at the 2007 Cheltenham he won the Sun Alliance Novice Chase. With his huge ground-devouring stride and seemingly boundless stamina he dominated the field and won by ten lengths.

Denman showed his wellbeing in preparing for Cheltenham 2008 by winning the Hennessy Gold Cup of 2007 under 11st 12lb on stamina-sapping soft ground. He gave 19lb and an 11-length beating to Dream Alliance, who later won a Welsh Grand National. But his hour truly came in the Gold Cup on 14 March 2008. Kauto Star, the 10-11 favourite, was defending the crown he had won in 2007. Denman was unbeaten over fences. The early pace was made by yet another talented stable compan- ion, Neptune Collonges, but while Denman was always travelling well, Kauto Star never quite found his rhythm and messed up a couple of fences. On the second circuit Denman took over and remorselessly ground out a pace to test titans. That was the way he won his races – not with a flashy finishing burst but with sustained, relentless pres- sure keeping others on the stretch.

Four fences out Denman, ridden by stable no. 2 Sam Thomas, stepped it up again and went ten lengths clear. From that moment he never looked in any danger and although Kauto Star eventually closed the gap to a more respectable seven lengths it was unquestionably Denman's day. Everyone in jumping wanted to see the rematch but the wonder was that Denman appeared at all in the 2009 Gold Cup.

Immediately after the 2008 race Paul Nicholls was inclined to believe that at Cheltenham over 3m 2f Denman would always prevail from then on, but would be beaten by Kauto in the King Georges on the sharper, flatter Kempton track. But Denman, who put everything into his races, took two hours to cool down that day and perhaps his Gold Cup exertions had taken more out of him than was realised at the time.

Denman, ridden by Ruby Walsh, goes to post in the Royal and
Sun Alliance Novices' Hurdle, Cheltenham, March 2006.

In August when Denman returned from his summer
break it was clear that all was not well. He was perma-
nently hot and had little interest in his work. It turned out
that he was suffering from an irregular heartbeat. He was
sent to Newmarket for treatment and although it worked,
Denman lost two months of activity. When he came back
it was a question of nursing him back to confidence rather
than returning to the formidable work regime previously
implemented to hone his raw strength to lean competi-
tiveness. He did not run for 11 months and looked a
shadow of himself in a comeback race at Kempton. It was
not until ten days before the 2009 Cheltenham Festival
that he began to bloom again and Nicholls let him take
his chance in the Gold Cup. He was nothing like the force
of 2008 but still he finished second as Kauto Star regained
his crown.

Preparing for the 2010 Gold Cup Denman showed

he was not ready for a gentle decline. Once again in the autumn he went to Newbury for the Hennessy Cognac Gold Cup. Again, though he had not been in the winners' enclosure since his Gold Cup at Cheltenham he was given top weight but he pounded his Grade One rivals into the ground. Ruby Walsh called it an outstanding performance but then came a blip when, with Tony McCoy riding, Denman fell in the Aon Chase at Newbury, having already looked out of sorts. Back at Cheltenham, though, it was a different story and once more he led from halfway. This time it was Kauto Star who made heavy weather of things and crashed out at the fourth fence. Could Denman too win back the Gold Cup crown? For a moment it looked likely as he wound up the pace. But then the younger Imperial Commander sailed past and Denman had to be content with second again.

In 2011 it was another younger generation story. Denman and Kauto Star were now both 11 and no horse older than ten had won since 1969. But as Kauto Star led from halfway and then Denman took over three out, the crowd cheered what they were beginning to see as the final battle for the crown between the two veterans. Denman got the better of Kauto certainly, but then at the last fence the latest young pretender Long Run appeared, smoothly handled by amateur rider Sam Waley-Cohen, and ran on up the hill to beat the old guard by seven lengths. Denman, second again, at least had the satisfaction of being seven lengths clear of Kauto.

While a rejuvenated Kauto Star then went on to beat Long Run twice, winning his fifth King George in the process, Denman was being aimed at the Lexus Chase but then sadly strained a tendon and was retired, staying on for a while though in the front yard box at Ditcheat in which he had become such a star fixture.

Career highlights:
2006: Challow Novices Hurdle, Berkshire Novices Chase
2007: Royal and Sun Alliance Chase, Hennessy Gold Cup,
      Lexus Chase
2008: Aon Chase, Cheltenham Gold Cup, Hennessy Gold Cup

36. DUBAI MILLENNIUM

Sheikh Mohammed, perhaps the world's most committed racehorse owner, is not a man afraid of giving hos-
tages to fortune. So impressed was he when he saw the
two-year-old Yaazer at exercise in trainer David Loder's
care in 1998 that he renamed him Dubai Millennium,
confident that this was the super-horse he needed to give
his Godolphin enterprise their first victory in the Dubai
World Cup – and in the millennium year of 2000.

No horse has ever come closer to the heart of the
Godolphin chief. Although the powerful, buzzy colt's
handlers used to find him pushy, even aggressive sometimes in his box, Sheikh Mohammed would spend hours
in there alone with him, the horse tucking his head under
the Dubai ruler's arm and Sheikh Mohammed fondling
his tongue. It was a very personal relationship and Dubai
Millennium proved every bit as good as 'Sheikh Mo'
had hoped, winning nine of his ten races including the
World Cup.

By the Mr Prospector stallion Seeking The Gold out
of Colorado Dancer, Dubai Millennium didn't seek a lot
of it in his first race, taking a humble event at Yarmouth
in the hands of Frankie Dettori, who eased him in the
final furlong and still won by five lengths. He was then
transferred from Loder, the two-year-old specialist for
Godolphin, to Saeed bin Suroor and wintered in Dubai.

Back in Britain for the 1999 season Dubai Millennium won his first race at Doncaster by nine lengths. A large Godolphin cadre turned out to watch his next performance in Goodwood's Listed Predominate Stakes, a recognised Derby trial over ten furlongs. The big, imposing colt was driven clear two furlongs out by Frankie and won by three and a half lengths – so it was on to Epsom.

There Dubai Millennium met with his only defeat. Pulling hard early on, he could not carry through his effort early in the straight and faded to finish ninth behind Oath. He did not stay the Derby distance of a mile and a half and from then on ran over shorter distances. In July he won the Group Two Prix Eugene Adam at Maisons-Laffitte unchallenged by three lengths and then went back to France to win the one-mile Prix Jacques Le Marois at Deauville. His final start of the year was on heavy ground at Ascot in the Queen Elizabeth II Stakes. After Dubai Millennium had pulled clear to win by six lengths Sheikh Mohammed announced that he was the best Godolphin had ever had and would be going for the year 2000 Dubai World Cup.

Following another winter in Dubai the apple of the Sheikh's eye came out to run on a dirt surface for the first time and looked just as impressive winning a round of the Sheikh Maktoum Challenge. Three weeks later it was the big night: in the Dubai World Cup, Dubai Millennium did everything his owner might have dreamed of. He led after a furlong, moving at such a high cruising speed that he had soon cracked all the field except Behrens. Over the final stages Dubai Millennium motored away from Behrens too, cruising home in a record time by six lengths. Frankie Dettori called the colt 'the best I've ever ridden, absolutely unbelievable'.

For the only time in his career an injured Frankie

did not ride Dubai Millennium in his next race. The American rider Jerry Bailey took over for an eagerly awaited clash with Sendawar, the French colt who had won four Group Ones and who had been rated on a par with Dubai Millennium as Europe's top miler. Bailey wound it up from the start and Sendawar proved unable to match him. It was the German challenger Sumitas who eventually finished second eight lengths behind the Godolphin star.

The racing world was excited then by Sheikh Mohammed's offer of a $6 million winner-takes-all challenge for a match over ten furlongs between Dubai Millennium and the King George and Arc winner Montjeu

Dubai Millennium, ridden by Frankie Dettori, winning the Queen Elizabeth II Stakes at Ascot, September 1999.

for the informal title of best horse in the world. But alas it was destined not to be. In August 2000 Dubai Millennium broke a leg in training and although he was able to walk back to his yard and was saved for stud duties his racing days were over. Then, as if there were some kind of curse attached to his talent, Dubai Millennium's stud career too was cruelly curtailed. Having covered 65 mares in his first year Dubai Millennium contracted grass sickness and after three operations had to be put down.

The winner of nine out of ten races, on turf and on dirt, Dubai Millennium was a champion in his prime when his racing career came to an end, and when his life at stud too was cut short Sheikh Mohammed was so distraught that he sent his team scouring the markets to secure every son or daughter of his great horse that could be bought, even making offers to owners of mares carrying unborn foals. In the end he secured 51 of Dubai Millennium's 54 live offspring, a remarkable testimony to one man's love of a horse.

Career highlights:
*1999: Predominate Stakes, Prix Eugene Adam, Prix Jacques
Le Marois, Queen Elizabeth II Stakes*
2000: Dubai World Cup, Prince of Wales Stakes

35. BULA

One sure sign for a jumper that entry to the hall of fame is beckoning is having a race named after you at Cheltenham. Bula was good enough to earn that accolade. An inmate of the little row of boxes in Fred Winter's Lambourn yard that was nicknamed 'Millionaires' Row' (at around the same time it also housed Pendil, Killiney,

Lanzarote and Crisp), Bula was possibly the most talented of them all, a natural jumper of hurdles who also proved to be a decent fencer although he did not even start over the bigger obstacles until he was nine.

Bula was bone idle on the gallops and did his own thing when he pleased. Amiable enough in his box, he would suddenly take it into his head to charge off in one direction or another. On his first racecourse outing Stan Mellor, who had picked him up as a spare ride when stable jockey Paul Kelleway was injured, was asked by Winter to find out if the horse was worth persevering with. After coasting to a six-length victory despite Bula kicking the first three hurdles out of the ground he came back and told the trainer he had a Rolls Royce in his equine garage.

At the 1970 Cheltenham Festival Bula won a division of the Gloucestershire Hurdle by the same margin and the next year, 1971, he dethroned the mighty Persian War, winner for the previous three years, to take the Champion Hurdle from him and Major Rose by four lengths. That was the 12th in a sequence of 13 races Bula ran without being beaten.

In the 1972 Champion Hurdle Bula doubled his victory margin to eight lengths as he came home ahead of Boxer and Lyford Cay. Paul Kelleway, holding up his mount as usual, had been tracking Dondieu but on instinct switched away to follow Boxer instead before the third last. It was just as well: Dondieu had a terrible fall and broke his neck. Bula escaped the melee as other horses fell too. He surged up to Boxer at the second last and went away up the final straight.

Crowds thrilled to the sight of the ice-cool Paul Kelleway sending his mount to sleep at the back of the pack in top hurdle races, confident that when he pressed the booster-rocket button after the second last his mount

Bula (*left*), under Paul Kelleway, takes the third last in
the Champion Hurdle, Cheltenham, March 1972.

would turn it on and power past his rivals. Sometimes
he left it agonisingly late, as in the Benson and Hedges
Hurdle at Sandown in which Bula sprinted past seven
horses after the last hurdle to win by two short heads in a
truly tight finish.

The brown horse, whose name was Fijian for 'hello',
won his first 13 hurdle races and only lost the 14th
because an uncharacteristic jumping error at the last left
him unable to rescue the situation with his habitual fast
finish. His 33-1 conqueror at Newbury that day was called
I'm Happy: few punters shared the feeling. In all Bula
won 34 of his 51 races and his career was far from over
after he lost his Champion Hurdle crown to Comedy of
Errors and turned to chasing. He won 13 of his 25 races
over bigger obstacles.

Bula may not have been quite so brilliant over fences but he was good enough to beat Tingle Creek over two miles one day at Sandown and brave enough to finish third in the 1975 Gold Cup in a quagmire that he hated. Connections believed that on better ground he would have won. The next year, aged 11, he was runner-up in the Mackeson Gold Cup carrying a massive 12st 1lb.

Even then it wasn't over. Bula was back at Cheltenham for the 1977 Festival in which he was made favourite for the two-mile Champion Chase. Tragically he fell and broke a shoulder. They got him back to Uplands but two months later he had to be put down. The sight of a set-alight Bula in full flight after the last is not one that those of us who saw it will forget.

Career highlights:
1970: Gloucestershire Hurdle
1971: Champion Hurdle, Benson and Hedges Hurdle
1972: Champion Hurdle, Welsh Champion Hurdle

34. MANDARIN

The first pseudonym I ever adopted as a writer was that of 'Mandarin' in my days as a trainee everything cum sub-editor cum racing columnist on the *Liverpool Daily Post* a couple of centuries ago. Nothing else would have done because the brave little chaser had already become my racing hero. He was the first to make me aware that race-horses are not just about speed but about courage, tenacity and fighting spirit too. Full of quality though not the biggest, patched up time and again from various injuries, he figured in one major steeplechase after another giving his all, and then with his incredible rider Fred Winter he put in the sporting performance that still to me defines the word.

The pair of them not only stayed in the Grand Steeplechase de Paris at Auteuil on 17 June 1962 after the rubber bit in the horse's mouth had broken as he jumped the fourth fence: with the rider deprived of brakes or steering they actually won the race. Rider journalist John Oaksey's report on that event, headed 'Triumph Over Impossible Odds', remains for me the most sublime piece of sporting copy ever written – I have read it 20 times or more.

But first back to earlier days. In 1957 the first Hennessy Gold Cup, later to become a fixture at Newbury, was run at Cheltenham. The favourite was the Gold Cup winner Linwell, carrying 12st 2lb. In the betting he and Mandarin, owned by the sponsoring family's Madame Killian 'Peggy' Hennessy and trained by Fulke Walwyn, were bracketed on 8-1 while the favourite in a field of 19 was local hero The Callant.

Ridden by the little-known Gerry Madden, Mandarin, the youngest horse in the race at only six, moved into the lead three out. Only The Callant, Hall Weir, Linwell and Bremontier remained in touch. Hall Weir fell at the second last and Linwell, cheered on by the crowd, came to challenge Mandarin at the last. Mandarin fought back, re-passed him up the finishing hill and won by three lengths a race that he was to take again four years later.

Mandarin, who had finished runner-up in the Whitbread Gold Cup both in 1956 and 1957, was given top weight for the 1958 Hennessy and finished fifth to his stable mate Taxidermist, ridden by the then Mr John Lawrence (who was to become Lord Oaksey). The mare Kerstin, who won the Hennessy the next year, was beaten a short head.

Mandarin, ridden by Fred Winter (*right*), just behind Fortria, before going on to win the Cheltenham Gold Cup, March 1962.

In 1961 Mandarin and Taxidermist were in the Hennessy field again against the Grand National winner Nicolaus Silver, the Irish Grand National winner Olympia and rising young second-season chasers – the kind who usually win the Hennessy – like Springbok and Blessington Esquire. Mandarin by now was an established star. He had been second a tantalising three times in the Whitbread, he had twice won the King George VI Chase at Kempton Park and he had been third in the Cheltenham Gold Cup. In between he had been a regular visitor to equine A&E. He had broken down and had his tendons fired and he had broken a bone in his stifle when finishing third in another King George.

In the 1961 Hennessy, while Nicolaus Silver jumped the obstacles as if he were still at Aintree, Mandarin under

Willie Robinson was fencing fast and cleverly. Blessington Esquire, going well, broke down and into the straight it was the top weights Mandarin and Olympia who led. With a big leap at the last Mandarin went away up the run-in with Olympia being passed by John O' Groats and Taxidermist for the places. Springbok, winner the next year, was in fifth.

Mandarin, despite his series of injuries, was now established as the most consistent and gutsy chaser in the land, a tribute to Fulke Walwyn's genius. But it was his next big victory that supplied the one key element still missing on his equine CV. At the age of 11, in his 18th victory since coming over from France and ridden by Fred Winter, he won the Cheltenham Gold Cup, passing Ireland's hope Fortria on the run-in after the last fence. Said Peggy Hennessy: 'This is the greatest day of my life. I have kept horses in training over here with only one object – to win the Gold Cup.'

After that great day there was to be one final hurrah in Paris in June of that year, contesting the 'French Grand National' (Mandarin never ran in the English version): the Grand Steeplechase de Paris. I wasn't there but thanks to John Oaksey I have always felt as though I was.

Mandarin, he wrote, was soon in front pulling like a train. Going to the fourth obstacle the bit broke in half: Fred Winter was left without any contact with the horse's mouth or head, his only hand-hold the reins that were still held by the Irish martingale round Mandarin's neck and the neck strap of the horse's breast-girth. The vital counterbalance of a rider had gone. 'The man, with no means of steering but his weight, had to rely entirely on grip and balance, the horse, used to a steady pressure on his mouth, had to jump 21 strange and formidable obstacles (round a figure of eight course) with his head completely free – a natural state admittedly but one to which Mandarin is wholly unaccustomed.'

As they negotiated four 180-degree turns Fred Winter could only sit or drive and match the horse's moves with natural rhythm. Some sporting French jockeys did what they could to help, 'Proving gloriously', said Oaksey, 'that the comradeship of dangers shared can in some sports at least count for more than international rivalry'.

Somehow, through Mandarin's good sense and the strength of Winter's legs, they got round, though a lurching swerve around some bushes at one stage put them back to fifth round the final bend. With two obstacles to jump they were some seven lengths behind the leader. Winter drove and Mandarin 'thrust out his gallant head and went for the Bullfinch like a tank facing tissue paper'. He passed three horses as if they were walking and landed first over the last. Then came a desperate challenge from the Frenchman Lumino through the last hundred yards. They crossed the line together but Mandarin got the verdict. It was truly a famous victory, especially as Mandarin's tendon had gone again three fences out. Fred Winter, literally speechless and suffering from stomach cramps, had virtually to be carried into the weighing room. Forty minutes later he came out and won the next race on Beaver II.

Unlike some great steeplechasers, incidentally, Mandarin had a long and happy retirement, with Whitbreads until the end of his days sending him a regular supply of the stout to which he was partial in his feed.

Career highlights:
1957: Hennessy Gold Cup, King George VI Chase
1959: King George VI Chase
1961: Hennessy Gold Cup
1962: Cheltenham Gold Cup, Grand Steeplechase de Paris

33. ALLEGED

Trainer Vincent O'Brien, owner Robert Sangster and jockey Lester Piggott made a formidable trio and perhaps their most successful enterprise together was the career of Alleged, the horse who achieved the rare feat of winning the Prix de l'Arc de Triomphe in successive years. Asked about the best horse he had trained, O'Brien once said: 'For brilliance Nijinsky. For toughness Sir Ivor', but then he felt compelled to mention Alleged in the same breath.

Sangster, with two partners Bob Fluor and Shirley Taylor, bought Alleged from horse-whisperer Monty Roberts, who originally made his name as a 'pinhooker' buying and selling-on yearlings. If the original plan had been adhered to, Alleged would never have qualified for this volume: he was to have raced in California. But when Sangster saw him in Kentucky he reckoned Alleged's forelegs would not stand the strain of racing on 'dirt' in the USA and persuaded his partners that they should send him to O'Brien in Europe.

Alleged never won a British Classic and his inability to cope with firm ground restricted his options even on this side of the Atlantic, but he won nine of his ten races and both his Arc victories were clear-cut.

Lester Piggott came to rate the horse highly, saying, 'You could do anything with him in a race and he had a lovely relaxed attitude', but Alleged took time to come to himself, not seeing the racetrack until November as a two-year-old. The next year, 1977, although Alleged had won his first two races Lester chose to ride Valinsky, the 5-4 favourite, in the Royal Whip at the Curragh, but it was Alleged with a stable work-rider on board who coasted to victory at 33-1. From then on he was Piggott's ride.

Dunfermline (*left*), ridden by Willie Carson, finishes ahead
of Alleged (Lester Piggott) in the St Leger, Doncaster,
September 1977.

Alleged had not participated in the earlier English
Classics (for which O'Brien had The Minstrel that year)
but he started as favourite for the St Leger after winning
York's Great Voltigeur Stakes from a top-class field by
seven lengths. Two furlongs out the 4-7 favourite looked
all over the winner but faded as the crowd cheered home
a 10-1 royal winner that day, the Queen's Dunfermline.
Hosting Prime Minister James Callaghan at Balmoral that
weekend, she must have been disappointed to miss the
race. Co-owner Bob Fluor, already miffed that Alleged
had not contested the Irish Derby against The Minstrel,
was so disappointed by the Leger result that he thereupon sold his share.

Even Lester could make misjudgements and O'Brien

was critical of his jockey's ride that day, uncharacteristically showing his anger in public outside the weighing room. Dunfermline had a pacemaker but Piggott kept Alleged ahead of the filly and took up the running when the pacemaker faded. Dunfermline, ridden cannily by Willie Carson, then outstayed him. Piggott's reaction to O'Brien's public ticking-off was in character: no words, just a shrug.

In the Arc only two weeks later it was a different story. Alleged showed that running in the Doncaster Classic need not be a bar to victory in Paris. He took the lead after only two furlongs and Piggott earned O'Brien's unstinted praise for the way he dictated the pace. On entering the straight he sprinted away to win easily from the New Zealand horse Balmerino. Dunfermline finished fourth and Alleged became European Horse of the Year. Piggott, much criticised for his rides in the Arc on Nijinsky and Park Top, was now a Longchamp hero.

Sangster and O'Brien cashed in that year on The Minstrel's success, syndicating him at stud for $9 million. They could have done the same with Alleged, but with O'Brien as the leading spirit they decided to risk keeping him in training for another year to aim at rich summer prizes like the Eclipse and the King George VI and Queen Elizabeth Stakes. He was after all a comparatively lightly-raced horse.

For a while it all seemed to have gone wrong. In 1978 Alleged made a winning debut at the Curragh but the ground was firm that day and he jarred himself badly. As he was getting over that the O'Brien yard was hit by a virus and he suffered more than most. The big summer occasions flicked by without Alleged's participation and it was the autumn before the colt could get back into action. He did so with a vengeance, winning the Prix du

Prince d'Orange in record time, quite some achievement for a horse who had not run since May.

Two weeks later he ran again in the Arc, this time on ground Piggott feared might be too soft to enable Alleged to unleash his finishing speed. On this occasion there were others to make the pace. With two furlongs to go, both Piggott and Freddie Head on the French champion filly Dancing Maid made their efforts but it was Alleged who triumphed and the filly eventually gave him best, being passed also by Trillion, ridden by the American Willie Shoemaker, before the winning post.

The last horse before Alleged to win back-to-back Arcs was the great Ribot in 1955 and 1956. The gamble had paid off and Alleged was duly syndicated for $13 million.

Career highlights:
1977: Gallinule Stakes, Royal Whip Stakes, Great Voltigeur Stakes, Prix de l'Arc de Triomphe
1978: Royal Whip Stakes, Prix du Prince d'Orange, Prix de l'Arc de Triomphe

32. SHERGAR

On Glint of Gold in the 1981 Derby, rider John Mathias, who could be described as a journeyman jockey, thought for a few seconds that his moment of fame and glory had come when they headed the pack of horses coming up the cambered Epsom straight. Then he noticed the sleek bay figure in the middle distance ahead of him and realised they were only in second place: the 19-year-old Walter Swinburn and Shergar had already scooted ten lengths clear of the field. Shergar's victory margin was the biggest in the 200-year history of the Derby.

That should have been Shergar's marker in history but instead he is talked about still because of a totally different and grisly event after his racing career ended. First things first, though.

Shergar, a bay colt with a white blaze and four white socks, by Great Nephew out of Sharmeen, was bred by his owner the Aga Khan and trained at Newmarket by Michael Stoute. He was lightly raced as a two-year-old, winning the Kris Plate at Newbury in September 1980 and running a good second to the more experienced Beldale Flutter in the Futurity at Doncaster in October. Those performances had him rated out of the first 30 in the Free Handicap and when the 1981 season opened you could get 33-1 about him for the Derby.

That soon changed. Shergar, whose style of racing was efficient rather than elegant, had clearly flourished over the winter. He won the Guardian Classic Trial at Sandown by ten lengths in April, going ahead at the three-furlong marker. He then demolished the field in the Chester Vase in May, storming clear the same way to beat Sunley Builds by 12 lengths, and on Derby Day he was an unchallenged 10-11 favourite.

Those who laid the odds never had a moment's worry. Shergar had the pace to keep close to the leaders early on and coming round Tattenham Corner was the only one still on the bridle. In those days as Epsom residents we used to picnic close to the rails about two furlongs out and as the field flashed past I couldn't believe how far he was in front. Swinburn didn't look behind him until he was into the final furlong – 'I couldn't believe how far clear we were' – and he could probably have won even further had he not then eased Shergar before the post.

With Swinburn serving a suspension Lester Piggott rode Shergar in the Irish Derby. Under orders not to let him down on the firm ground unless he really had to, he rode the Aga Khan's colt cheekily and still won by a four-length margin that he could have easily doubled.

Shergar was then aimed at the King George VI and Queen Elizabeth Stakes at Ascot, Britain's answer to the Arc, where he took on older horses. He was boxed in for a while but once extricated by Swinburn and given the go he drew away and won by four lengths again, maintaining his unbeaten record as a three-year-old.

Then came the one blot on his career. Shergar was being aimed at the Arc but it was decided all the same to run him in the St Leger. Although stories about training difficulties had circulated, he looked in great condition on the day but had little to offer in the race. He was

Shergar with Walter Swinburn in the saddle, September 1981.

nicely poised behind the leaders four furlongs out but then seemed to run out of petrol quite suddenly, in the end finishing in fourth place some 11 lengths behind Cut Above, whom he had trounced in Ireland. Maybe Shergar didn't stay, maybe there was an undiscovered problem. Either way connections decided, to the fury of some in the racing media, not to risk a repetition in the Arc and the dual Derby winner was retired to the Aga Khan's Irish stud at Ballymany.

There had been much publicity about the £10 million post-Derby syndication of Shergar, the most expensive deal of its kind ever. The Aga Khan split Shergar into 40 lots of £250,000 each, keeping six for himself and selling the other 34. Criminal antennae quiver at news like that, and in Shergar's second year at stud his groom Jim Fitzgerald was raided at gunpoint one night by eight men. He was forced to lead the gang to Shergar, who was loaded into a stolen horsebox and abducted. Ransom approaches were made to the Aga Khan but the kidnappers had not understood that syndication meant they were negotiating not with one but with 34 owners. Most of those were determined not to pay any ransom for fear that if they did every decent racehorse would then become a criminal target.

The police handling of the case was a joke, epitomised by the declaration from the trilby-wearing detective 'Spud' Murphy, 'A clue is something we do not have', and Shergar was never seen again.

Many conspiracy theories circulated but the circumstantial evidence makes it look like an IRA fund-raising plot that went awry. It was widely reckoned in Ireland that the event had been a public relations disaster for that grim organisation.

One version from insiders was that Shergar became

agitated in the stolen horsebox, that the vet the gang had hoped to bring along to cope with him had been dissuaded from participation by his wife and that, unable to handle a distressed animal, the gang shot and buried the horse. The most recent newspaper investigation on the 30th anniversary of his disappearance suggests, tragically, that Shergar was messily and incompetently executed by machine gun in a stable, dying eventually from loss of blood. Whatever the precise form of his demise it was a tragic ending to the life of a sublimely talented horse.

Career highlights:
1981: Guardian Classic Trial, Chester Vase, Derby, Irish Derby,
*   King George VI and Queen Elizabeth Stakes*

31. DESERT ORCHID

Desert Orchid, one of the most popular horses of all time, was lucky to survive his very first race. Dessie, as the grey came to be known by his horde of adoring fans, fell heavily at the last in a Kempton novice hurdle in 1983. The dreaded green screens were erected but after an age the wounded horse finally got to his feet. He went on to win 34 of his remaining 69 starts, including among his victories a Cheltenham Gold Cup, an Irish Grand National and no fewer than four King George VI Chases – a record that seemed unbeatable until the arrival on the National Hunt scene later of Kauto Star.

Desert Orchid was owned by the Burridge family and trained by David Elsworth at Whitsbury Manor in Wiltshire. His hurdling career was not particularly distinguished – he fell three times over the smaller obstacles – but when he was switched to fences it was a different matter. His flamboyant style, his durability – he was in the top flight of jumpers for nine seasons – and his sheer charisma helped to make Desert Orchid one of the best-loved horses who has ever been in training. His colour helped too: the racing public has a thing about greys, perhaps because they are so easily identifiable when they race. But with Dessie it was more than that. Crowds loved his enthusiasm for the job and his sheer versatility.

He swiftly ran up a series of four wins in the 1985–86 season, capped with his first victory in the King George, by 15 lengths from Door Latch and beating horses of the quality of Wayward Lad, Forgive'n'Forget and Combs Ditch. It was the first race in which he was partnered by Simon Sherwood, who rode him to nine successes in their ten races together.

In 1988 after being beaten by Pearlyman in the Queen Mother Champion Chase, Desert Orchid went to Aintree and won the Martell Cup over three miles (his first victory on the left-handed tracks he did not favour). He then led all the way to win the Whitbread Gold Cup over 3m 5f. The next season he won the two-mile Tingle Creek and Victor Chandler chases, the King George and the Gainsborough over three miles. One of his bravest efforts came in the Victor Chandler Chase when he took on Panto Prince and Vodkatini. He gave them 22lb and 23lb respectively and just got up to beat Panto Prince by a head. But the race that will never be forgotten was the 1989 Cheltenham Gold Cup over 3m 2f.

So bleak were the conditions that year that they nearly didn't race. But when readers of the *Racing Post* were asked to vote on the Hundred Greatest Races this one finished on top. Not only, the paper pointed out, because it was won by a hugely popular horse but because it was a great contest too.

The weather was vile. It was a day of heavy rain, sleet and snow. Only after a midday inspection was the ground ruled fit to race. Many worried that Desert Orchid, who never seemed to like the Cheltenham track anyway and was regarded as at his best over two and a half miles, would be pulled out. Trainer David Elsworth was made of sterner stuff. He declared him to run, saying: 'The ground is horrible and conditions are all against him, but he is the best horse.' 'Elzee' even increased his bet as Desert Orchid drifted to 3-1.

Team Dessie went for boldness in the race too, rider Simon Sherwood taking him out into the lead, his easy jumping helping to conserve his energy. On the second circuit he was joined by Elsworth's other runner Cavvie's Clown, second the previous year, and Fulke Walwyn's talented Ten Plus, who passed Desert Orchid at the 14th of the 22 obstacles. Tragically, three out Ten Plus fell, fatally injured.

Approaching the second last, the tough, mud-loving Yahoo came through on the inside to take the lead. But Desert Orchid was ready for battle and set out after him. By the last they were almost level and somehow Desert Orchid and a jockey who admits he was 'knackered' summoned up what was, in the dire conditions, the equivalent of a burst. Simon Sherwood said afterwards: 'I have never sat on a horse that showed such courage. By hook or by crook he was going to win.' With Desert Orchid drifting left to eyeball Yahoo, the mud-spattered pair's surge took them clear. In the end Desert Orchid won by one and a half lengths with the two eight lengths clear of Charter Party, the previous year's winner. Horse and jockey were applauded every step to the winners' enclosure. John Francome rated Simon Sherwood's performance as good as he had seen from a National Hunt jockey.

Desert Orchid, with Simon Sherwood aboard, races to victory
in the Cheltenham Gold Cup, March 1989.

Sherwood had a remarkable understanding with Desert Orchid. He lost only one of the ten races he rode on him and entitled his autobiography *Nine out of Ten*. Others were equally impressed. Former champion jockey Richard Dunwoody, who partnered many jumping stars, called Desert Orchid 'without doubt the best horse I rode'.

After Desert Orchid's eight consecutive victories he fell in the 1989 Martell Cup, won by Yahoo. But that Christmas he again won the King George at Kempton, following up with victories at Wincanton and back at Kempton for the Racing Post Chase, where he carried the massive burden of 12st 3lb. From there he went on to win the Irish National with 12 stone by 12 lengths, despite an uncharacteristic blunder at the final fence.

Desert Orchid made history by winning the King George for the fourth time in 1990 and his last race came when he fell in his attempt to win that contest for an unprecedented fifth time.

With a tendency to jump to his right Desert Orchid was always better at right-handed tracks like Kempton, Sandown and Ascot. But few cared about such trivialities. The athletic and determined winner of 27 of his 50 races over fences was the most popular jumper for decades. His exhilarating jumping and front-running gave him huge box office appeal and though he retired in 1992 his racecourse parade reappearances were cheered to the echo. Often the old gentleman seemed to want to stay on for the race as well.

Career highlights:
1986: King George VI Chase
1987: Gainsborough Chase
1988: Martell Cup, Whitbread Gold Cup, Tingle Creek Chase, King George VI Chase
1989: Gainsborough Chase, Cheltenham Gold Cup, Victor Chandler Chase, King George VI Chase
1990: Irish Grand National, Racing Post Chase, King George VI Chase

30. OH SO SHARP

Only five fillies in the whole of the 20th century won three English Classics and Oh So Sharp, one of the first horses that Dubai's Sheikh Mohammed bred at his Dalham Hall establishment, joined an exclusive list including Sceptre, Pretty Polly, Sun Chariot and Meld when she collected her three victories in the 1,000 Guineas, Oaks and St Leger of

1985. At the same time she gave her rider Steve Cauthen an enviable record: he became the first jockey ever to win a Triple Crown both in the USA and in Britain. Not surprisingly he called her the best filly he ever rode.

As a daughter of the champion miler Kris the lengthy Oh So Sharp, who was trained by Henry Cecil, turned out to have more stamina than might have been anticipated. She won her three races as a two-year-old, in the last of them beating Helen Street, later an Irish Oaks winner, in the Fillies Mile at Ascot.

At three she debuted successfully in the Nell Gwyn Stakes and went on to contest the 1,000 Guineas as the 2-1 favourite. Her chance appeared to have gone but suddenly in the last 100 yards she made up two lengths and snatched victory on the line by two short heads from Al Bahathri and Bella Colora in one of the most exciting finishes the race has ever seen.

The Oaks at Epsom was won in an entirely different manner: after a slow early pace Oh So Sharp was majestic in coming home six lengths clear of the classy Triptych, later that year the winner of the Irish 2,000 Guineas and the Champion Stakes.

When his Derby winner of that year Slip Anchor was injured, Henry Cecil ran Oh So Sharp as a substitute in the King George VI and Queen Elizabeth Stakes. She was not suited by the fast ground or the breakneck pace but a furlong out she looked likely to win until Petoski, galvanised by Willie Carson into running the race of his life, came storming through at the end to beat her a neck, with Rainbow Quest, the subsequent Arc winner, in third. Cauthen said Oh So Sharp was beaten because she had not seen the fast-finishing Petoski coming; others, including BBC commentator Julian Wilson, raised a question mark about her stamina.

Oh So Sharp, ridden by Steve Cauthen (*second left*), coming home
ahead of Lanfranco (*right*) and Phardante (*centre*), in
the St Leger, Doncaster, September 1985.

Oh So Sharp showed her class again in what was a
tough campaign for a filly by running a close second to
the Piggott-ridden Commanche Run in the Benson and
Hedges Gold Cup, and it was probably class rather than
stamina that got her home the winner in the St Leger,
her third Classic, again as a substitute for the injured Slip
Anchor. Steve Cauthen was forced to take the lead sooner
than he had wanted and the filly drifted off her line up
the Doncaster straight as she held on by three-quarters
of a length to win from Phardante and her stable companion Lanfranco, ridden by Lester Piggott. The winning
combination had to survive a stewards' inquiry.

Oh So Sharp was a major contributor to Henry Cecil that year becoming the first trainer to win more than £1 million in prize money in a season. It was a major training feat and racegoers sometimes forget just how fine the fine-tuning has to be. Cecil said of Oh So Sharp after the St Leger: 'Another week and it might have been too late. She was beginning to go and I was just hanging onto her.' Piggott, who had been Cecil's stable jockey until the end of the previous season, would love to have ridden Oh So Sharp, whose career ended with seven victories from her nine races and second place in the other two.

Career highlights:
1984: Fillies Mile
1985: 1,000 Guineas, Oaks, St Leger

29. ROCK OF GIBRALTAR

Thanks to a dispute between two high-profile figures over the precise terms of his ownership, Rock of Gibraltar became as famous off course as he did on the racetrack. It is a pity because this tough horse's record of seven consecutive Group One/Grade One victories deserves to have been celebrated without any trailing clouds of disgruntlement.

Trained by Aidan O'Brien at Ballydoyle, Rock of Gibraltar was part of the Coolmore operation headed by the former Irish senator John Magnier, possessor of the best business brain ever applied to making money out of horseracing. Once the biggest shareholder in Manchester United, Magnier became friends with another man who is a major force in his own world, the club's long-time manager Sir Alex Ferguson, famous both for the high-level results he achieves on the pitch and for his 'hairdryer' roastings of players who fail to come up to the standards he has demanded. Neither are compromisers by nature.

Ferguson was in and out of part-ownerships with several Coolmore horses as Magnier fed his growing interest in racing. He was publicly presented as a joint owner of Rock of Gibraltar with Mrs Sue Magnier, the great trainer Vincent O'Brien's daughter and John Magnier's wife, and for the two seasons he ran in 2001 and 2002 Rock of Gibraltar competed not in her plain dark blue colours but in Sir Alex's red and white. What was never plain to the public, and under racing's rules never had to be, was whether he was literally a 'gift horse' for a while or in perpetuity, whether Ferguson was paying half his training fees, what sort of percentage of Rock of Gibraltar's prize money he was banking and what percentage of his future stallion fees he was to receive.

Rock of Gibraltar lost two of his first five races. Having won his maiden over five furlongs at the Curragh he suffered in a rough race for the Coventry Stakes at Ascot and was only sixth of 20. He then won the Group Three Railway Stakes at the Curragh and the Group Two Gimcrack at York before losing out in the Group Two Champagne Stakes at Doncaster over seven furlongs when 'mugged' in the final stages by Frankie Dettori riding a clever race on Dubai Destination. After that Rock of Gibraltar ran in seven consecutive Group Ones, including two Classics, and won every one of them, breaking a 30-year-old record held by the great Mill Reef.

First there were two more races as a two-year-old, winning the Grand Criterium at Longchamp and the Dewhurst Stakes at Newmarket. At Longchamp Rock of Gibraltar signalled his quality with an exhilarating injection of pace two furlongs out to coast home by three lengths. At Newmarket it was a rather different story. With Aidan O'Brien out to win a record number of Group Ones in a season there were three other entries from Ballydoyle, and Rock of Gibraltar, ridden as nearly always by Mick Kinane, only squeezed home ahead of two of them, Landseer and Tendulkar, by a short head and a head. Just 13 days after the Grand Criterium it revealed what a tough and gritty horse he was.

In 2002 Sir Alex's horse, for that is how the public had been encouraged to see him, opened his campaign at Newmarket in the 2,000 Guineas with the worst draw in the field, stall 22 on the outside of the field. That was one reason why he was allowed to start at the generous odds of 9-1. The other was that O'Brien was also running

Rock of Gibraltar, ridden by Mick Kinane at Royal Ascot,
June 2002.

the exciting and supposedly invincible 6-4 favourite Hawk Wing. Again O'Brien had the first three, but it was Rock of Gibraltar, not Hawk Wing who was in the no. 1 slot. With Johnny Murtagh deputising for the suspended Kinane, the two O'Brien horses were on opposite sides of the track and Rock of Gibraltar just held on the better to win by a gritty neck.

The Rock's next race was the Irish 2,000 and in a now familiar pattern he once more led home two stable companions for an O'Brien 1-2-3. This time it was Century City and Della Francesca in the minor placings.

A mile was always going to be his distance and the next two triumphs in his roll call of Group Ones were the St James's Palace Stakes at Ascot and the Sussex Stakes at Goodwood. The Ascot race was effectively Europe's mile championship with the winners of five 2,000 Guineas equivalents taking part. Rock of Gibraltar settled the argument by comprehensively beating Landseer, the winner of the French 2,000.

Down in Sussex, taking on his elders for the first time, Rock of Gibraltar whooshed by the opposition when Kinane pressed the pedal and his jockey emphasised how easy it was by looking back through his legs for the non-existent opposition in the final furlong. Most of O'Brien's horses had the virus at the time but Rock of Gibraltar's constitution somehow enabled him to fight it off.

To break the existing record for the number of consecutive Group Ones he then went on a foray to Longchamp for the Prix du Moulin where, despite a brave effort by the French-trained Banks Hill and an accidental blow in the face from Banks Hill's jockey Richard Hughes, Rock of Gibraltar once again did the business. The French jockeys, Kinane revealed, were referring to his mount as 'The Monster'.

There was to be just one more race in this extraordinarily consistent career – in the Breeders' Cup Mile at Arlington Park, Chicago. Sadly it fell just short of the fairytale ending. In a field of 14, Rock of Gibraltar was making his forward move in the straight when poor Landseer broke a leg and fell ahead of him, checking his effort. Domedriver, the 26-1 French outsider, had waited for a gap on the inside, got it when he needed it and won the race on a burst that Rock of Gibraltar might not have been able to match anyway. So there was no eighth consecutive Grade One but an honourable end to a superbly consistent career as he finished the runner-up. Rock of Gibraltar raced 13 times, winning on ten occasions and finishing second twice. Only in the Coventry Stakes scrimmage had he failed to make the first two. He ended his career as the highest-rated horse in the world.

The sadness came afterwards in the semi-public spat between Ferguson and Magnier over the breeding rights to Rock of Gibraltar. Rock of Gibraltar earned more than £1 million in his career but his potential earnings as a stallion would have been a hundred times that sum at least. When Sir Alex started asking for his money and was told there wouldn't be any and that he had no stake in the breeding rights, he threatened to sue. The dispute need not concern us here at length and it was in the end settled out of court. But it left a sour taste and didn't do either man's reputation any good. Agreements involving superstars from other worlds in 'prestige' horse ownership are likely to be much more accurately drawn up in future.

Career highlights:
2001: Gimcrack Stakes, Grand Criterium, Dewhurst Stakes
2002: 2,000 Guineas, Irish 2,000 Guineas, St James's Palace
Stakes, Sussex Stakes, Prix du Moulin

28. SEA PIGEON

There cannot be too many horses who have run both in the Epsom Derby and in the Champion Hurdle but Sea Pigeon, trained from 1976–81 by Peter Easterby at Habton Grange in Yorkshire, was one of them. The son of the great Sea-Bird had class and a turn of foot and it was his capacity for a well-timed burst of speed at the end of his races that made him a Festival hero at the level of his old rival Monksfield and his stable companion Night Nurse.

Racegoers admire courageous front-runners who grit their teeth and strike for home, defying the others to catch and pass them, but they thrill even more to the 'hold-up' horses who swoop like a falcon from a crag to snatch the prize on the line.

Twice, in 1978 and 1979, Sea Pigeon was brought too early to tackle Monksfield in the Champion and twice the courageous little Irish horse responded by fighting him off and battling on to win. But Sea Pigeon too was to win his brace of Champion Hurdles, and a small change in the Champion Hurdle course was probably the clincher.

Known as 'Pidge' in the Great Habton yard, Sea Pigeon ran seventh in the Derby for Jeremy Tree. He was a good performer on the Flat, collecting two Chester Cups, three Vaux Gold Tankards and famously winning an Ebor Handicap under the hefty burden of ten stone with Jonjo O'Neill in the saddle. If, as they say, champagne was flowing down the York stands when he won that Ebor in a photo-finish (after Jonjo had uncharacteristically 'dropped his hands' too early) Sea Pigeon's victory in the Champion Hurdle at his fourth attempt threatened to have the roof lifted off the Cheltenham stands.

Jonjo had obtained medical clearance to ride in the

Ebor only when he kidded the course doctor into examining his uninjured foot, not the one with the crushed toes. But no subterfuge was needed for his Champion Hurdle victory on Sea Pigeon in 1980, just shrewd calculation. That year a change in the course layout reduced the Champion Hurdle by 200 yards to exactly two miles and for Sea Pigeon, whose stamina was stretched to the limit by the hill finish, that may have made all the difference, O'Neill believes.

That year Sea Pigeon had had an interrupted preparation after an injury and was only 90 per cent fit. At the top of the hill he was gasping. So Jonjo switched him off, gave him time to get his second wind, and on this occasion he jumped the last not upsides Monksfield but a length down. Then Sea Pigeon produced such a surge of power that they were clear half way up the run-in. Even that was sooner than the jockey had intended. But he need not have worried. He had never felt such speed under the saddle in a jumper and with the crowd roaring encouragement they went clear to win by seven lengths.

The Cheltenham crowd loved the classy, quirky Sea Pigeon and they loved Jonjo, whose cherubic grin and twinkling eyes were accompanied by an iron will and a competitive spirit second to none once in the saddle. In riding terms he was the smiler with the knife. Sadly, when Sea Pigeon came back to defend his crown in 1981 it was without his usual partner. Jonjo's leg had been shattered in 36 places in a fall at Bangor and his efforts to get back in time to ride Sea Pigeon exacerbated the injury, requiring a further operation. This time it was John Francome who provided a silk-smooth ride, delivering Sea Pigeon half way up the run-in to beat Pollardstown and Daring Run. 'Pure class', said Francome. He too said he had never ridden a jumper with such acceleration.

Sea Pigeon (*right*), ridden by John Francome, before going on
to beat Pollardstown and Daring Run in the Champion Hurdle,
Cheltenham, March 1981.

Sea Pigeon lived on in his Yorkshire retirement
to the ripe old age of 30. He and Night Nurse won 70
races between them and the pair are buried side by side
at Habton Grange with a plaque that reads 'Legends in
their Lifetime'. No tombstone bears truer words.

Career highlights:
1977: Chester Cup, Scottish Champion Hurdle
1978: Chester Cup, Fighting Fifth Hurdle, Scottish Champion
*   Hurdle*
1979: Ebor Handicap, Welsh Champion Hurdle
1980: Champion Hurdle, Fighting Fifth Hurdle
1981: Champion Hurdle

27. NIGHT NURSE

Particular races at the Cheltenham Festival seem to go through periods when a special lustre attaches: Festival aficionados talk of a 'golden age' of hurdling from 1968 to 1981. During those 14 years the Champion Hurdle was won by just seven horses – Persian War, Bula, Comedy of Errors, Lanzarote, Night Nurse, Monksfield and Sea Pigeon – every one of them an outstanding champion. Of the seven only Lanzarote failed to win the title more than once. All were Cheltenham favourites but the ultimate accolade goes to Night Nurse. Sired by a sprinter, he not only went on to be a successful chaser too, like the mare Dawn Run, but, more importantly, he won his Cheltenham crowns against the specially tough competition of dual winners Monksfield and Sea Pigeon.

A bold front-runner who was ridden for most of his career by Paddy Broderick and latterly by his great admirer Jonjo O'Neill, Night Nurse not only won races because of his indomitable will but because of his speed and precision over the obstacles. In 1975–76 he was unbeaten in eight races including the English, Irish, Welsh and Scottish champion hurdles.

An inmate of the remarkable hurdlers' academy run by Miles Henry Easterby, known to all as Peter, Night Nurse started his career by winning three races on the Flat. He swiftly achieved a dominant position among juvenile hurdlers in the 1974–75 season and in 1976 he won his first Champion Hurdle at the age of only five, making all the running under Paddy Broderick to come home ahead of Bird's Nest.

Some horses make the running because they are tearaways who cannot be taught restraint. Night Nurse was not one of those. He was a gutsy horse and was encouraged to run that way not because he was unrestrainable but because he was comfortable out in front, a natural jumper. Like See You Then, like Istabraq, he skimmed his hurdles and was quickly away from them.

Bird's Nest, a brilliant hurdler when in the mood, was made favourite for the 1977 renewal of the Champion Hurdle on very heavy going. Bookmakers didn't reckon Night Nurse would handle it and he was pushed out from 5-2 to 15-2 to the delight of his owner Reg Spencer, who doubled his bet. He knew that Night Nurse had been for a secret racecourse gallop on soft ground and handled it well. Also in the field were two more outstanding hurdlers whose careers were to be interwoven over the next few years and who were both, like Night Nurse, to be adored by the Festival crowd: Sea Pigeon and Monksfield.

Despite the appalling conditions, Ron Barry still opted to make the pace as usual on Night Nurse, hoping that way to find the best ground. He was briefly headed mid-way through the race by Beacon Light, then challenged in turn by Fulke Walwyn's Dramatist, by Bird's Nest, Monksfield and Sea Pigeon. The race was really on as they came to the hurdle at the bottom of the hill. Monksfield hit it hard, Night Nurse jumped cleanly and was off up the rise to the winning post to record an authoritative win by two lengths. Tommy Kinane rallied Monksfield but he didn't have time to get to the leader. Dramatist and Sea Pigeon were next. It was probably the highest-quality Champion Hurdle ever and Monksfield and Sea Pigeon won the next four Champion Hurdles between them.

Seventeen days after the 1977 Champion came what has been described as the best performance ever by a hurdler: in Aintree's Templegate Hurdle Night Nurse was set to give Monksfield six pounds. Drawing upon every equine reserve, both horses gave everything in an epic

Night Nurse, ridden by Alan Brown, taking the last fence to win the Buchanan Whisky Gold Cup Chase at Ascot, November 1979.

duel. They raced head-to-head from three out and finished in a dead heat. It was enough to have wrecked many a horse but Night Nurse went on to win another Welsh Champion Hurdle. Timeform gave him a rating of 182, the highest it has ever awarded to a hurdler since it began its jump ratings in 1962–63.

After finishing third in the 1978 Champion Hurdle Night Nurse was sent over fences. Only his stablemate Little Owl beat him in the Cheltenham Gold Cup of 1981 and he was favourite when he failed to finish the next year. His chase victories included the Buchanan Whisky

Gold Cup in 1979 and the Mandarin Chase in 1982. In all he won 32 of his 64 races through nine seasons, with a record of 19 out of 32 over hurdles, and he even beat Red Rum's earnings record for a British jumper. Bold, tough, versatile and durable, he was the epitome of the National Hunt horse and few champions have been better loved.

Career highlights:
1976: Champion Hurdle, Irish Sweeps Hurdle, Welsh Champion Hurdle, Scottish Champion Hurdle
1977: Champion Hurdle, Templegate Hurdle (dead heat with Monksfield), Welsh Champion Hurdle
1979: Buchanan Whisky Gold Cup
1982: Mandarin Chase

26. HYPERION

The *Dictionary of National Biography* noted of the 17th Earl of Derby, the 'King of Lancashire' as he was known: 'Derby possessed what Englishmen admire: geniality, generosity, public spirit, great wealth and successful racehorses.' In their authoritative collection *A Century of Champions* (Portway Press) John Randall and Tony Morris made Derby their 'Man of the Century', arguing that without the stallions and broodmares that he bred with the aid of experts like trainer George Lambton the modern thoroughbred as we know it would not exist.

It was Hyperion's triumphs, they wrote, that provided the high-water mark of the century's most important racing and breeding operation. But although Hyperion was to score runaway victories in the Derby and St Leger of 1933 before becoming champion sire six times, we were lucky that he was ever born and even luckier that he made it to the racecourse.

His dam Silene had been barren for two years and her mating with Gainsborough was to be her last chance before being retired. When he was born, the colt named after a Greek sun god was small and weak with the four white socks that some see as a bad omen in a chestnut. When his contemporaries left Side Hill Stud to be trained the tiny chestnut was left behind and it is said that some urged Lord Derby to geld or even destroy him. Instead he was left to develop in his own time, and trainer George Lambton took a fancy to him when he did start training a horse who was still no bigger than a child's pony and who never grew to more than a fraction over 15 hands. He liked Hyperion's intelligence. After an early April gallop, stable jockey Tommy Weston delivered himself of the opinion that Hyperion was 'either dead lazy or next to useless'. It must have been the former because within weeks Weston was calling him 'a real good colt'.

As a two-year-old Hyperion dead-heated with the filly Nancy Stair in the Prince of Wales Stakes at Goodwood and he was beaten next time out by Manitoba before winning the Dewhurst in heavy ground. At three, still small, he was not entered in the 2,000 Guineas and did little at home on the gallops. He made his seasonal debut in the Chester Vase and after winning that by two lengths despite a sluggish start he was made favourite for the Derby.

Came the day at Epsom and Hyperion won stylishly, beating King Salmon and Statesman by four lengths. After his next race Hyperion dislocated his kneecap and missed his prep run for the St Leger. The three-month layoff did not seem to matter as Hyperion won that race from the winners of the French and Irish Derbies (those were the kinds of horses who habitually contested the St Leger in those days) by an easy three lengths after leading most of the way.

A sticky moment followed. Lord Derby felt that Lambton was too old and too sick to carry on training and called him in. The version leaked from the house before Lambton told his team the next day went like this: "'It's time for you to retire and give way to a younger man.

Derby winner Hyperion, with Tommy Weston in the saddle, is led in by victorious owner Lord Derby, May 1933.

I have decided to settle a sum of £100,000 from which you can enjoy the income for your lifetime." The old man seemed very put out and said straight off "I don't want your money" and stumped off out of the room.' Derby and Lambton parted ways, although Lambton went on training until he was 85 and they were eventually reconciled.

With Colledge Leader taking over his training, Hyperion won his first two races at four. He missed the Coronation Cup because of hard ground and although home trials had revealed doubts about his stamina he contested the Gold Cup at Ascot. In the parade ring before that race Hyperion encountered George Lambton, now in a wheelchair. Touchingly, he stopped dead and refused to move for some minutes.

The race conditions could not have been worse for him. After heavy rain the course was a bog and he finished a tired third. Hyperion's final race was in the Dullingham Stakes over a mile and a half. It was a two-horse race and he carried 142lb to the 113lb carried by his rival Caithness. In an epic nose-to-nose struggle up the straight Hyperion fought all the way but went down by a short head before quitting the racecourse for his stellar career as a stallion. His 527 foals included seven winners of 11 British Classics and he was champion sire in 1940, 1941, 1942, 1945, 1946 and 1955.

Lord Derby was once offered a blank cheque for Hyperion by American movie mogul Louis B. Mayer. His response was, 'Even though England be reduced to ashes, Hyperion shall never leave these shores', and he kept his word.

Career highlights:
1932: Prince of Wales Stakes, Dewhurst Stakes
1933: Chester Vase, Derby, St Leger

25. ISTABRAQ

He may be an instinctive genius with horses, a meticulous planner and a ruthless executioner, but trainer Aidan O'Brien is a gently spoken, almost shy man given more to understatement than braggadocio. Jockey Charlie Swan was therefore startled to hear Aidan declare before Istabraq tackled Cheltenham's Champion Hurdle for the first time in 1998: 'Istabraq will destroy them.' But never was a truer word spoken.

Swan had won the 1997 Sun Alliance Novice Hurdle at the Festival on Istabraq but he reckoned that his mount, having won over two and a half miles, might be short of a true Champion Hurdler's speed. He resolved to ride him for stamina, forcing the pace. But he need not have worried. By the time they got to the top of the hill and began the descent Istabraq's high cruising speed had demolished his rivals. He simply crushed them body and spirit with his sustained pace and came home 12 lengths clear. Jockey Chris Maude, asked by an owner the next year if his horse had a chance of beating Istabraq, replied: 'Only if he kicks him at the start.'

Istabraq was a phenomenon who won 18 of his first 20 contests over hurdles. The most respected of all racing assessors, Timeform, gave Night Nurse a rating of 182 in 1976–77. The only other horse ever to make 180 in Timeform was Istabraq in the 1999–2000 season. Was O'Brien's horse the best of all? The inter-generational comparison game is fun but can often be misleading. All we really know is that Istabraq, owned by J.P. McManus and handled by O'Brien before he began concentrating on the Flat, soared above his contemporaries. He was never tested in handicaps but in championship races involving Istabraq we did not get the 'duel factor' with regular rivals. There was simply no one around capable of duelling with him. His winning margins over his three Champion Hurdle victories totalled nearly 20 lengths compared to 15 for See You Then and nine and a half for Persian War.

Despite the way he raced, Istabraq was highly strung and easily upset. Before his first Cheltenham victory in 1997 he got himself into a mucksweat that could have ruined the chances of a horse with a smaller talent reserve. O'Brien and his team had to devise a schedule that kept Istabraq happy without letting him get too boisterous and edgy, as he was inclined to do when approaching race-fitness.

Originally owned by Hamdan al-Maktoum and trained at Newmarket by John Gosden, Istabraq had won only twice from 11 starts on the Flat. But a change of game and of training scenario can work wonders. He rapidly showed O'Brien what he could do over obstacles and was soon holding his own at home with any of O'Brien's Flat stars over a mile and a half. All Ireland seemed to know it and he was the banker for their Festival punters for four years.

Istabraq's 12-length margin in winning the Champion Hurdle of 1998 was the biggest since 1932. When he came back to the Festival the next year O'Brien said he was heavier, stronger and quicker and a record first-day crowd of 46,470 turned out to see him defend his crown at 9-4 on. Some thought French Holly might have given him a race but at the second last Istabraq asserted and won as he liked, with O'Brien's Theatreworld eventually finishing second nearly four lengths down. The previous year O'Brien had put the stable staff money each way on Theatreworld at 40-1. This time they had to be content with the return from 25-1.

In theory the 2000 contest should have been a lot tougher for Istabraq. Among those lining up against him was Hors La Loi III who had won the Supreme Novices Hurdle the year before in a time three seconds faster than Istabraq's in the Champion. There was, too, a scare the day before racing. At the course, Istabraq had bled from one nostril. If it was an internal haemorrhage that could be serious, but it could equally be just a knock on

Istabraq, ridden by Charlie Swan, on the way to winning the first of his three Champion Hurdles, Cheltenham, March 1998.

the nose. So close to a race he could not be sedated and 'scoped' (i.e. the mucus from his lungs examined) and, because it was the Champion Hurdle with a third consecutive title involved, Team O'Brien chose to run.

In the event there was no problem. Make A Stand, back from injury, tried to repeat his all-the-way win from three years before but faded after the fifth. Nicky Henderson's runners Katarino and Blue Royal then took it up. But by the turn for the straight every whip except Charlie Swan's was in action. Istabraq won by four lengths from Hors La Loi in a new record time. O'Brien commented that Istabraq probably hadn't been at his best but he was so superior to the other horses that that had not mattered. The tragedy is that the foot-and-mouth epidemic in Britain, which produced far more serious repercussions for many farmers, wiped out the Festival of 2001 and so gave Istabraq no chance that year of becoming the first four-time champion.

He was back for the Festival of 2002 but by then rumours were flying that all was not well with him. The thousands of Irish fans wearing rosettes in McManus's green and gold colours demanding 'Gimme Four' backed the champion down to favourite once again. But soon after they set off Charlie Swan sensed something was amiss and before the second hurdle he pulled up Istabraq. The impressive thing was the way the crowd responded. Much like the reaction when Kauto Star was pulled up in his final Gold Cup in 2012 they applauded the pulling up of a well-backed horse. Many of those who signalled their approval of the jockey's action would have lost their betting money for the week, but they did not want risks taken with a great horse who had given so much pleasure. The reaction was a tribute to the sporting crowd of true enthusiasts that Cheltenham draws. It was also a sign of massive respect and affection for a remarkably talented horse.

Career highlights:
1997: Sun Alliance Novices Hurdle, Hatton's Grace Hurdle, Punchestown Champion Novices Hurdle, December Festival Hurdle
1998: Champion Hurdle, Irish Champion Hurdle, Hatton's Grace Hurdle, December Festival Hurdle
1999: Champion Hurdle, Irish Champion Hurdle, Aintree Hurdle, Punchestown Champion Hurdle, December Festival Hurdle
2000: Champion Hurdle, Irish Champion Hurdle, December Festival Hurdle
2001: Irish Champion Hurdle

24. GALILEO

Ask top trainers to sum up the essence of what they do and most find it impossible to put into words. One response that always sticks in my mind, though, was Aidan O'Brien's when we questioned him after one of Galileo's victories. How did he know when the horse was ready? 'You know by his behaviour, the expression on his face, how he carries on with himself.' So that's it ...

Galileo was beautifully bred. His sire Sadler's Wells produced more than 130 Group One winners. His dam Urban Sea was an Arc winner who was the dam also of Sea The Stars. Galileo, a bay with a thin white blaze and a white sock on his near hind, has himself become a highly successful sire, responsible among others for the mighty Frankel. But in his comparatively short career he was no mean performer on the racetrack too.

Trained by O'Brien at Ballydoyle for Sue Magnier and Michael Tabor, Galileo did not make it to the course as a two-year-old until October 2000 but he did not appear unnoticed, being made the even money favourite of 16 runners in a Leopardstown maiden despite good-looking entrants from John Oxx and Jim Bolger. With Mick Kinane in the saddle Galileo tracked the leaders early on, moved into the lead in the straight and extended the margin to 14 lengths before he reached the line.

Mick Kinane on Galileo leads the field home to win the Derby, June 2001.

At three he took the Derby trial route, heading back to Leopardstown to contest the Listed Ballysax Stakes over a mile and a quarter. As the 1-3 favourite he raced smoothly, led two out and coasted to an easy victory by three and a half lengths. Runner up Milan was to win the St Leger and the third-placed Vinnie Roe went on to win the Irish version four times. With O'Brien having announced that his horses were still 'as big as bulls' after that outing Galileo was not surprisingly odds-on also for the Derrinstown Stud Derby Trial back at Leopardstown in May. Seamus Heffernan had to put Galileo under a little pressure but he went on to beat John Oxx's Exaltation by one and a half lengths.

Next stop was Epsom and Galileo was the 11-4 favourite for the Derby too, despite the presence in the field of 2,000 Guineas winner Golan. Mick Kinane brought Galileo round Tattenham Corner with just Mr Combustible and Perfect Sunday ahead of him. Two furlongs out he moved past Mr Combustible and went clear for a three and a half length victory over Golan and Tobougg. 'The best I have ridden', was Kinane's verdict. 'There is no weakness to him.'

Galileo continued to confirm that verdict, winning the Irish Derby as an odds-on favourite four lengths clear of Italian Derby winner Morshdi with Golan another four lengths away in third. After that the next test was to take on the older horses in the King George VI and Queen Elizabeth Stakes at Ascot.

It was here that Galileo began his famous rivalry with the older Fantastic Light, winner of a string of Group Ones across the world. Mick Kinane made his usual move two out. Frankie Dettori followed him on Fantastic Light, but though they matched strides for a while it was Galileo who went away at the end to win by two lengths.

It was Fantastic Light, however, who took away Galileo's unbeaten record at their next meeting in the Irish Champion Stakes over two furlongs shorter. Fantastic Light committed early this time, Galileo tackled him and edged past but in one of the greatest race finishes seen in Ireland Fantastic Light came back once more to beat him a head in a photo finish. O'Brien felt he had got the tactics wrong.

For Galileo there was to be just one more race, in the Breeders' Cup, though sadly it was not against Fantastic Light, who was at the last minute switched by Godolphin from the Classic to the Turf. Tackling dirt for the first time, Galileo tracked the leaders but proved unable to quicken in the final straight, finishing sixth of 14 to Tiznow. It was the only blemish on an otherwise spotless career.

Career highlights:
2001: Derby, Irish Derby, King George VI and Queen Elizabeth
     Stakes

23. DAWN RUN

Only one horse in the history of the Cheltenham Festival has won both the Champion Hurdle and the Gold Cup, the mare Dawn Run. Ireland's heroine wasn't a friendly mare or an attractive one. She was built on masculine lines and bad-tempered with it. Even getting her rug on or off took two people to ensure no one was savaged.

Dawn Run's owner, Charmian Hill, who had insisted on trainer Paddy Mullins 'jocking off' his son Tony and putting up Jonjo O'Neill to ride her in the Gold Cup, was an awkward cuss too. She had to be forcibly retired from riding herself at 62. But what horse and owner both had was fighting spirit. That was why Dawn Run was adopted by the Irish nation and the way she won her Gold Cup was an inspiration to anyone who has ever faced adversity. It had looked all over, but it wasn't – thanks to a jockey who never gave up and a horse prepared to reach to the uttermost limits to get her nose back in front.

When Jonjo first rode the mare in her hurdling days he told Paddy Mullins: 'She's no Champion Hurdle mare, you know, she's slow!' After riding her in a few more races Jonjo changed his mind about her quality and he was on board when she won the 1984 Champion Hurdle as the 5-4 on favourite, the first mare to do so since 1939.

Dawn Run may have benefited from the 5lb allowance for mares participating in the race but her racing qualities had more to do with character than strict handicap ratings. She was one of those horses who hated to be passed and who was always ready to fight back.

The 1984 Champion Hurdle had been expected to be a virtual match between her and Gaye Brief, the 1983 Champion Hurdle winner whom Dawn Run had defeated in the Christmas Hurdle at Kempton Park after the Rimells' horse had suffered an interrupted preparation, but then Gaye Brief was withdrawn injured. Only the novice Desert Orchid was at less than 14-1 to beat her on the big day and she had a two-length margin entering the straight. She lost concentration at the last and landed flat-footed but when she heard the lone pursuer, the 66-1 outsider Cima, coming she ground her teeth and powered up the hill to win. With Tony Mullins back on board two victories in France followed and Dawn Run's success in the Irish, English and French Champion Hurdles amassed record stakes for a season of a few pounds short of £150,000.

But hurdles are one thing, fences quite another. When

she came to Cheltenham for the Gold Cup it was only Dawn Run's fifth race over the bigger obstacles and she had unshipped Tony Mullins in the fourth. Irish money had made her the ante post favourite after she had won chases at Punchestown and Leopardstown but when Jonjo went over to school her he was appalled how novicey she was, quite apart from being 'a moody old devil'. He told her trainer she shouldn't be in the race.

Dawn Run's opponents on Gold Cup day were proven quantities. The classy Wayward Lad had three times won the King George VI Chase, Forgive 'n' Forget had won the previous year's Gold Cup and Run And Skip had proved his stamina by winning the Welsh Grand National.

It is exhilarating still to hear her rider tell the story of that extraordinary race. Says Jonjo: 'Coming down the hill we were after going a right gallop. I missed the water jump and that kind of messed us up a little bit. There were three or four front-runners. There was Cybrandian, herself, and Run And Skip and I think another [Forgive 'n' Forget] all going for the lead, all good horses. We were going so fast I missed the water and I couldn't give her a breather when I wanted to. Then she got headed. She didn't like being headed and I had to motivate her out of it, motivate her from every angle.

'We were going some lick. She missed the fence after the ditch going up the hill – she walked through that one – and then I was in trouble trying to get her back as the race was really on at that stage. I was lucky enough that Run And Skip missed the one at the top of the hill and so I got upsides – we were back on top again.

'We were flying down the hill and I could hear them coming behind us. I thought we'd gone a right gallop and couldn't believe they were so close to us. We jumped the third last and they were jumping up my backside and I

Dawn Run, ridden by Jonjo O'Neill, jumps ahead of Run And
Skip in the Cheltenham Gold Cup, March 1986.

thought "Jesus, if we don't ping the second last we're going
to get beat". She did ping the second last but they passed
me as if I was stopped. I couldn't believe it. I thought "Oh,
we're beaten" so I left her alone for a few strides. Then,
just between the second last and the last I could feel her
filling up and I thought "We ain't done yet".

'We rallied to the last and we were flying and she
picked up, she picked up outside the wings herself in fair-
ness to her. Wayward Lad was in front of me and he hung
in across. I thought "He won't get home" because I'd ridden him the year before and Forgive 'n' Forget had had
enough of it at that stage. I just kept going across the track
on her now, and the more on her own she was, the better

she was. She came up the hill like a tyrant. The funny thing was that halfway going down to the last I knew I was going to win. I just knew she'd keep going once I'd got her motivated. I know it didn't look that way but I knew she'd get up the hill.'

Dawn Run came level with Wayward Lad in the last 40 yards and went by to win by a length. Their epic contest was a test as much of character as of racing ability and Dawn Run had that in bucketloads. No horse has ever appeared so beaten in a big race and yet gone on to win, and at the moment Peter O'Sullevan declared, 'The mare's going to get up', a small nation rose to its feet. Festival regulars have never heard a noisier reception for a winner and no clips of any Cheltenham Festival finish have ever had so many replays.

On the course there was pandemonium, with souvenir hunters grabbing hairs from Dawn Run's tail and Jonjo terrified he would lose his tack before weighing out. 'It was a magical day. It was fantastic. The whole of Ireland wanted her to win and knew she could win. It was great that she did it and it was great how she did it. I've met a lot of people since who've told me what inspiration it gave them at times when they were down in their lives.'

Dawn Run had her own way of doing things. Says Jonjo: 'If you hit her before she was ready to be hit she'd pull up, and she would let you know. But if you got her motivated and motivated then once you had her up and running she'd go through fire – no problem.'

Go through fire she did in that 1986 Gold Cup. It was the finest recovery ever. But the sequel was sad. A few weeks later Charmian Hill insisted against her trainer's advice that the mare should be sent back to Paris to run over hurdles once again. At Auteuil she fell and was killed. But she is never forgotten and her Cheltenham statue remains a favourite meeting point, especially for Irish fans.

Career highlights:
1983: Christmas Hurdle
1984: Irish Champion Hurdle, Champion Hurdle, Grand
        Course des Haies d'Auteuil (French Champion Hurdle)
1986: Cheltenham Gold Cup

22. TUDOR MINSTREL

When Tudor Minstrel ran in the 2,000 Guineas of 1947 I was of an age more concerned with catapults and sherbet lemons but it is said that no racing enthusiast who saw his display that day will ever forget it. So spectacular was his early speed that everybody knew the winner before half-way. A side-on photograph of the field at that stage shows Gordon Richards perched up cantering on the hard-held Tudor Minstrel with virtually every other jockey already hard at work simply to keep in touch. The official victory margin was eight lengths: many thought it was more, and had Gordon Richards wanted he could probably have doubled the gap.

Many the next morning hailed Tudor Minstrel in print as the best there had ever been. Phil Bull wrote later: 'The memory of Tudor Minstrel's strolling home the length of a street in front of everything else will remain with me for the rest of my life. I don't expect to see such a thing in a Classic race again.' As seasoned a judge as Quintin Gilbey declared that Tudor Minstrel could beat any horse in the country at any distance from five furlongs to five miles.

He wasn't quite that good. Tudor Minstrel had come to hand particularly early despite a bad winter. His trainer

Fred Darling had another horse he rated for the Derby and so went all out for the Guineas with Tudor Minstrel, holding nothing back. Come Epsom on Derby Day the hopes of a super-horse took a huge dent. Although Gordon Richards had insisted that as a two-year-old Tudor Minstrel was as tractable as you could wish, on that day he fought his jockey for his head all the way and was a spent force by the time they reached the straight. Richards put down his whip and accepted the fourth place that was the best he could do as the French-trained outsider Pearl Diver went on to win. Newspapers the next day greeted the defeat of the 4-7 Derby favourite as a national tragedy.

Tudor Minstrel, with Gordon Richards in the saddle, leaves the paddock at Bath after winning the Somerset Stakes, April 1947.

Because Tudor Minstrel would not give himself the chance to settle, from then on a mile was his limit. Every race he had run up until then he had been able to run his own way, blasting off as the tapes went up and never easing, but you can't do that in a Derby. As Phil Bull's Timeform noted: Tudor Minstrel had always been a free runner; from the Guineas on he was a puller, determined to tear up the course from the word go.

Tudor Minstrel, a brown colt by Owen Tudor, went on from the Derby to win the St James's Palace Stakes at Royal Ascot. He then ran second in the Eclipse, failing to stay the ten furlongs at Sandown, and concluded his short racecourse career by winning the Knight's Royal Stakes (the Ascot contest that became the Queen Elizabeth II Stakes) when he injected an extraordinary burst of speed into the race just after the turn, which carried him clear of his field. Overall he won eight of his ten races. His Guineas display and the sheer brilliance he showed as a two-year-old, running away with four races including the Coventry and the National Breeders Produce Stakes in effortless style, have maintained his position among the all-time greats.

Career highlights:
1946: Coventry Stakes, National Breeders Produce Stakes
1947: 2,000 Guineas, St James's Palace Stakes, Knight's Royal
   Stakes

21. NASHWAN

Dick Hern, who trained 16 Classic winners in his 40-year career, said of Nashwan: 'Although he had a shorter career than many of the other top horses I have been fortunate to train, I still regard Nashwan as the best.' Nashwan was a favourite too with Willie Carson. The former champion jockey, who nicknamed the horse 'Nash the Dash', said: 'He had that lovely long stride that would grab the ground and enable him to quicken in an instant.' More excitedly, Willie said once: 'Riding Nashwan is like making love. It is absolutely fantastic. Whatever you are thinking, the horse does' – although we didn't get to hear Mrs Carson's view of that comparison.

Nashwan, a son of Blushing Groom out of Height O'Fashion, may have run only seven races but his was a glorious career. As a two-year-old he won two not particularly fashionable races at Newbury and Ascot. He strengthened over the winter and word soon spread that the big colt had been leaving vapour trails on the gallops in the approach to the 1989 2,000 Guineas, resulting in his installation as favourite. All did not progress smoothly, though, and after a setback Nashwan missed the Guineas trials, arriving at Newmarket without a preparatory race. You would not have known it from his performance in the first Classic, and Willie Carson says that he was never more confident of winning a race than he was that day.

Hamdan al-Maktoum's colt won like a favourite should, taking the lead two furlongs out and impressing all with the fluency of his action. He won by a length from Exbourne, the result never in doubt, with Danehill in third, and in the process he clocked the fastest showing since the arrival of electrical timing. It was as smooth as an otter's glide through water. Some then wondered if such a big long-striding horse would be suited by Epsom's gradients and camber, but Hern and Carson expressed no doubts and he was made favourite for that race too. In the event it was a romp. With the French champion Old Vic staying at home for the Parisian Derby the main danger was Cacoethes, who had looked good in winning the Lingfield Derby Trial by four lengths.

A fast pace was set by Cacoethes' pacemaker Polar Run. Early in the straight Willie momentarily had to get to work on Nashwan, who was switched to the inside. But after a couple of cracks of the whip he simply strode away from his field, with Clive Brittain's underrated 500-1 outsider Terimon running on to be second five lengths behind him and Cacoethes third.

Then it was on to the Eclipse at Sandown, which produced another spectacular performance. Starting as the 2-5 favourite, Nashwan was opposed again by Cacoethes and the pair were taken on by Sheikh Mohammed's Champion Stakes-winning mare Indian Skimmer and Opening Verse, by the good miler Warning and by

Nashwan, ridden by Willie Carson, is led into the winners' enclosure at the 2,000 Guineas, Newmarket, May 1989.

Greensmith and Spring Hay. Turning for home Opening Verse, ridden by Nigel Day, had beaten off the latter pair and went six lengths clear but with a phenomenal burst of speed Nashwan closed down the leader and swept past him, winning in the end by five lengths. It looked like a romp but Carson, often his own fiercest critic, says he gave Nashwan too much to do in letting the leader get so far ahead, making life much harder for him in a fortnight's time.

Nashwan already had a burgeoning trophy cupboard – the 2,000 Guineas, the Derby and the Eclipse. No horse yet had won those three and gone on to collect the King George VI as well, but that was the next task assigned to Hamdan al-Maktoum's champion. Again his rivals included Cacoethes and this time his old rival battled him all the way to the line in a struggle reminiscent of that between Grundy and Bustino. Nashwan, says Willie, was a tired horse and they only just got away with it by staging a slowly-run race. 'We bottomed him in the Eclipse and after that I was having to look after him in the King George.'

His quartet of victories gave Nashwan a racing first, and the public yearned for him to go on to the St Leger and become the first Triple Crown winner since Nijinsky in 1970. Perhaps with modern breeding trends in mind, his owner decided to go for the Arc instead. But from then on things went awry. In his prep race in the Prix Niel in France Nashwan was unexpectedly beaten into third behind Golden Pheasant. To some puzzlement, particularly after a sparkling gallop ten days before the race, he was then withdrawn from the Arc and targeted instead at Newmarket's Champion Stakes. In the end he missed that race too, suffering from a fever, and so a great year and a great career ended with a damp squib.

Career highlights:
1989: 2,000 Guineas, Derby, Eclipse Stakes, King George VI
  and Queen Elizabeth Stakes

20. L'ESCARGOT

If ever a horse was inappropriately named it was
L'Escargot. After his first Cheltenham Gold Cup win his
owner, the polo-playing Raymond Guest, America's millionaire Ambassador to Dublin, was wandering about the
parade ring muttering, 'He's no snail … he's no snail',
and he was absolutely right: his fine chestnut chaser is the
only horse apart from Golden Miller to have won both
the Cheltenham Gold Cup and the Grand National.

Trained by Dan Moore at Fairyhouse, L'Escargot
landed a betting coup for his yard by winning his first
outing in a bumper (a Flat race for jumping horses) at
Navan at 100-7 in 1967. At the Cheltenham Festival in
1968 he won the Gloucester Hurdle but he failed to figure in the 1969 Champion Hurdle and embarked on a
chasing career.

His owner sent him to the USA where he won the
Meadowbrook Chase and in 1970, on the insistence of
Raymond Guest, L'Escargot ran as a 33-1 shot in the
Cheltenham Gold Cup. Despite some doubts about his
stamina he out-battled French Tan up the run-in to score
by a length and a half, although only after the favourite
Kinloch Brae had tipped up three out when going well.

The next season L'Escargot took a while to find his
best form but came good in time for Cheltenham, where
he won by ten lengths from Leap Frog on heavy ground.
This time he benefited when Glencaraig Lady, who was to
win the race in 1972, knuckled over when going well at

the third last. Tommy Carberry was adamant L'Escargot would have won anyway but Raymond Guest was not exactly an unlucky owner – there were seven fallers when his Larkspur won the Derby!

Mr Guest, who won a Derby too with Sir Ivor, badly wanted a Grand National to add to his brace of Derby and Gold Cup victories and he sent L'Escargot on to Aintree three weeks later, but the Gold Cup winner was brought down at the third fence.

In 1973 it was an even tougher ask. Having finished fourth in the Gold Cup L'Escargot was asked to run again at Aintree only 16 days later. The good to firm going that year was ideal for the duel between Crisp and Red Rum and it did not suit L'Escargot. Nevertheless he finished third as the pair fought out an epic finish ahead of him.

In 1974 his connections made Aintree the focus and swerved Cheltenham. Red Rum carried an extra 23lb, giving 1lb to L'Escargot, but it was not enough of a turnaround in the weights: L'Escargot finished second but Red Rum was still seven lengths ahead of him at the line.

After that trainer Dan Moore told Raymond Guest that L'Escargot's only hope of winning the National was to go to Aintree as a comparatively fresh horse. He did run at Cheltenham in 1975 but this time only in the two-mile Champion Chase. At Aintree the handicapper clearly believed that at the age of 12 and with only one success in the past four seasons L'Escargot was past his prime, and he set him to receive 11lbs from Red Rum. On soft ground that made all the difference Red Rum on this occasion could not shake off L'Escargot and Tommy Carberry. The two horses jumped the last together but up that long elbow run-in L'Escargot this time forged 15 lengths clear. Lucky Raymond had his National too and he immediately announced that L'Escargot would be

L'Escargot, ridden by Tommy Carberry, comes home to win
the Grand National, April 1975.

retired and spend the rest of his days with Dan Moore and
his wife.

They found the old boy so lively still that autumn that
they could not resist running him in the Kerry National,
in which he lost by only a head. That was not what Guest
had intended: L'Escargot was thereupon shipped to
Virginia where he spent the final decade of his life without facing the starter again.

Career highlights:
1968: Gloucester Hurdle
1970, 1971: Cheltenham Gold Cup
1975: Grand National

19. PRETTY POLLY

Sometimes you wonder why more breeders don't go mad. Pretty Polly, the outstanding racemare of her century and probably of all time, was sired by Gallinule, who had a breathing problem that made him a 'roarer' and who was also a 'bleeder' prone to breaking blood vessels. Her dam was Admiration, who had won two insignificant races in Ireland before being tried without much success as a steeplechaser. Their daughter ran in nine races as a two-year-old in 1903 and won them all – including the Cheveley Park and Middle Park Stakes with just one day between the two contests.

One jockey who rode against her then declared: 'If you continue to race after her with the courage of despair all you can win is a bad headache. It is her nature to be first past the post.'

The races won at two were a mere prelude. As a three-year-old Pretty Polly, trained by Peter Purcell Gilpin and ridden in each race by Billy Lane, won the Fillies' Triple Crown. First she took the 1,000 Guineas, scoring easily by three lengths in record time. She won the Oaks at Epsom and the St Leger at Doncaster. But for good measure she added the Nassau Stakes at Goodwood and the Park Hill Stakes. The only pity is that her connections didn't take on the colts in the 2,000 Guineas and Derby. Both those races were won by St Amant, whom she beat on every one of the five occasions when they met.

To the delight of the racing public, owner Major Eustace Loder, who had bred the filly on the Curragh, kept Pretty Polly in training as a four- and five-year-old. She won the Coronation Cup back at Epsom in both 1905 and 1906. In all she won 22 of her 24 races and there were explanations for the two defeats. When Pretty Polly was beaten in Longchamp's Prix du Conseil Municipal in 1904 (the Prix de l'Arc de Triomphe was not then even a glimmer in a race-planner's eye) a bad train journey, heavy going and the substitution of Danny Maher for Billy Lane, who had been injured in a fall, did not help her chances. Then in her final race, the Gold Cup at Ascot in 1906, Pretty Polly went down only a length to a proven stayer with a pacemaker. She was out of sorts, having had a boil on her stomach lanced in the racecourse stables, and yet she still ran Bachelor's Button to a length as he set a new course record.

It is not surprising that Pretty Polly has races named after her both at Newmarket and the Curragh. Her range

Bernard Dillon on Pretty Polly, winner of the Fillies' Triple Crown in 1904: the 1,000 Guineas, the Oaks and the St Leger.

was extraordinary. She won over distances from five furlongs to two and a quarter miles and was champion of either sex at two, three and four. Competing in an age when racing truly was the people's sport, attracting a level of attention now given only to overpaid and oversexed footballers, the chestnut filly was adored by the public. Thousands of postcards of her were sold before she took the third leg of the Triple Crown and men and women wore rosettes and ties proclaiming their allegiance like the Kauto Star scarves of recent years.

The media and racing fans loved it too when they discovered that (like those other great racemares later, Petite Etoile and Pebbles) Pretty Polly had an inseparable companion for whom she displayed obvious affection, a cob named Little Missus who used to be there waiting for her in the winners' enclosure – an area that at Newmarket became known as 'Pretty Polly's corner'. On the day Pretty Polly lost at Ascot her friend Little Missus was absent sick.

Pretty Polly's immediate progeny did not win on the same scale but her four daughters, each by a different sire, all proved to be successful broodmares, founding a Classic-winning family (14-C) with a vital place in the stud book. John Randall and Tony Morris argue that Pretty Polly's racing record is unapproached, let alone unsurpassed. In their *A Century of Champions* they had no hesitation in awarding her the title of 'Mare of the Century'.

Career highlights:
1903: Champagne Stakes, Cheveley Park Stakes, Middle Park Stakes
1904: 1,000 Guineas, Oaks, St Leger, Nassau Stakes, Park Hill Stakes, Coronation Stakes
1905: Coronation Cup, Champion Stakes, Jockey Club Cup
1906: Coronation Cup

18. PEBBLES

The racing public adores a quality filly, especially a filly who demonstrates a flash or two of feminine temperament. Clive Brittain's Pebbles, the best filly we saw in the second half of the last century, was all girl.

Clive likened the bright chestnut foal with the white splash on her forehead and a big bold eye to a lissom French model rather than the more masculine fillies who have often prevailed in top races. What is more, Pebbles had a stable love affair with the gelding Come On The Blues, who accompanied her around the world. That made her tabloid property too, so she was always 'news'.

It did no harm to the story that she was handled by a trainer widely perceived as the nicest man in racing, famous for his winners' enclosure dances, his quick quips and for aiming his horses at seemingly impossible targets and then achieving them. But there can be no belittling what Clive and Pebbles achieved together.

She won a 1,000 Guineas with total authority and humbled two outstanding colts in a Champion Stakes. She was the first filly in history to win the Eclipse Stakes and the first British-trained winner of a Breeders' Cup – it was six years before any other British trainer secured a follow-up – and she won more money in a season than any other British horse had done before her.

Not only was that a fair list of advertisements for Clive Brittain's abilities as a racehorse trainer but he had to be a horse psychiatrist too. Pebbles was the nervy sort, easily upset by racecourse preliminaries, and he had to pull every kind of stroke to spare her those whenever he could. As he puts it: 'It was a question of working out her break level. All that pent-up power and emotion had to be saved and directed.'

Pebbles' career began down the field in a Sandown maiden before she then won a better race at Newbury. She was fourth in the Lowther Stakes at York, disappointed next time out at Goodwood and then finished her juvenile season by figuring in a three-way photo for the Cheveley Park.

Pebbles opened her three-year-old career in 1984 by winning the Nell Gwyn Stakes at Newmarket and it was then on to the 1,000 Guineas. There Pebbles, ridden by Philip Robinson, did more than win: she stamped her authority on the fillies of her generation, beating Meis El-Reem by three lengths, the widest winning margin for 11 years. The story behind the story should have put Clive Brittain in line for a Hollywood Oscar.

To stop Pebbles fretting through the parade in front of the stands he led her up himself, then pretended to fall over, letting her go off to the start while anxious officials clustered to see he wasn't injured.

After the Guineas Clive Brittain aimed Pebbles at the Oaks, declaring: 'She is a very good filly – the best I have ever trained. I am sure she will stay a mile and a half. She's like a cat, so agile. She can change legs in mid-air. The Epsom hill should be no problem.' But her owner-breeder Marcos Lemos accepted a huge offer for the filly from Sheikh Mohammed. Since he already had two fancied runners scheduled for the Oaks, Pebbles was instead aimed at Royal Ascot's shorter Coronation Stakes, where she was beaten by Mick Ryan's Katies – with Philip Robinson aboard.

Said Clive: 'She's the sort of animal that you wouldn't want to gee-up in a hurry. She went there having been trained for the Oaks but still ran a game race to be second to Katies.' After that, injury kept Pebbles off the course until the Champion Stakes in the autumn. There she

Trainer Clive Brittain with Pebbles, winner of the 1,000 Guineas
at Newmarket, May 1984.

accelerated impressively and came with a great late run, only going down to the talented French raider Palace Music by a neck. After the race Brittain told Sheikh Mohammed: 'I'll bring her back and win it for you next year.' He kept his promise in formidable style in a year in which Pebbles proved herself the best in the world.

In 1985 Pebbles won a comeback race at Sandown and was beaten at Ascot before coming out again in the Eclipse to tackle that year's Coronation Cup winner Rainbow Quest, later to win the Arc. Again, a little Brittain subterfuge involving some shoe-checking by a compliant blacksmith kept Pebbles from participating in the preliminaries and bubbling over. In the race Steve Cauthen was on Pebbles and he made a decisive move past Rainbow Quest's pacemaker three furlongs out. Just one tap with the whip and Pebbles stretched away from Rainbow Quest to become the first filly to win the race in its 99 years of existence. Rainbow Quest never looked like having the speed to match her acceleration.

A month or two later the *Daily Mirror* ran a big story with a picture of Pebbles and her amour Come On The Blues, the two horses seemingly cuddling. Tim Richards wrote: 'A rich and special young lady has fallen for a poor boy. Wonder filly Pebbles, who is worth in excess of £6 million, took one look at Come On The Blues, worth a mere £50,000, and she lost her heart to the four-legged lad. When two horses find happiness together, who are the humans to argue? A special grille was put between their adjoining boxes and Clive said: "They spend hours looking at each other. Their relationship is like a happy marriage."'

Her next race, the Champion Stakes, was astonishing. Although it contained six Group One winners it was widely seen as a duel between two outstanding colts – the runaway Derby winner Slip Anchor and Commanche Run, being ridden by Lester Piggott. Steve Cauthen took Slip Anchor to the front at the start but was never allowed to go clear.

Pat Eddery had trouble settling Pebbles at first and switched her off at the back. They were still last at halfway. Three furlongs out as Commanche Run dropped back, unable to go the gallop any longer with Slip Anchor, she began to waltz through the field on the stands rail. Everyone else was hard at work but Eddery was perched up with a double handful. With majestic acceleration Pebbles went clear as if the others were plodding home in a three-mile chase and won by three lengths from Slip Anchor and Palace Music. It was an almost contemptuous victory, one of those electric moments in racing we all live for, and Clive Brittain had made good his promise to Sheikh Mohammed.

Pat Eddery's comment as he dismounted was succinct: 'Next stop Breeders' Cup' – and off they went to Aqueduct racetrack, New York. There in the Breeders' Cup Turf she was made favourite.

British jockey Tony Ives, on Lord Derby's Teleprompter, the winner of the Budweiser Arlington Million, set a scorching pace for the 14 runners. To conserve Pebbles' suspect stamina on her first attempt at a mile and a half, Pat Eddery took the risky course of anchoring her at the back and hugging the rail. Turning for home, America's Greinton swept past Teleprompter with several runners still forming a potential wall ahead of the filly. But at that moment a chink of light appeared inside Teleprompter on the far rail and Pebbles pounced like a cat.

Immediately displaying the famous acceleration that had won her the 1,000 Guineas and taken her past Rainbow Quest in the Eclipse, Pebbles went through the gap and took the lead. Steve Cauthen, on Daniel Wildenstein's Strawberry Road, then launched a power-ful attack but Pebbles kept pulling out more for a clever win. When the time was announced, lowering the course record by a massive 1.2 seconds, there was an audible gasp from the crowd. Americans called her 'the British super-filly' and Pebbles had proved herself one of the toughest and bravest racemares ever seen.

Sheikh Mohammed kept Pebbles in training for the 1986 season but after suffering inflammation of a shoul-der cartilage she was retired that July without getting back on a racecourse.

Career highlights:
1985: Nell Gwyn Stakes, 1,000 Guineas
1986: Sandown Mile, Eclipse Stakes, Champion Stakes, Breeders'
    Cup Turf

17. DANCING BRAVE

There are perhaps three races that I would have been will-ing to endure an eye-tooth extraction to have seen live: Mandarin's triumph in the 1962 Grand Prix de Paris with-out brakes or steering, Sea-Bird's effortless triumph in the 1965 Derby, and Dancing Brave's arrival at the end of the 1986 Prix de l'Arc de Triomphe with the velocity of an arrow to rocket past the best Europe had to offer. Those who saw it doubt that any horse has ever travelled so fast over the last one and a half furlongs of Longchamp turf, and Dancing Brave's victory that day was important not only because of the dramatic way in which it was achieved but because without that extraordinary race one of the best horses we have seen might have been remembered more for one unlucky defeat than for the series of top-class races he won. Poor Greville Starkey, a truly talented rider, probably went to his grave regretting what appeared to be his over-confidence on Dancing Brave on Derby Day 1986.

Khalid Abdulla's colt, trained at Pulborough by Guy Harwood, was hardly handsome, having a parrot mouth. He didn't spend his two-year-old days tussling with the best of his generation through the traditional trial races. Instead he picked up two late-season contests over a mile at Sandown and Newmarket. Even though he was rated outside the top 50 two-year-olds that year, it was enough to ensure that this son of Lyphard headed some books as a winter favourite for the 2,000 Guineas.

At three he soon demonstrated his wellbeing. Dancing Brave won the Heidsieck Champagne Craven Stakes over the Guineas course and distance at Newmarket. His jockey never even had to show him the whip in all three prep races. In the first Classic he looked in magnificent shape in the parade ring and won equally handsomely, quickening up the hill in the way El Gran Senor had done two years earlier to beat Green Desert by three lengths. Then began the usual debate about whether a horse demonstrating such class over a mile could be expected to last the Derby distance. His trainer contributed by declaring at Newmarket: 'He's got such speed that we'd always thought of today as his race.'

Harwood had other potential Derby entries for Khalid Abdulla including Bakharoff and Armada, but in the end Dancing Brave started favourite at 2-1 despite having been temporarily displaced when Shahrastani won the Mecca Dante and he had been reported as having disappointed in a gallop.

Lester Piggott, winner of the race nine times, has

always held the view that in the Derby you have to keep handy throughout and use a horse's speed to maintain a good position. Few come from the back of the pack round Tattenham Corner to win the race. But that is what Greville Starkey tried to do.

Some restraint might have been understandable: doubts had been expressed over Dancing Brave's stamina and he hadn't been tested over more than a mile either on the gallops or on the racetrack. But coming down Tattenham Hill Starkey had his mount 12 lengths behind the leaders, third from the back. When they came into the straight Starkey moved him out for a clear run, unbalancing the colt slightly as he did so, and then began riding him hard.

Dancing Brave, ridden by Greville Starkey, winning easily from Triptych and Teleprompter in the Eclipse, Sandown, July 1986.

At first the response was limited, then Dancing Brave began grabbing the ground. He was closing down the leader at a furious rate over the last two furlongs, but on Shahrastani Walter Swinburn showed once again what a brilliant jockey he was for the big occasion, riding a text-book race. For all the astonishing pace he showed, there just was not the time for Dancing Brave to get there and Shahrastani held on by half a length.

It is always easy for punters who have been burned to blame the jockey. This time there was no other obvious explanation. The media saw Dancing Brave as the moral winner and lumped the blame on his rider. That year's Derby was in danger of being remembered as the Derby Dancing Brave lost rather than the Derby Shahrastani won. Starkey himself was so sensitive about it that he even refused interviews a month or so later after riding Dancing Brave to a brilliant victory in the Coral-Eclipse Stakes at Sandown.

A week before that race Shahrastani, the victor at Epsom, had won the Irish Derby by eight lengths. In the Eclipse Dancing Brave and Clive Brittain's Bold Arrangement, who had run second in the Kentucky Derby on Guineas day, were the only two three-year-olds but Dancing Brave ran a cracker to beat the Classic-winning French filly Triptych, who had gone down by just a short head in the Coronation Cup, and Teleprompter, later a big winner in America.

This time, in a smaller field and over a lesser distance, Dancing Brave was kept closer and made his challenge earlier. Shown the whip in the final furlong by Starkey, he stretched out well and left the others like posts up a driveway as he won by four lengths. With both horses on an upward curve it was then on to a showdown with Shahrastani in the King George VI and Queen Elizabeth

Diamond Stakes at Ascot, a prospect that saw the biggest betting on that race for years. Shahrastani was made 11-10 favourite and Dancing Brave was at 6-4, with Shahrastani's stable companion Shardari drifting to 14-1, as was the 1985 winner Petoski.

Expected 'match' races do not always work out that way and it was not Shahrastani but Shardari who this time provided the test. With Greville Starkey injured, Khalid Abdulla had chosen Pat Eddery to ride Dancing Brave and his mount gave another superlative display. He slashed through the field a furlong and a half out. Shahrastani, who was to finish fourth, was toiling and it was Shardari who then rallied to fight back, cutting Dancing Brave's one-time lead of two lengths to three-quarters of a length at the line. Triptych confirmed the Eclipse form by finishing four lengths back in third.

The final test in Europe then had to be the Arc, the crucial all-age contest for the Continent's best over the classic distance of a mile and a half. It was a measure of the test that only Ribot, Ballymoss and Mill Reef had won a King George and an Arc in the same season. The great Sir Noel Murless used to argue that the Arc came three weeks late for British horses that had undergone a Classic preparation for the Guineas, the Derby, the Eclipse and the King George. Thanks to the timing of their programme French middle-distance horses can generally afford to peak later in the season than their English equivalents. As the Arc preparations went on there was a lively debate in Britain about whether or not Dancing Brave was the equal of Mill Reef. Bookmakers, though, were taking no chances. When he had a warm-up race for the Arc in Goodwood's Select Stakes there was no betting and no starting price recorded despite the presence of five other runners.

When the 1986 Arc field assembled racing writers hailed

it as the strongest and most representative yet seen for the contest (begun in 1920) with the most expensive collection of bloodstock that had ever faced the starter in Europe.

This was what Dancing Brave was up against: the two other three-year-old colts were Shahrastani and Bering, winner in record time of the 'French Derby', the Prix du Jockey Club, who was unbeaten in four races that year. Then there was the filly Darara, a five-length winner of the Prix Vermeille.

Older horses included Triptych and Shardari, the Coronation Cup winner St Estephe, the French St Leger winner Mersey and the German Derby winner Acatenango, unbeaten in his last 12 races which included the Grand Prix de Saint-Cloud.

On firm going (Dancing Brave might not have run if it had turned soft) the field were led into the straight by Baby Turk, Nemain, Acatenango and the four runners in the Aga Khan's colours: Shardari, Dihistan, Darara and Shahrastani. Two furlongs out Shardari hit the front with Shahrastani and Darara poised behind him to challenge. Making his run on the outside, Bering then accelerated to join the battle. A furlong out he led from Shahrastani. But halfway up the straight Pat Eddery had urged Dancing Brave to go and suddenly there was this streak on the wide outside in the Abdulla green and pink as he arrived to take the bunch. In a few strides it was all over.

It was only half a furlong out when Dancing Brave caught the flat-out Bering but by the line his winning margin was (at least) a length and a half. He had passed the cream of Europe's middle-distance performers like Usain Bolt tackling the over-forties in a school parents' day contest. It was a simply electrifying burst after a race that had been run throughout at a testing pace and not surprisingly it set a course and distance record. Triptych, who must by then have grown heartily tired of viewing Dancing Brave's backside, stayed on to snatch third. Fourth, fifth and sixth were the Aga Khan's trio Shahrastani, Shardari and Darara with Acatenango next.

So fast had been Dancing Brave's finish and so obsessed had the French TV director and cameramen been with the idea that Bering had sewn up the race when he passed Shahrastani a furlong out that they missed Dancing Brave's charge and there is no film record of the key moments when he seemed to be travelling twice as fast as his rivals.

Nobody claimed any hard luck stories, virtually all present united in greeting a true championship performance. There was no longer any doubt about who was the boss of his generation and the Derby second could now be relegated to a footnote.

After that it seemed there was no middle-distance horse in the world who could take him on. But you can only go to the well so often and Dancing Brave's career was to end with another rare defeat. He was sent to contest the Breeders' Cup Turf, held that year at Santa Anita. The race had been taken by European candidates the last two years in the shape of Lashkari and Pebbles and the only question in European minds was how much he would win by. But it was not to be. Like all the other European contestants in that year of high expectations he was beaten, and well beaten, by two classy American grass horses: Manila and Theatrical. It was an anti-climax but after the quality of the main course who cared that much if the dessert had disappointed?

Career highlights:
1986: Craven Stakes, 2,000 Guineas, Eclipse Stakes, King George VI and Queen Elizabeth Stakes, Prix de l'Arc de Triomphe

16. BEST MATE

If Ireland had her favourites at the Cheltenham Festival
– Prince Regent, Cottage Rake, Arkle, Danoli, Doran's
Pride, Moscow Flyer and Florida Pearl, horses that tugged
at racegoers' hearts as well as helping to fill their wallets
– so too has England in the shape of Golden Miller, Mill
House, Desert Orchid and One Man. But if there was one
single horse who became the public property of English
racegoers it was surely Best Mate, the winner of three
Gold Cups from 2002 to 2004. The last of them was a race
I will never forget.

Best Mate was owned by a flamboyant showman in
the person of Jim Lewis, who would lead a team into the
parade ring all wearing the claret and blue colours of his
beloved Aston Villa Football Club. But it stirred far more
that Best Mate's career was overseen by a contrasting
pair who encapsulate the colour, the quirkiness and the
enduring 'animals-first' honesty of character that gives
National Hunt racing such a wide appeal.

Henrietta Knight and her husband and assistant Terry
Biddlecombe, otherwise known as Hen and Terry or, with
affection, as 'the Odd Couple', are for jumping folk the
best double act in town since Morecambe and Wise. The
combination of Henrietta, the well-connected ex-deb,
ex-schoolmistress and ex-Olympic three-day-event selec-
tor with Terry, the battered, earthy three-times champion
jockey from the cavalier era who lost some early rounds
with the bottle and then came through to a new life, has
proved a potent one.

Henrietta, whose apparent mild dottiness conceals a
formidable strength and ambition, is an excellent judge
of a horse. Terry, who rode as well as he celebrated, can
read a race like few others and planned the tactics for

their jockeys. They acquired Best Mate from Tom Costello in Ireland after Terry had spotted him running unplaced in a point-to-point. By the time his racing days ended Best Mate, a handsome, well-balanced bay by Un Desperado out of Katday, had competed in 22 races, winning 14 of them and finishing second in seven (five of those were Group One races, the others Group Two). He won the Cheltenham Gold Cup for three years running, as well as a King George, and was the best horse his recently-retired trainer ever handled.

Best Mate would have been fancied to win the Arkle Chase at Cheltenham in 2001 but the meeting was cancelled after a foot-and-mouth disease outbreak. When racing resumed in 2002 Best Mate was the baby of an unusually large field of 18. Having been beaten by Florida Pearl in that year's King George, he started as the 7-1 third favourite. The previous year's winner Looks Like Trouble was at 9-2 and Nicky Henderson's Bacchanal was at 6-1.

Approaching the last few fences it was the Irish outsider Commanche Court, trained by Ted Walsh and ridden by his son Ruby, who first came to dispute the lead with the former winner See More Business. There too was the improving Best Mate and the young horse quickened impressively on the inside rail. He drew away from Commanche Court up the run-in to win by one and three quarter lengths with the 12-year-old See More Business in third. Jim Culloty, who had given the horse a dream ride, went on to complete a rare double, winning that year's Grand National on Bindaree.

The next year, 2003, it was even easier. Best Mate was a stronger horse and this time he came to Cheltenham having won the King George VI Chase at Kempton on Boxing Day, beating Sir Robert Ogden's Marlborough. The young pretender this time was Beef Or Salmon, trained in Ireland by Michael Hourigan and only a seven-year-old as Best Mate had been the year before. Sadly Cheltenham was never to be his happy hunting ground and he fell at only the third fence. This time at the top of

Trainer Henrietta Knight with Best Mate before his third and final Cheltenham Gold Cup victory, March 2004.

the hill it was Valley Henry who made a move along with Best Mate's stable companion Chives. But Best Mate had been playing with them. To the cheers of the crowd Jim Culloty sent him on at the second last and up the hill he surged clear of Truckers Tavern to win by ten lengths. It was the first time since L'Escargot in 1971 that a champion had successfully defended his crown.

Best Mate's third and final Gold Cup victory was the one in which he proved himself a rough-house fighter as well as an athlete.

Technique is vital but the best jump racing requires bravery too, in the saddle and underneath it. In his first two victories Best Mate had demonstrated his high cruising speed, his natural fencing ability and his sheer class. On his third appearance in the Gold Cup, which tragically turned out to be his last, it was to be his courage and the nerve of his rider Jim Culloty that was tested to the ultimate. 'We knew he had the class and the ability', said Culloty after the race. 'Now we know he's got the bottle too.'

The course having suffered a late drenching, Culloty and Terry Biddlecombe had decided the best ground was down the inside. But going round the inside at Cheltenham you are gambling on getting a clear run.

Best Mate had been flicking over his fences in his usual neat way, maintaining a nice rhythm. But others were determined he was not going to be allowed to have things his own way. At the last ditch he was tightened up by Sir Rembrandt (Andrew Thornton) on his outside with Harbour Pilot (Paul Carberry) deliberately hemming him in at the front.

They did nothing outside the rules of racing. Nor did Jim Culloty resent the tactics. He admits he would have attempted some boxing-in had he been in their place: 'You wouldn't get many rides in this game if you were a perfect "after you, Sir" gentleman.' But if Best Mate was unamused he never became flustered and was ready to force his way out of the scrimmage. At the second last Culloty pulled him out and they jumped it with élan. But going for safety rather than the spectacular at the last they were a little slow, a touch flat-footed. Best Mate's usual fluency was not there and Sir Rembrandt was battling.

It was no time for kindness and Jim Culloty was as hard on his old partner as he had ever been driving up the hill. Best Mate had the courage to respond up the lung-bursting slope and in the end they prevailed, though only by half a length. For Henrietta, Terry and all of England. As owner Jim Lewis said, his class animal had shown he could be a streetfighter too. A 'drained' Henrietta Knight said afterwards: 'Everyone wanted him to win. He has been taken over by the country and I just couldn't bear the thought of letting anybody down.'

The final testimony to Best Mate's quality is that only in his final race at Exeter, when he was pulled up and died after a heart attack, did he fail to finish in the first two. He never ever fell at a hurdle or a fence, and the memory of that last Gold Cup will keep us all warm in our beds for many years to come. Arguments about the respective merits of Best Mate and Arkle are largely inappropriate because Best Mate, unlike his great predecessor, rarely ran in handicaps and so never earned a handicap rating to match Arkle's. What is for sure is that both were adored by the racing public of their days.

Career highlights:
2002: Cheltenham Gold Cup, Peterborough Chase, King George VI Chase
2003: Cheltenham Gold Cup, Ericsson Chase
2004: Cheltenham Gold Cup

15. BAHRAM

Any horse that has won the Triple Crown (the 2,000
Guineas over a mile, the Derby over a mile and a half, and
the St Leger over 1m 6f) merits a high place in the top
100. Bahram was probably the best of those few who have
performed this feat: he was unbeaten throughout his
career and no horse ever really extended him. It seems
that he knew how good he was: I would love to have seen
Bahram in what was apparently a favourite position, lean-
ing against the wall of a stable with his legs crossed looking disdainfully around him at lesser beings.

Precise positions in racing's Hall of Fame are often
affected by politics, sometimes otherwise known as sour
grapes, and there were plenty in his time who were ready to
cast doubt on the true value of his achievements. Bahram
was owned by the Aga Khan, who had five major studs in
Ireland feeding into his equine empire and who was the
leading owner in Britain seven times between 1924 and
1937. That enabled those who wanted to crab Bahram's
achievements to suggest that his owner, who had several
of the other best horses around, made sure that Bahram
never encountered them and that his title was too easily
earned. It is true that he only ever raced against his contemporaries, but that hasn't stopped others to whom that
applied being hailed as worthy champions.

So what was the record? Bahram was a powerful
good-looking colt by Blandford who raced five times
as a two-year-old and won every time. In his very first
contest, Sandown's National Breeders Produce Stakes,
he faced the Aga's strongly-fancied stable companion
Theft and beat him by a neck at 20-1. There was never
again a price like that. In his four other victories at two,
including the Gimcrack and Middle Park Stakes, Bahram

Bahram went undefeated in his racing career and won
the 1935 Triple Crown. (June 1935)

started odds-on. At the season's end Theft and another
Aga Khan colt, Hairan, were rated at 9st 6lb in the Two
Year Old Free Handicap and Bahram was on 1lb more at
9st 7lb.

It was Theft he battled with again in the 2,000
Guineas, in which Bahram was making his seasonal debut

after being off colour and missing the Craven. This time he beat his stable companion by one and a half lengths. In the run-up to the Derby again his market rivals were Theft and Hairan, and Bahram was allowed to start at 5-4 because some doubted his stamina for the longer trip. It seems that connections did not share those doubts: Prince Aly Khan, no wilting flower in the betting ring, confessed to having had the biggest wager of his life.

Bahram was trained at Newmarket by Frank Butters, who declared that he never really knew how good the horse was because he was so lazy on the gallops and did no more on the racecourse than he needed to win his races. There was, too, one controversial note about his convincing win at Epsom. At one stage Bahram's rider Freddie Fox found himself chopped for room and shouted to Harry Wragg on Theft, who eventually finished fourth, to pull over. Wragg did so and was later called in by the stewards to explain his action.

Bahram was made 11-4 on to take the third leg of the Triple Crown and did so in comfort by five lengths, ridden by Charlie Smirke after Fox met with an accident on the eve of the race. It was the first time the feat had been performed since 1903 and it was what followed Bahram's retirement that probably led to some carping about his record.

The Aga Khan sent his star performer to the breeding sheds immediately after the St Leger, paying him lavish tributes and declaring he would never sell his Triple Crown winner. But in 1940 the Aga did sell Bahram to America for £140,000 before leaving wartime Britain for neutral Switzerland. Since he also sold his Derby winners Blenheim and Mahmoud to the USA, British breeders understandably didn't have much time for Bahram's owner. It is sad, though, if that has led to his horse's

remarkable achievements on the racecourse being
under-valued.

Career highlights:
1934: Gimcrack Stakes, Middle Park Stakes
1935: 2,000 Guineas, St James's Palace Stakes, Derby, St Leger

14. FLYINGBOLT

Racing folk are apt to talk of Arkle as if there was never
a horse to touch him, but by extraordinary coincidence
there was one – Flyingbolt – in the very same yard, Tom
Dreaper's establishment at Greenogue near Dublin, at
the very same time. The two never met on the racecourse
but they did once race each other in a contest witnessed
only by their two riders, an appalled trainer and a handful
of goggle-eyed stable lads.

It was the first time Arkle and Flyingbolt were exercised together over fences. One moment the feisty young
Flyingbolt, with Paddy Woods aboard, was eyeing his older
rival and jostling a little. You could even see the curl of
his lips as he ranged upsides his great stable companion,
said Arkle's rider Pat Taaffe. The next minute, the horses'
competitive instincts had taken over and the two were flying at breakneck speed over a string of four fences, their
riders helpless passengers as the horrified trainer yelled
at them unavailingly to pull up their mounts. No winner
was declared but Flyingbolt was certainly not worsted and
Dreaper made sure the two never jumped fences together
again.

Flyingbolt's very existence was something of a minor
miracle. His sire, the 1946 Derby winner Airborne, had
been retired from his stud career in the belief that he

was impotent. He was retired to a paddock as companion to the supposedly barren 19-year-old mare Eastlock, who had not conceived for four years, but something clicked between the old couple and the result was a chestnut foal born in 1959.

Mr Nice Guy he was not. Flyingbolt was not an amenable sort like the good-tempered Arkle. No man would ever step willingly into his box, not a second time anyway, if he valued life and limb. But he was possessed of a precocious ability. Had he not lived at the same time as Arkle and had he not tragically picked up a cattle disease in his prime he would have been more widely acknowledged as one of the all-time greats.

At the Cheltenham Festival of 1966, the year Arkle collected his third Gold Cup, Flyingbolt contested the two-mile Champion Chase and won it in a canter. The big chestnut had scarcely had to change into second gear, said his owners, and they ran him again that week in the Champion Hurdle. For once his jockey, the great Pat Taaffe, seemed to be at fault for going the long way round and for not making enough use of Flyingbolt's staying power, but he did also lose ground when getting too close to one of the late obstacles. He still managed to finish third to Salmon Spray.

Such a performance in his second race at the meeting took nothing away from Flyingbolt's fine Festival record. Before that 1966 Champion Chase victory Flyingbolt had stamped himself as the best novice hurdler of his year by winning a division of the Gloucestershire Hurdle in 1964 and had won the Cotswold Chase (now the Arkle) in 1965. Peter O'Sullevan puts him firmly among the all-time greats, and outside the Festival Flyingbolt put up an incredible performance in the Massey Ferguson Gold Cup in 1965.

Flyingbolt, ridden by Pat Taaffe, winner of the Champion Chase,
Cheltenham, March 1966.

Before the drainage improvements Cheltenham
could be a very testing course, and that year the ground
was heavy. Flyingbolt, though he was unbeaten over
fences, was only six and was set to carry 12st 6lb, giving
25lb and more to ten rivals. That probably was why he was
offered, unusually, at odds against. The layers regretted
it: Flyingbolt came home a majestic 15 lengths in front
of Solbina and Scottish Memories. What the knowledgeable Cheltenham crowd didn't forget was that Scottish
Memories, given a similar weight concession, had twice
met Arkle in the previous season and had stretched him

on both occasions. Arkle had beaten him only by a length or two. Now Flyingbolt had beaten the same horse by 16 lengths.

Flyingbolt followed that by winning the Thyestes Chase at Gowran Park from Height O'Fashion and Flying Wild, who was in receipt of 29lbs, by 'a distance' (at least 30 lengths) and 25 lengths. Arkle had tried in the Massey Ferguson to give Flying Wild 32lb and had been beaten by a length.

That season's Irish Grand National was another weight-carrying triumph for Flyingbolt, a spectacular powerhouse who out-jumped and out-muscled his opponents and won it by two lengths under 12st 7lb, beating Height O'Fashion and the previous year's winner Splash while conceding them 40lb and 42lb respectively. When Arkle took on Height O'Fashion in that same race he beat her two lengths too, but he was giving her only 30lb. Said Pat Taaffe: 'Once again I was reminded that I was alternating between the king and the crown prince of chasing. It seemed only a matter of time before he took over from Arkle.'

After that Irish National season Flyingbolt was the unbeaten winner of 11 chases. In all he had won 17 of his 20 races. His owners, the Wilkinsons, were looking forward, even if Dreaper was not, to him taking on Arkle in the 1967 Gold Cup. But when he made his seasonal return in October 1966 Flyingbolt could finish only third in a moderate field. Something was wrong and eventually tests revealed that, probably when turned out with cattle in a field in the summer, he had contracted brucellosis, a cattle disease that causes inflammation of the joints.

The great challenge match was never to be. Within two months Arkle's career was over with a fractured pedal bone at Kempton. Flyingbolt eventually returned to racing a year later despite Dreaper's wish that he should be retired. Sent first to Ken Oliver and then to Roddy Armytage, he did win another handicap and was even second in the King George as a ten-year-old, but in the few races he ran he was never the same horse again. The lacklustre end to his career in the post-brucellosis days sadly dimmed the memory of his spectacular earlier achievements.

Career highlights:
1964: Gloucestershire Hurdle
1965: Cotswold Chase, Massey Ferguson Gold Cup
1966: Champion Chase, Thyestes Chase, Irish Grand National

13. NIJINSKY

Horses with the speed to win over a mile in May, the agility and temperament to perform over one and a half miles of Epsom's undulations in June, and the stamina to cope with 1m 6f at Doncaster in mid-September do not come around that often. Even if they do, the Americanisation of the breeding industry and the enhanced focus on speed has meant that fewer owners of Derby winners are willing to run their stars in the third leg of the traditional Triple Crown – which requires winning the 2,000 Guineas, the Derby and the St Leger. (There has been talk of making the one and a half mile King George VI and Queen Elizabeth Stakes at Ascot the third leg, though there seems no great momentum behind it and Doncaster would have a few things to say.)

There were 17 years between Gainsborough's wartime Triple Crown (with the September Stakes substituted for the St Leger) and Bahram's attainment of that objective in 1935. Racegoers had to wait twice as long for the next Triple Crown winner to come along and perhaps inevitably it was an inmate of Vincent O'Brien's Ballydoyle stable who achieved the feat in 1970, the fleet-footed Nijinsky, owned by the minerals multi-millionaire Charles Engelhard.

The O'Brien team purchased the son of Northern Dancer, then an unproven sire, as a yearling in Canada in 1968, the year of Sir Ivor's victories, and it was Nijinsky's success that persuaded O'Brien and his associates to concentrate on Northern Dancer blood, so helping to make him the most influential sire of modern times.

Nijinsky, though something of a neurotic, was probably the best horse O'Brien ever trained. He started by winning a predictable series of races in Ireland including the Railway Stakes, the Anglesey Stakes and the Beresford Stakes. With his reputation swelling, the unbeaten Nijinsky came to Newmarket for the Dewhurst and immediately impressed both with his looks and his performance. Lester Piggott, riding him for the first time, scarcely had to move a muscle as Nijinsky saw off England's best. In 1970 he came back to Newmarket as a 4-7 favourite for the 2,000 Guineas – the shortest-priced in the race since 1934 – and won as he pleased.

Northern Dancer himself had not seemed to stay 1m 4f. Would Nijinsky do so, because he faced in the Derby the impressive Sea-Bird colt Gyr, whom Etienne Pollet had postponed his retirement to campaign as a three-year-old and who could certainly be expected to stay? The question was answered emphatically. The big, leggy Gyr coped well with the Epsom track but Nijinsky coped with it even better. As the long-striding Frenchman began to draw away from his field in the Epsom straight Nijinsky ranged alongside, engaged an extra gear and

Nijinsky, ridden by Lester Piggott, the day they triumphed
in the King George VI and Queen Elizabeth Stakes, Royal Ascot,
July 1970.

coasted past him for a two-length victory. The time of the
race almost equalled Mahmoud's record, always a little
suspect because that was a hand-timing.

For the proud owner Charles Engelhard the only
difficult moment of the day came when he and Vincent
O'Brien were invited to the Royal Box. In the excitement
of the race the portly Engelhard's braces had broken.

He was presented to the Queen Mother clutching his hat and stick while endeavouring to keep up his trousers with his elbows. 'You seem to be having some difficulty, Mr Engelhard', she said, 'can I hold something for you?' Had he altered his pose, the American later confided to Jacqueline O'Brien, his trousers would have come down.

For Nijinsky there was plenty more to come. Although he sweated up in the preliminaries back at the Curragh for the Irish Derby he once again accelerated away from his rivals for another comfortable victory there. His popularity was obvious: few in the crowd that day would have backed a horse available only at odds of 1-3, but when they saw jockey Liam Ward invite him to go and Nijinsky began charging though the classy field there was a cheer of triumph from a knowledgeable crowd who knew they were seeing rare quality.

His next task was to take on the older horses in the King George VI and Queen Elizabeth Stakes at Ascot. A furlong out he left for dead both Karabas and the hard-ridden Blakeney, the previous year's Derby winner, and again he won in some comfort. Lester Piggott scarcely had to move in the saddle.

It was already a phenomenal record but the Ballydoyle team decided to include on Nijinsky's engagement list not just the Prix de l'Arc de Triomphe but the St Leger as well. The Triple Crown was on. Through no fault of Nijinsky's that may have proved an ambition too far. A week after the King George the colt developed a virulent case of ringworm. His hair dropped out and there were raw patches on his skin. O'Brien favoured a longer rest: Engelhard fancied owning a Triple Crown winner and Nijinsky was pronounced ready to run in the St Leger. He passed that test as stylishly as ever. Seventh of nine into the straight, the 2-7 favourite picked off his rivals one by one and came home one and a half lengths clear of Meadowville and Politico. But what price did he pay for it? In winning the St Leger, Nijinsky, who lost a lot of weight after the race, may have left behind an Arc.

Not one but two races were to follow the first Triple Crown for 35 years: first the Arc and then the Champion Stakes. Sadly Nijinsky won neither. He went to Longchamp undefeated in his previous 11 races. As usual he turned on the speed in the closing stages but it was not on this occasion as devastating or as sustained as before. Nijinsky did take the lead a furlong out but his acceleration petered out, he hung left and Sassafras went past him to win by a head. Some, including Vincent O'Brien, criticised Lester Piggott for giving Nijinsky too much to do, but that seems unfair. It had been a long, long season for Nijinsky and he was without the usual spark in the Champion Stakes, too, when he contested that a fortnight later and was beaten by the clearly inferior Lorenzaccio. When he dismounted Piggott said defiantly: 'He is still the best horse I have ever ridden.' When horses win as easily as Nijinsky had won his first two Classics it is easy to be supremely confident, but even Triple Crown champions can be taken to the well once or twice too often.

Career highlights:
1969: Dewhurst Stakes, Gladness Stakes
1970: 2,000 Guineas, Derby, Irish Derby, King George VI and
*   Queen Elizabeth Stakes, St Leger*

12. PERSIAN WAR

The heroes in Dick Francis's racing novels always come through in the end. We would be upset if they didn't.

But nearly all of them get knocked about pretty badly on the way – injured by trip wires in races, locked away in deserted yards, beaten up by thugs in racecourse car parks. Persian War was a bit like that. If he had been a film star he would have reached the fade-out not with a martini at his lips and a blonde on his arm but in a blood-stained head bandage gruffly acknowledging the thanks of his company commander. Persian War was adopted by the Cheltenham crowds who loved him not just for his honesty and courage but for his ability to come back patched up from one injury after another to deliver his best at the track he clearly relished.

He finished third in one race despite biting through his tongue and losing two teeth. Another time Persian War was given up for dead after knocking himself out for some minutes by hitting his head on the top bar of a hurdle. When his opinionated owner had him handled by an eccentric Frenchman in Chantilly he returned a very sick horse.

The three-times Champion Hurdle winner did little on the Flat for Dick Hern but was bought by Henry Alper after showing winning form over hurdles for Tom Masson. Brian Swift then won a Triumph Hurdle with him before Alper sent the horse to France, but it was Colin Davies who rescued Persian War from Chantilly and prepared him for his first title bid in 1968. He began by winning the Schweppes Gold Trophy with him under a massive 11st 13lb.

Persian War, who won on every kind of going from firm to heavy and who usually forced the pace, was faced in his first Champion field by the two previous winners Salmon Spray and Saucy Kit. The favourite, though, was the in-form Chorus, who was known to relish the prevail-ing firm ground.

Taking over from his stable companion Straight Point, Persian War, ridden by the stylish hurdles specialist Jimmy Uttley, led them down the hill to the second last where the challenging Saucy Kit landed awkwardly and so left Henry Alper's horse, the 4-1 co-second favourite, to come home in his claret and blue West Ham colours a comfortable winner, pursued by Chorus.

In 1969 Persian War came to defend his crown with a question mark or two against him. He had fallen and injured himself on his seasonal debut, fracturing a femur and being off the course for three months. He had also been beaten in a prep race at Wincanton after running a temperature. This time Drumikill with Barry Brogan aboard took up the running three flights out. Rounding the bend for home Persian War was still four lengths behind, already being hard driven, although by the last he was gaining ground. There Drumikill sprawled and Persian War had enough left to drive up the hill and win by four lengths. He beat Drumikill again in the Welsh Champion Hurdle.

Coming to the 1970 Festival, Persian had not won a race since the previous Easter although he had been placed in top company, finishing third in the new Irish Sweeps Hurdle. On this occasion Colin Davies, who used to ride the horse himself in all his work, had tied down Persian War's tongue to prevent the champion swallowing it as he had become prone to do – an affliction that leaves a horse short of air and effectively running on an empty tank. Jimmy Uttley took the tough old campaigner into the lead at the fifth hurdle and they stayed in that position until the winning post, resisting the challenge of Josh Gifford on Major Rose.

Following his third victory Persian War had an operation on the 'soft palate' condition that had been inducing

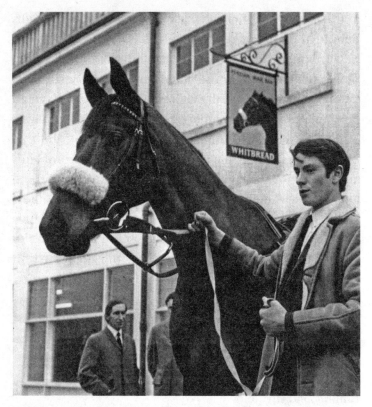

Persian War, three times Champion Hurdler, at the opening
of the Persian War Bar, Chepstow, December 1969.

his tongue-swallowing. In the course of that it was discovered he had a broken wolf tooth, which must have been
causing him severe pain. Before he ran again in the
1971 Champion Hurdle, differences between owner and
trainer saw him removed from Davies to the Epsom yard
of Arthur Pitt.

From his new Epsom base Persian War won the Irish
Sweeps Hurdle at Christmas, but a new generation was on
the way. Persian War ran down the field in the Schweppes
and was beaten ten lengths by Bula at Wincanton. At
Cheltenham he responded to the crowds again and once
more he beat his old rival Major Rose. But Bula, produced

at the last by Paul Kelleway, left Persian War four lengths behind as he stormed up the hill.

A popular reign was over, although the former champion passed through the hands of two more trainers before he was allowed the retirement he deserved. In all Persian War, a good-tempered horse with a decent turn of foot, won 18 of his 51 hurdle races. It was a tribute to the courage of a horse plagued with respiratory problems and to the fortitude of handlers plagued by an opinionated owner who changed trainers as often as some others changed their suits. Persian War was handled by no fewer than eight trainers through his racing life and thanks to Henry Alper, who liked to campaign him in France in summer and run him on the Flat in the autumn, the gutsy horse literally didn't get a break. Colin Davies memorably commented: 'When we put a tongue strap on Persian War a few people said it was a pity we didn't put it on the owner.'

Career highlights:
1967: Triumph Hurdle
1968: Schweppes Gold Trophy
1968, 1969, 1970: Champion Hurdle
1969: Welsh Champion Hurdle
1970: Irish Sweeps Hurdle

11. LAMMTARRA

Not many Derby winners succeed at Epsom after 300 days off the track. Sired by Nijinsky II out of the Oaks winner Snow Bride and bred at the Maktoum family's Gainsborough Stud in Kentucky, Lammtarra had a short career but a glorious and undefeated one. That he was a top-class horse is uncontested but just how he rates on the all-time scale is hard to gauge with an animal who raced so infrequently.

The story surrounding Lammtarra, though, is not only one of a horse's quality. Lammtarra began his racing career in the hands of the young Newmarket trainer Alex Scott, who was so convinced of his outstanding ability that he took a £1,000 bet with Ladbrokes at 33-1 that the colt would win the 1995 Derby, a bet struck before Lammtarra had even seen a racecourse. At only 34 Scott was then tragically shot dead by a disgruntled former employee and Lammtarra was sent to Sheikh Mohammed's Godolphin trainer Saeed bin Suroor to continue his preparation.

Lammtarra made just one winning appearance as a two-year-old in the Washington Singer Stakes at Newbury. When he arrived at Epsom for the 1995 Derby it was his seasonal debut and his first run for 302 days: during the early season he had been a very sick horse with an abscess on the lungs and it was touch and go whether he could be readied for the Derby.

In the big race he took on Pennekamp, with whom André Fabre had won the 2,000 Guineas, and Spectrum, whom Peter Chapple-Hyam had trained to win the Irish equivalent. Not surprisingly after his long absence, Lammtarra, who was ridden by Walter Swinburn, was at 14-1. Coming round Tattenham Corner you would have thought even that too low a price as Lammtarra was pinned on the rails at the rear of the pack. However, there was no big-race jockey cooler than Swinburn who eased him clear and set out in pursuit of Tamure, on whom Frankie Dettori had set sail for the winning post looking likely to win. Lammtarra, though, showed great finishing speed, making up six lengths in the last furlong to win going away by a length. So impressive had his finishing

Frankie Dettori wins the Prix de l'Arc de Triomphe on
Lammtarra at Longchamp, June 1995.

been that Lammtarra broke the Derby record by 1.53 seconds and his time of 2 minutes 32.21 seconds stood until
bettered by Workforce in 2010.

With Alex Scott's fate in mind it was an emotional
winners' enclosure afterwards, and there was a nice
touch too from the bookmakers Ladbrokes. Normally a
bet is cancelled if the person placing it dies, but they let
his wager on Lammtarra stand and paid the winnings to
Scott's widow.

The next eagerly anticipated outing for Lammtarra
was in the King George VI and Queen Elizabeth Stakes.
To the surprise of most of the racing community, including the two jockeys, Sheikh Mohammed took Walter
Swinburn off the horse and gave the ride to his weighing
room friend and neighbour Frankie Dettori, who sat on

him for the first time just minutes before the big race well aware of what wagging tongues would say if he lost.

Swinburn had told Frankie that with Lammtarra the more his jockey asked of him in a race, the more he gave. But the still inexperienced Lammtarra could be wilful on the gallops and his playboy streak was showing before the race. Dettori had wanted to cool him down under the trees, instead his mount kept larking about.

Aware that Ascot's short straight makes it unwise to rely on one sharp burst of speed, Frankie wanted to build up the pace steadily but was alarmed as they came into the straight to see Michael Hills on the gutsy and experienced Pentire simply coasting alongside him. Remembering Walter Swinburn's advice, Frankie kept asking Lammtarra for more – and got it. With Dettori throwing everything at him, Lammtarra battled back in the final furlong to win by a neck. His horse, said Dettori, had the heart of a lion and it was probably his own best ride.

France provided the backcloth for Lammtarra's final racecourse appearance in the Prix de l'Arc de Triomphe. Many Epsom Derby winners have taken the Longchamp test at the end of the season and failed. Lammtarra did not. Dettori rode him just off the pace and drove him into the lead two furlongs out. Several challengers, including Swain, had a crack at him but Lammtarra, the 21-10 favourite, beat them off one by one and still had three-quarters of a length to spare over Freedom Cry at the line. Reflecting the scintilla of doubt that will remain as a result of his mount's comparatively light programme, Frankie declared that Lammtarra was 'possibly' the best horse he had ridden.

Whatever precise position he is allotted, a horse who won the Derby in record time after a 300-day layoff, who showed the fighting qualities he did in Ascot's all-age showpiece, and who signed off with an Arc against the best Europe could produce is entitled to be stabled with the greats.

Career highlights:
1995: Derby, King George VI and Queen Elizabeth Stakes, Prix
de l'Arc de Triomphe

10. RED RUM

On Grand National mornings I like to walk the Aintree course, as much as anything to remind myself of the courage and stamina required by the jockeys and horses who will a little later soar over those still formidable fences. Call me an old sentimentalist if you will, but for a good few years now I have started the ritual by visiting Red Rum's grave close to the winning post, with the memorial stone that proclaims: 'Respect this place, this hallowed ground. A legend here his rest has found. His feet would fly, our spirits soar. He earned our love for ever more.'

There is normally a bunch of flowers or two, occasionally a few cards, some Polos strewn around. And every year I am in company with hundreds of others who still marvel at the record on the headstone. Grand Nationals won in 1973, 1974 and 1977, second place in the same great race in 1975 and 1976. No wonder that 11 years after his death in 1995 at the age of 30, Red Rum still comfortably topped the poll with 45 per cent when people were asked in a nationwide survey what horse's name they could recall. (For the record, Black Beauty was second and Shergar third.)

Other jumpers may have had greater class or speed. But no other horse can match Red Rum in terms of the public affection he engendered and, as Tony McCoy has declared, while records are made to be broken (he should know) no horse surely will ever again achieve Grand National statistics to match Red Rum's.

'Rummy', as he came to be known, was bred to be a miler, not a staying chaser, and ran his first race at Aintree on the Flat over a mere five furlongs. It was a marvel too that he was able to go on racing. Quite early in his career he developed pedalostitis in his feet, normally a progressive affliction. But the irrepressible Ginger McCain, a one-time permit trainer who combined his originally small-scale seaside training operation with running a taxi service and car showroom in Southport, sorted out Red Rum's feet because he exercised his horses in the shallows lapping over Southport Sands.

Owned by octogenarian Noel Le Mare, whom Ginger had first met in the back of his taxi on regular trips to a Southport dinner dance, Red Rum swiftly gave them a return for the £6,000 Ginger had paid for him after seeing him run unsuccessfully in the Scottish Grand National at Ayr. He won his first five races in Ginger's care and rose from 10 stone to 12 stone in the handicap. By the time of the 1973 National, Red Rum was joint favourite for the big race with the giant Australian chaser Crisp, who was giving him 23lb. Although Red Rum was already a local hero that year he was also in a sense the national villain, running down the brave top weight Crisp after the last when Crisp and Richard Pitman had given the bravest-ever front-running display in the history of the race. At Doncaster that autumn when the two met again at level weights Crisp beat him by eight lengths. Red Rum showed he was no one-track horse, though, when losing the Hennessy Gold Cup at Newbury only by a head.

The next year, 1974, having won another four races,

Red Rum wins his third Grand National, ridden by Tommy Stack,
April 1977.

Red Rum himself was the top weight for the National
with 12 stone and he won again in the hands of Brian
Fletcher despite having to give weight to the Gold Cup
winner L'Escargot. For good measure he then went on
with 11 stone 13lb to win the Scottish Grand National too.

At Aintree in 1975, having to give the dual Gold Cup
winner L'Escargot 11 pounds and on the soft going he

didn't like, Red Rum finished second; and in 1976, now ridden by Tommy Stack, Red Rum was second again. Although he had not won since the 1975 season Red Rum ran another great race back at Aintree. Five horses jumped the second last together and Red Rum was the first of them to touch down over the final obstacle. He fought like a tiger but giving 12lbs to 'Teasy Weasy' Raymond's Rag Trade proved too big a task and he lost by two lengths.

Some had begun to suggest that it was time for Red Rum to be retired (Brian Fletcher's suggestion that the horse had 'gone' was the reason for him falling out with Ginger McCain the previous season) and when he followed a winning seasonal debut at Carlisle with four defeats, more felt the writing was on the wall. They were wearing the wrong kind of wall-reading glasses: in the 1977 Grand National at the age of 12 Red Rum not only won, he put 25 lengths between himself and the second. He was even prepared for another run at Aintree in 1978 but on the eve of the race suffered a hairline fracture of a small bone in his foot, which did ensure his immediate retirement. It was, however, retirement only from the racecourse: Red Rum became a major participant on the celebrity circuit, doing everything required of a modern celebrity except getting out of taxis in short skirts. He led racecourse parades, opened supermarkets, switched on the Blackpool Illuminations and appeared on *This Is Your Life*.

He left his racing days behind him with an incredible record, having run 100 times over jumps and fallen only once. At Aintree, where he jumped 150 Grand National fences often carrying lumps of weight and was only ever beaten by two horses in the process, he displayed great courage and stamina but adaptability too. Red Rum was a skilful horse in the way he measured his fences and kept out of trouble as the birch was flying around him. As his long-time partner Brian Fletcher said: 'He was thinking all the way round.'

Career highlights:
1973, 1974, 1977: Grand National
1974: Scottish Grand National

9. SCEPTRE

Asked which horse has won four English Classics most racing buffs would reply: 'Don't be silly. With the Oaks and the 1,000 Guineas confined to fillies, surely you mean three?' But they would be wrong because in 1902 the remarkable filly Sceptre not only won the St Leger and the Oaks, she collected both the 1,000 and 2,000 Guineas. No other British racehorse has won four Classics outright – and she might have won five. What is even more extraordinary is that because her often impecunious owner Robert Sievier (a serial womaniser who was three times made bankrupt) needed funds, Sceptre had opened her three-year-old season running in the Lincoln Handicap carrying 6st 7lb. He had backed her to win £30,000 and she lost by a head.

The bay Sceptre, a daughter of the Derby and St Leger winner Persimmon out of Ornament, a full sister to the 1885 Triple Crown winner Ormonde, was bred by the first Duke of Westminster. Sievier bought her for 10,000 guineas when the Duke's bloodstock was auctioned on his death. As a two-year-old she went to Charles Morton at Wantage and he trained her to win the Woodcote Stakes at Epsom and the July Stakes at Newmarket. When

Morton became a private trainer to Jack Joel at the season's end, Sievier decided to train the filly himself at a Wiltshire yard he leased from John Porter, and by modern standards the programme he imposed on his hardy filly was extraordinary.

After that outing in the Lincoln she went to Newmarket and won the 2,000 Guineas in a then record time. Two days later she won the 1,000 Guineas. Her next target was the Derby, no less, but having bruised a foot ten days before and got left at the start she could only finish fourth behind Ard Patrick. In all these top races Sievier used an inexperienced jockey, seemingly because he did not trust the top professionals. Just two days later Sceptre was turned out against the best of her own sex for the Oaks and won that. Sievier had to ask for her prize money in cash to pay the bookmakers for his losses on the Derby.

Sceptre must have been a horse with an iron constitution, with muscles like whipcord, because Sievier ran her next in the Grand Prix de Paris and then twice at Royal Ascot, where she was fourth in the Coronation Stakes and won the St James's Palace stakes over a mile. Sceptre ran twice also at Glorious Goodwood. She was beaten in the Sussex Stakes but won the Nassau Stakes against other fillies three days later. In case she was finding that too easy Sievier galloped her both days in between.

At Doncaster he wasn't content with winning the St Leger: he turned her out again two days later over the same distance in the Park Hill Stakes, where she was beaten. Her thanks for all that was to be sent for auction at the end of the season, but she failed to reach her reserve.

Always short of cash, Sievier started Sceptre's 1903 season too with the Lincoln. This time she carried 9st 1lb and could only finish fifth. After the race her eccentric owner sold her for £25,000 to Sir William Bass, who sent her to be trained at Manton by Alec Taylor Jr. He too kept this remarkable filly busy. She won the Hardwicke Stakes at Royal Ascot and then lost the Eclipse to Ard Patrick by only a neck, with that year's Derby winner Rock Sand behind them in third. Her remaining four runs that season brought four victories in the Jockey Club Stakes (where she walloped the Triple Crown winner Rock Sand), the Duke of York Stakes, the Champion Stakes and Limekiln Stakes.

In her final season in 1904 Sceptre did not win but was placed in all three runs, taking second place in the Coronation Cup and third in the Hardwicke Stakes and Gold Cup at Ascot. She thus ended her career with 13 victories. Only Formosa, running back in 1868, had a record

Sceptre, winner of four Classics in 1902: the 2,000 Guineas, the 1,000 Guineas, the Oaks and the St Leger.

to compare. She too won the Leger, the 2,000 Guineas and the Oaks but her first place in the 1,000 Guineas was shared in a dead heat.

As a broodmare Sceptre changed hands several times, being variously owned by Edmund Somerville Tattersall, John Musker and Lord Glanely. There was a public outcry when Glanely planned to sell her to a Brazilian breeder despite having promised to keep her in Britain. He scrapped his plan and she lived on in Britain until her death in 1926.

Career highlights:
1901: July Stakes
1902: 2,000 Guineas, 1,000 Guineas, Oaks, St James's Palace
*   Stakes, Nassau Stakes, St Leger*
1903: Hardwicke Stakes, Jockey Club Stakes, Duke of York Stakes,
*   Champion Stakes*

8. MILL REEF

On the last day of August 1972 the racing world held its breath, praying for the survival of a national hero. During a strong canter in preparation for a race at Ascot to ready him for another tilt at the Prix de l'Arc de Triomphe, Mill Reef had fractured his near foreleg. He broke a chunk off his cannon bone, shattered the inner sesamoid and damaged the main pastern. They were injuries that would normally have resulted in a horse being put down, but a team of specialists operated and Mill Reef was saved for an enjoyable retirement and what turned out to be a highly successful stud career.

Paul Mellon's colt, who was trained by Ian Balding at Kingsclere, took with him into the breeding sheds an outstanding record that had included winning a Derby, taking the King George VI and Queen Elizabeth Stakes by a record margin of six lengths, and a thrilling victory the previous year in the Prix de l'Arc de Triomphe.

There might have been even more lustre surrounding his name if he had not been running at the same time as Brigadier Gerard. The only time they met, in the 2,000 Guineas, the Brigadier, a specialist miler, beat Paul Mellon's little colt, but then Mill Reef moved up in distance and was never beaten again. The racing world had yearned to see the two of them clash again over a mile and a quarter and Ascot had changed the distance of the Cumberland Lodge Stakes that year in the hope of engineering such a head-to-head, but it was not to be.

As a two-year-old the speedy Mill Reef, whose constant partner in the saddle was the irrepressible Geoff Lewis, won the Coventry, Gimcrack and Dewhurst Stakes by wide margins. His only defeat came when he went to France and was short-headed by My Swallow. In the 2,000 Guineas of 1971, having tuned up by winning the Greenham, he had his revenge on My Swallow but in an outstanding year Brigadier Gerard beat both of them. After that Mill Reef won every one of his remaining 12 races.

Mill Reef's secret was fluidity. Though he may have been small he was a beautiful mover who seemed to glide across the turf. When Ian Balding took him over three days early for the 1971 Arc and galloped him with Aldie, a travelling companion, the trainer walked up the gallops afterwards. Aldie's footprints were cut deeply into the turf; where Mill Reef had exercised you could scarcely see a mark – it was as if he had floated over the ground.

Mill Reef's 1971 Derby victory was an emphatic one. Linden Tree set the pace and led into the straight under Duncan Keith. Homeric and Lombardo were also ahead

Mill Reef with trainer Ian Balding at Kingsclere before
his victorious Derby, May 1971.

of Mill Reef coming into the straight but they soon wilted.
Mill Reef was cruising under Geoff Lewis and he went past
Linden Tree in the final furlong to win by two lengths.

Then it was on to the Eclipse in which he faced the
French star Caro, who had won the Prix d'Harcourt, the
Prix Ganay and the Prix Dollar. The two principals shed
the others in the straight and battled for supremacy – and
then Mill Reef accelerated away two furlongs out to sustain the growing excitement of the British racing public
and win by four lengths in a new course record.

The King George VI was another remarkable race.
Nobody had ever won it before by such a margin as the
six lengths that Mill Reef put between himself and his
nearest pursuer, the Italian Derby and Hardwicke Stakes
winner Ortis. As jockey Geoff Lewis put it: 'Daylight
was second.' But it was in the Arc of that year that Mill
Reef totally stamped his greatness on his generation.

Some great horses have run in England's final Classic, the St Leger, and the Arc but Ian Balding reckoned that Nijinsky might have lost his Arc by running in the Leger. He gave Paul Mellon a choice – he could train Mill Reef to win the St Leger or the Arc but not both. Mellon chose the French race, which no English-trained horse had won for 20 years.

On the day his 17 rivals included Caro, the Irish Derby winner Irish Ball, the US challenger One For All, plus Pistol Packer and Cambrizzia who had finished first and second in the Prix de Diane.

Geoff Lewis always insisted Mill Reef was an easy horse to ride, but that day reflected great credit on his intelligent jockeyship too. As the field turned into the straight Mill Reef was pocketed on the rails in about sixth place. Because he was so small his trainer couldn't even see him. Ahead of Mill Reef were Ortis, ridden by Duncan Keith, and Hallez, under Lester Piggott. Lewis knew that when Duncan Keith went past a horse he would customarily move his mount to cover the one he had passed. Lester, he reckoned, would be keen to keep straight because he had had plenty of trouble with the French stewards. Lewis had tracked Hallez and calculated Keith's and Piggott's mounts would split. They did, and he and Mill Reef had the gap they needed.

One smack and the white noseband of the little hero was in sight. Mellon's gold and black colours were in the clear. Pistol Packer gave chase and momentarily reached his tail but no one could live with Mill Reef in full stream and he was three lengths clear by the post, setting a new course record. 'Like Sea-Bird, but quicker' read the headlines in the admiring French press the next day.

Connections were hoping for at least one repeat of that Arc success, and two days before Mill Reef's accident

Paul Mellon had announced he would stay in training as a five-year-old. He had certainly looked as good as ever on his seasonal debut back at Longchamp for the Prix Ganay, the most important early-season race for older horses in France. He was prominent from the start, grabbed the lead early in the straight and went away to win by ten lengths, which could have been plenty more had his jockey wished. One French trainer called him the best horse to have raced in his country since the Second World War.

In what turned out to be his final race, the Coronation Cup, Mill Reef won again at Epsom, although his margin over Humorist was the surprisingly narrow one of a neck. He missed the Eclipse because Balding's horses were under a cloud with a virus at the time, and then he had to pull out of the Benson and Hedges Gold Cup at York, where he might have met Brigadier Gerard, because of an injured hock. He was just back in full training when he shattered his leg, and the dreams of many English supporters of a follow-up Arc.

Career highlights:
1970: Coventry Stakes, Gimcrack Stakes, Dewhurst Stakes
1971: Derby, Eclipse Stakes, King George VI and Queen Elizabeth
*   Stakes, Prix de l'Arc de Triomphe*
1972: Prix Ganay, Coronation Cup

7. GOLDEN MILLER

For many aficionados there will never be a jumper to rival Arkle. Many more recent racegoers who never saw the great Irish champion reckon Kauto Star's five King Georges and two Cheltenham Gold Cups make him worthy of the top spot. But anyone hovering with the laurel crown should not forget the chaser who reigned supreme before either of those two came along: Golden Miller not only won five Gold Cups, he won a Grand National too.

In early days Basil Briscoe, who trained Golden Miller for most of his career, nearly gave up on the horse. In desperation he took him hunting, only to declare: 'I doubt if I ever experienced a worse day's mount. We went through the roots of every fence he jumped and try as hard as I could to coax him to take an interest my efforts were all in vain. Not only that – he appeared to me so slow that we could not even keep up with the hounds.'

But Golden Miller grew into his frame, learned his job, and was sold on to Dorothy Paget in a package deal with Insurance for £6,000 after Briscoe promised her one would win the Gold Cup and the other the Champion Hurdle.

Paget, who inherited a vast chain-store fortune, was one of the great characters of racing. She hated men, dressed like a drab and later lived a reclusive life in Chalfont St Giles, the floors stacked with yellowing copies of the *Sporting Life*. She slept by day and worked at night, telephoning her trainers at all hours. Bookmakers would allow her to bet long after races had been concluded, trusting her not to have found out the results. But many who worked for 'DP' would not hear a word against her. Her trainer Gordon Richards said: 'I never want a better owner and she was the best loser I have ever known.'

There were plenty of winners, 1,534 of them, to go with her losers by the time she died in 1960 and the best of them was Golden Miller. Basil Briscoe kept his promise. Golden Miller won his first steeplechase in Dorothy Paget's blue and yellow hooped colours, landing a stable coup, although he was subsequently disqualified for carrying the wrong weight. He then won two of his next three chases as he prepared for his first Gold Cup in 1932. There he was not given much chance against the 10-11 favourite Grakle. But Grakle lost his jockey in swerving to avoid a faller, and Golden Miller, ridden by Ted Leader, was left to win his first Gold Cup easily. Later that afternoon Insurance won the Champion Hurdle, delivering the second half of Basil Briscoe's promise.

Golden Miller was not seen out again until December. He won chases at Kempton, Lingfield and Hurst Park before defending his title at Cheltenham in 1933, this time ridden by Billy Stott. Golden Miller, now a six-year-old, was an odds-on 4-7. He was a lazy horse who did not do more than he had to and usually had to be niggled throughout his races to keep his place. His jumping was economical rather than spectacular but he possessed a high cruising speed and a big stride. He was the epitome, say those who saw him, of the horse who 'gallops his opponents into the ground'. He was also strong: he not only survived mistakes that would have felled others, he did not even seem to lose momentum in recovering.

On heavy ground the running in the 1933 Gold Cup was made by Delaneige. Jock Whitney's Thomond II jumped the third last fence in front but that was the end of the race. At that point Stott let Golden Miller take command and he strode away from his field to win by ten lengths. One previously doubting correspondent recorded: 'It was done in the style of a great horse. At last he must be admitted to be that.'

In 1934 Golden Miller, now a seven-year-old and being ridden by Gerry Wilson, was 6-5 favourite for the Gold Cup. One pretender after another took him on and all were rebuffed in turn. The champion, ears pricked,

Dorothy Paget's Golden Miller, five-times winner of the Cheltenham Gold Cup, here ridden by Gerry Wilson, April 1935.

galloped up the hill alone to the cheers of the sporting crowd. This time the margin was six lengths but it could easily have been more.

This was the year Basil Briscoe and Dorothy Paget had decided to make a priority of the Grand National.

Carrying the welter weight of 12st 2lb and with Southern Hero and Thomond II among his rivals, Golden Miller was among the leaders all the way at Aintree. Delaneige jumped the last ahead of him but Golden Miller motored away to win by five lengths in a then-record time of 9 minutes 20 seconds. His long-time rival Thomond II was third. The crowds were delighted and three cheers were delivered for the painfully shy Dorothy Paget in her usual misshapen tweed coat, utility stockings and squashy hat.

That Grand National victory by a horse who was to demonstrate that he didn't like Aintree was superb, but Golden Miller's greatest race was not there. It was at Cheltenham where in 1935 he won his fourth successive Gold Cup. Golden Miller, now a public hero, was again being aimed at the Grand National, taking in the Gold Cup as a useful warm-up. His most dangerous rival Thomond II was apparently being aimed instead at the two-mile Coventry Cup since his owner Jock Whitney already had the useful Royal Ransom in the Gold Cup field.

Whitney flew in for the meeting and changed his mind, switching Thomond to contest the Gold Cup. Briscoe had not been expecting to take on anything of Thomond's ability. With the National in mind he did not have Golden Miller fully wound up, and, he told the American millionaire, a protracted battle on the prevailing firm ground wouldn't do either horse any good with the Grand National to come. But Whitney remained adamant and the public, scenting a historic duel, arrived in record numbers. On a glorious sunny day people fought for places on Paddington race trains. Roads were blocked for miles around the course and many failed to get their bets on.

Dorothy Paget flew in in time to see Southern Hero set the early gallop. The pace was fast and unrelenting.

Basil Briscoe declared afterwards: 'If either horse had hit a fence he would never have stopped rolling.' By the third last Southern Hero could do no more as the two principals passed him, stride for stride.

The brave little Thomond, with Billy Speck on board, was relishing the fast ground, the bigger Golden Miller much less so. Over the second last, with Gerry Wilson driving the Miller for all he was worth, the two were level, but Thomond had the inside and Golden Miller had extra ground to cover. Coming into the last Golden Miller's bigger stride had him inching in front but Speck, going for his whip, got such a great leap from Thomond that the two touched down together. With the crowd on tiptoe screaming home their selection the two great horses battled every inch up that final hill. But though Thomond clung to him the Miller's superior strength just gave him victory by three parts of a length.

The *Sporting Life* declared of Golden Miller's fourth Gold Cup: 'There has never been anything like the performance of the Miller on any racetrack throughout the world.'

Both horses went on to Aintree. There were rumours of a plot to nobble Golden Miller and he was closely guarded. Rider Gerry Wilson told Briscoe and Paget a week before the race that he had been offered money to stop the horse. Coming to the fence after Valentine's, Golden Miller wandered and seemed to want to refuse. Still driven into it by Gerry Wilson, he somehow scrambled over but ejected his jockey. Basil Briscoe, who had allegedly backed Golden Miller to win £10,000 and told his owner weeks before that he was a certainty, took exception to her comments that the horse looked too light and had been over-galloped. If that was the way she felt she could find another trainer.

Two vets brought in by Briscoe could find nothing wrong and they ran Golden Miller again the next day in the Champion Chase. He galloped to the first, hit it hard, and ejected his jockey, although once again he did not fall himself – he never did come down in 52 races.

Dorothy Paget sent her horses to Owen Anthony to be trained and Golden Miller came out the next December at Sandown. He ran third there, won a chase at Newbury and then in February ran off the course in a three-mile chase intended as his last race before the 1936 Gold Cup, where the young Evan Williams took over the ride on this now puzzling public hero. Golden Miller had never failed to win the Gold Cup. There didn't seem to be any-thing wrong with him physically, but what was going on in his mind?

When it came to it, Williams proved fully up to the task. So did Golden Miller. He jumped with all his old power, moved into the lead three fences out and was 15 lengths clear approaching the last. The crowd went silent: would something now snap, would the Miller refuse as he had done at Aintree or run out as he had done at Newbury? The nine-year-old did neither. He took the fence well. The stands erupted with a great roar of relief and encouragement that echoed back off the hills and Golden Miller strode on. At the post he was 12 lengths clear of Royal Mail.

Surprisingly, with hindsight, he was sent again to Aintree that year. Knocked over at the first fence, he was remounted and got as far as the fence after Valentine's, where he refused.

In 1937, when Golden Miller would almost cer-tainly have added to his tally of Gold Cups, there was no Cheltenham Festival thanks to bad weather and once again connections sent him to Aintree. Now ridden by

Danny Morgan, he jumped well to begin with. But as soon as his rider came to Valentine's he could sense Golden Miller would refuse at the next, which he duly did. Driven into the fence a second time, said his rider, 'he jumped down instead of up'. Golden Miller was never again sent to Aintree. But his Cheltenham efforts were not over.

Before the 1938 Gold Cup the Miller won a couple more chases but he was twice beaten and the writing was on the wall. At the Festival this time he was ridden by Frenchie Nicholson, up against old rival Southern Hero, Macaulay and Morse Code.

With his age and the very hard ground against him Golden Miller still gave his all. Coming round the bend towards the last he was still in front, but Nicholson was having to work hard to keep him stoked up. Morse Code, ridden by Danny Morgan, had been tracking him through the race and now drew level. He landed half a length up over the last and though Golden Miller drew almost level with him, that was his final effort. His courage had got him to the leader, but he did not have the acceleration any longer to pass him. Morse Code became the only horse ever to beat Golden Miller at Cheltenham, drawing away to win by two lengths.

The public still cheered in their old hero and fortunately, after he ran poorly in his only race the next season he was retired with Insurance to The Paddocks, Dorothy Paget's stud at Stanstead. The two old horses seemed to enjoy each other's company and their owner, who visited regularly, ensured they had regular health checks and plenty of apples.

Career highlights:
1932, 1933, 1934, 1935, 1936: Cheltenham Gold Cup
1934: Grand National

6. KAUTO STAR

In racing the best things come in fives, like Golden Miller's Gold Cups, and when on 26 December 2011 Kauto Star won the King George VI Chase at Kempton Park for the fifth time he joined the racing immortals. Even Desert Orchid, the best-loved chaser in Britain until Kauto Star, had only managed four King Georges. It was the point at which some stopped asking, 'Is he the best steeplechaser since Arkle?' and inquired instead: 'Is he the best steeplechaser ever?'

It is at least worth serious debate. On his wins-to-runs ratio Kauto Star does not rival Arkle but his career extended far longer and he had to fight off second and third waves of pretenders. Kauto Star lost and won back his Cheltenham Gold Cup crown. He was fast enough to win two Tingle Creek chases over two miles as well as durable enough to drive up the Cheltenham hill at the end of three miles plus. He won no fewer than 16 Grade One races and he was still winning top-class chases at the age of 11, eight years on from his debut in a modest hurdle in France. Against that you would have to say that Kauto's record of crossing his fences did not always match Arkle's and jumping is the name of the game. Nor did Kauto hump huge weights to success in major handicaps.

That King George record, though, is a remarkable testimony to Kauto's quality. Kauto first won the three-mile Kempton Classic in 2006, just three weeks after beating Voy Por Ustedes to win the Tingle Creek, a specialist event for speed chasers, over two miles at Sandown. He took the lead three out from Exotic Dancer and pulled clear, although he nearly blotted his copybook with a jumping blooper at the last fence which probably quintupled the usual number of cardiac arrests on the traditional hang-over day.

In 2007 Kauto won the King George in a stroll from Our Vic, blasting into the lead four out, and in 2008 he came home eight lengths clear of Alberta's Run, again taking over with four to jump, and again taking liberties with the last.

In 2009 he was sublime. Those of us who saw it will long remember him finishing 36 lengths clear of Madison du Berlais, who had won the previous year's Hennessy. Few Grade Ones have ever been won with such ease and authority. The victory margin was on a par with Bob Beamon's long jump leap in Mexico City which rewrote his sport's record books.

In 2010 Kauto Star had fallen heavily in the Gold Cup and, with hindsight, took a long time to recover from the experience. In that year's King George he could only finish third behind Long Run, who went on to beat him too in the next Gold Cup. But if anybody had thought that was the moment for Kauto to walk off the stage in honourable retirement they were wrong. It was merely a sabbatical. At the age of 11 he came back as good as ever, giving Long Run a jumping lesson in the Betfair Chase at Haydock Park and then a tactical lesson at Kempton as the canny Ruby Walsh dictated a slow pace in the lead. As Kauto Star's elated trainer Paul Nicholls declared in the winners' enclosure after the 2011 King George: 'He's come in and he's not even having a blow. He was like that at Haydock. Last year he bled here and he was out on his feet.'

At that point Kauto Star had run in 30 chases and won 19 of them, including 16 Grade Ones. And his Cheltenham races too will long be part of racing's folk memory.

Kauto Star and Ruby Walsh jump the last to win the Commercial
First Ascot Chase, February 2008.

Paul Nicholls probably knew he had the 2007 Gold Cup in his grasp when he saw the grin on stable jockey Ruby Walsh's face as he rode towards the winners' enclosure at Haydock Park on 18 November 2006. That was the day trainer and jockey tested their theories by running Clive Smith's chaser over three miles for the first time in a Grade One chase, the Betfair. They faced a cluster of top horses lured to Lancashire by the £1 million bonus Betfair were offering to any horse that won their race plus either the King George or the Lexus Chase in Ireland and the Gold Cup. But Kauto Star did not just win that day against the likes of Kingscliff and L'Ami: he demolished them, striding home 17 lengths clear of Beef Or Salmon.

The King George duly followed, although twice in that race and once in his Cheltenham prep race in the spring Kauto Star alarmed his connections by making jumping errors – not just small ones but mistakes that would have led to many other less well-balanced horses falling as a result. In particular he seemed to be developing a habit of panicking at the final fence and tending to dive through it. Since he had rapidly become a famous name, this foible was given ample coverage in the media: once again the public had what they liked best – a spectacular hero with just a hint of fallibility about him, likely to turn every race he ran into a drama.

In the 2007 Cheltenham Gold Cup, Kauto Star did not disappoint his admirers or his detractors. With an electric acceleration round the final bend he went clear of his pursuers, but then he lost concentration, got too close and launched himself at rather than over the final fence. Somehow he got through it and somehow Ruby sat tight. They were pursued up the hill by Tony McCoy on Exotic Dancer but once Kauto Star had found his feet the result was clear. He duly collected his £1 million bonus to add to the £242,335 first prize.

As Kauto Star and his stablemate Denman prepared to meet in the 2008 Gold Cup they took different routes to Cheltenham. When Kauto Star returned to action in the Old Roan Chase at Aintree in October he suffered a shock defeat. He had been unusually uninterested in schooling before the race and at Aintree Ruby Walsh had to chase him along to keep him involved in the race at all. The grey Monet's Garden, always hard to beat first time out, defeated him clearly by one and a half lengths. With Ruby out injured and Sam Thomas in the saddle Kauto Star then ran more like his old self when winning the Betfair Chase at Haydock, beating his old rival Exotic Dancer. But it was the huge Denman who really sparkled when he contested the Hennessy Gold Cup at Newbury. Under top weight of 11st 12lbs and after an eight-month layoff he simply slaughtered a field of top-class handicappers, winning by 11 lengths from Dream Alliance.

Kauto Star then reaffirmed his credentials with his King George victory and Denman further burnished his by flying to Ireland to win the Lexus Chase. Then Denman powered his way to victory at Newbury again in the Aon Chase and Kauto Star put in a flawless performance winning the Commercial First Ascot Chase. It was game on, with Paul Nicholls predicting: 'Whatever beats Kauto Star will have to be a superstar.' Come Gold Cup day one of those turned up: the horse in the box next door. At his most menacing and dominant, in a masterclass of power-jumping Denman turned the screw on the rest of the field. Taking over a circuit from home and steaming on like a rail express, Denman forced Kauto Star into jumping errors as he drove on to an emphatic victory. It was a glorious day for his connections but Paul Nicholls told everybody not to write off Kauto Star, and his owner Clive Smith declared: 'We'll have him in the re-match.' So they did, but in different circumstances. Perhaps as a result of his Gold Cup power display, Denman developed heart trouble and spent much of the year off the track. It was touch and go whether he would even get to that re-match in 2009 and when he did he earned enormous credit by ploughing on to be second to a revivified Kauto Star, albeit 13 lengths in arrears.

Kauto had followed his 2008 Gold Cup failure by losing by a nose to Our Vic at Aintree when the wrong riding tactics were employed. In that year's Betfair Chase in November he and Sam Thomas parted company. But reunited with Ruby he won the King George again and was back to his classy athletic best in the 2009 Gold Cup.

We all looked forward to 2010 as the ultimate showdown, hopefully with Kauto Star and Denman both fully fit. But warning signs started flashing when in the 2009 Betfair Chase Kauto was only a nose ahead of Imperial Commander, and in the 2010 Gold Cup it was the younger Imperial Commander who took the honours. Denman, who had won another Hennessy in the meantime, slugged on again to be second but Kauto Star took a horrible fall, the kind that can often lead to maiming or death. Thankfully, he survived and in the 2011 Gold Cup the two old stablemates were there again. This time it was Robert Waley-Cohen's Long Run, ridden by his amateur son Sam, who was seen as the next generation's threat. Had any scriptwriter pencilled it in it would have been rejected as too impossibly perfect but racegoers saw the three best chasers in the country – Kauto Star, Denman and Long Run – rise as one at the second last. Long Run then forged ahead at the last and powered up the hill ahead of Denman, second for a third successive year, with Kauto Star in third.

Cue misty-eyed retirement statements, summaries of two great careers and fade-out? Not a bit of it. Denman and Kauto remained in training. Denman then, alas, suffered a tendon injury that did lead to his retirement but Kauto Star, incredibly, became the comeback king with those stunning victories over Long Run in the Betfair and the King George in 2011. In the 2012 Gold Cup Kauto Star was, of course, pulled up after Ruby felt something was amiss and at the time of writing no decision has been taken about whether he will race again. Whichever way that decision has gone by the time you read this, no one who saw him in his prime will ever forget a jumper who was the ultimate equine athlete with the highest cruising speed I have ever seen in a chaser.

Career highlights:
2005: Tingle Creek Chase
2006: Old Roan Chase, Betfair Chase
2007: Cheltenham Gold Cup, Betfair Chase, Tingle Creek Chase, King George VI Chase
2008: Lexus Chase, King George VI Chase
2009: Betfair Chase, King George VI Chase
2011: Betfair Chase, King George VI Chase

5. SEA-BIRD

Every few decades we get a Special One: Sea-Bird was one of those horses who has passed into legend, as beloved by handicappers, historians and statisticians as by those who experienced the tingle of seeing him in action. I had contemplated excluding him from this volume since we are celebrating horses that made an impact on the British scene and Sea-Bird ran only one of his eight races in Britain. In the end I could not because those who witnessed his 1965 victory in the Epsom Derby were in no doubt it was then the most commanding Derby performance ever seen, a performance by which other Derby performances have been judged ever since.

Owned and bred by Jean Ternynck and trained by Etienne Pollet at Chantilly, Sea-Bird, a chestnut by Dan Cupid out of Sicalade, had been beaten twice in his three races in 1964 as a two-year-old. In his Classic year, though, he came to Epsom as a warm favourite having won the Prix Greffulhe by three lengths and the Prix Lupin by six. His Epsom victory was not a surprise, but it was the way he won in an era when many French horses seemed to find

Sea-Bird, ridden by Pat Glennon, cruises home to win the Derby from Meadow Court under Lester Piggott, May 1965.

it a problem coping with the Epsom gradients and cambers that stamped Sea-Bird onto the retinas of a racing generation.

In their essay in which they hailed Sea-Bird as the 'Horse of the [last] Century' John Randall and Tony Morris declared: 'The Derby performance had to be seen to be believed. In a field of 22 he came to the front still cantering one and a half furlongs from home, then was just pushed out for a hundred yards before being eased again so that runner-up Meadow Court was flattered by the two lengths deficit.' Within weeks Meadow Court, the horse whom Sea-Bird toyed with, had become an authoritative winner of both the Irish Derby and the King George VI and Queen Elizabeth Stakes.

Sea-Bird won the Grand Prix de Saint-Cloud just as easily and then in his finale in the Prix de l'Arc de Triomphe he trumped even his Derby victory. In a glittering field he was facing the American champion Tom Rolfe, the unbeaten Russian Anilin, and Reliance, impressive winner of the French Derby and another horse yet to taste defeat.

Sea-Bird and Reliance drew away from the other 18 early in the straight at Longchamp. Reliance then moved up a gear and sought to move away, only to find instead that Sea-Bird simply sprinted past him. Had the champion not veered away off a straight line in the final stages he could have doubled the official victory margin of six lengths. It was quite astonishing. If only we could have seen him against Dancing Brave, Shergar or Sea The Stars.

Career highlights:
1965: Prix Greffulhe, Prix Lupin, Derby, Grand Prix de Saint-Cloud, Prix de l'Arc de Triomphe

4. SEA THE STARS

When jockey Mick Kinane, then approaching 50 and with a lifetime's experience of riding top horses, dismounted from Sea The Stars after winning the Epsom Derby he whispered six words in the ear of trainer John Oxx: 'This is one of the greats.' In his racing career Sea The Stars, by Cape Cross out of Urban Sea, was a magnificent looking horse, a horse who exuded masculinity and athleticism. He was a horse of presence and intelligence. Kinane once said: 'Every morning as he goes out on the Curragh I swear he counts the sheep – he would know if one was missing.' At the racetrack he was composed, almost sleepy sometimes in the preliminaries. But in his races he was the personification of balance and power, a horse with the ability to change a race in an instant with a powerful injection of pace.

Crucially, though he never won his races by the extravagant margins achieved by some great horses, Sea The Stars was a battler with a strong will to win: if Mick Kinane's whip cracked the instant answer was a thrusting forward of the neck, a bunching of those muscled hindquarters to intensify the forward drive, an instant willingness to search for and destroy the enemy. Above all, Sea The Stars had the physical constitution and mental strength to cope with a three-year-old season that was unparalleled. Racing once a month over half a year he won the 2,000 Guineas, the Derby, the Coral Eclipse, the Juddmonte International, the Irish Champion Stakes and the Prix de l'Arc de Triomphe. He won six top Group One races off the reel against the best horses in Europe, scoring victories at a mile, a mile and a quarter, and a mile and a half against specialists at each distance without a single defeat – a remarkable display of speed, stamina, courage and consistency.

Ling Tsui, of the Hong Kong Chinese family who bred and raced him, put it like this: 'In Chinese history emperors were all looking for a "Thousand Miles Horse". The criterion was that the horse had to be calm, strong and tireless. He had to have a champion's spirit and he had to have speed. However, they never mentioned the change of gear, the conformation and the beauty, so Sea The Stars has more qualities than the Thousand Miles Horse that our emperors so wanted.'

The 2008 season was the first since the 1980s in which Mick Kinane hadn't ridden a Group One winner. Retirement was beckoning, but it was a prospect he postponed once he had sat on Sea The Stars – the only horse he had ever believed capable of winning both the 2,000 Guineas and the Derby, a feat performed only by Nijinsky and Nashwan in four decades.

Although he never lost a race in the season that mattered, Sea The Stars was not unbeaten. In his very first race at the Curragh on 13 July 2008, running for a prize of 13,000 euros in the Jebel Ali Stables and Racecourse European Breeders Fund (C&G) Maiden, three horses came home ahead of Galileo's half brother, who started at 6-1. Tony O'Hehir noted in the *Racing Post*: 'Sea The Stars improved to chase the leaders towards the inside over two furlongs out … running on quite well in the closing stages.'

No horse ever beat him again. On 17 August at Leopardstown on heavy ground, which he coped with but which did not suit him, Sea The Stars, this time the 2-1 favourite, duly won a similar seven-furlong maiden, and immediately was offered at no better than 12-1 for the Derby by Ladbrokes. His trainer commented: 'Sea The Stars is a nice colt who is half asleep most of the time at home.'

Mick Kinane on Sea The Stars after winning the Derby,
June 2009.

Next time out Sea The Stars won the Group Two one-mile Beresford Stakes at the Curragh, a route often taken by those with Classic pretensions. John Oxx was pleased with his progress but warned that you could not be absolutely certain about Sea The Stars getting the Derby trip of a mile and a half.

It was the Derby, however, that he nominated as the next target after Sea The Stars, having been allowed to start at a generous 8-1, was an impressive winner of the 2,000 Guineas at Newmarket, beating Delegator. He accelerated smoothly past the favourite in the final furlong after tracking the leaders for the previous two. It was all the more meritorious since Sea The Stars had been held up in his work after running a temperature in March. Ireland provided four of the first five home.

No horse since Nashwan 20 years before had completed the 2,000 Guineas/Derby double but in a small field of only 12, six of them provided by Aidan O'Brien and Coolmore, what was impressive about Sea The Stars was not just the way he ran his race, travelling beautifully for Mick Kinane and having the measure of the field from three furlongs out, but his calm and composure before the race when many of his rivals were sweating up.

Kinane, who had ridden Sea The Stars' half brother Galileo to victory at Epsom, said he had been winning every step of the way, his main worry that Sea The Stars was finding the pace too slow. 'He has a very high cruising gear. He had improved enormously from Newmarket – we had to chase him hard to get there. Only a horse of his constitution would have taken what we threw at him, but since then it has been a coast.'

So where next after his one and a half length defeat of O'Brien's Fame and Glory? The Irish Derby, conceded

John Oxx, was unlikely. 'It hasn't stopped raining in Ireland for about two and a half years.' Nor were there any dreams of the Triple Crown, taking in the St Leger. The Eclipse and York's Juddmonte International, two mile-and-a-quarter races, were both mentioned as possibles and in the end Sea The Stars contested both.

Sea The Stars was now a horse who generated real excitement – so much so that owner Christopher Tsui fainted at Sandown on Coral Eclipse day. At Sandown that day he wasn't able to run the race Mick Kinane had planned, sitting in behind the leaders and taking them a furlong out. Sea The Stars broke so well that he had to be anchored ahead of the horses he had planned to track. He was forced to step things up at the two-furlong marker, which gave O'Brien's Rip Van Winkle a target, but one crack of the whip when Sea The Stars idled a furlong out was enough to see him home. He won without over-exerting himself and yet it was the fastest time for the race in 40 years.

At that stage the Irish and Newmarket Champion Stakes were higher on Sea The Stars' agenda than the Prix de l'Arc de Triomphe and his next contest was the Juddmonte International in August. There once again it was Aidan O'Brien who provided the opposition. All three of the Derby winner's opponents came from Ballydoyle and it was O'Brien's improving Mastercraftsman who gave Sea The Stars' supporters the first nail-biting moments they had endured all season. At the two-furlong pole Mastercraftsman was in full flight and Sea The Stars was initially slow to respond when Kinane pressed him. His rider had to get serious, but after a couple of smacks Sea The Stars went into overdrive and it became clear he would get up, which he did by a length at the line in a course record time. Said Oxx: 'Mick says he will never win anything by much more than a length but as long as he keeps winning we'll be happy.'

Keep winning he did, but it looked like an even tougher test next time when Sea The Stars ran on Irish soil for the first time in his championship season. Once again the challenge came from Ballydoyle, this time in the Irish Champion Stakes at Leopardstown, and once again it came in the shape of Mastercraftsman and Fame and Glory, who since Epsom had collected the Irish Derby and who had a couple of pacemakers to help him make the race a true test of stamina.

Sea The Stars' connections, who had pulled out of a run in the Irish Derby with the ground too soft, were praised for not ducking the race when the track had been deluged two days before and the ground was yielding. Kinane was cool enough when the pacemakers dropped away and Mastercraftsman faded to let Johnny Murtagh have first run on Fame and Glory. When Kinane pressed the button it was all over. A furlong out he swept past Fame and Glory and won by two and a half lengths. 'Quite easily for him', smiled Oxx.

If everything else was the same there was now a significant change of target. Suddenly Sea The Stars' connections were talking seriously about the Arc. Said Oxx: 'You wouldn't call running in a Group One every month since May as being a typical Arc preparation but Sea The Stars has taken all his races really well this year and seems to be thriving. He is heavier now than he was earlier in the season and he showed us today that he is really on top of his game.' That, of course was a tribute not just to the horse but to his remarkable trainer.

So it was that on 4 October 2009 Sea The Stars lined up at Longchamp for the Qatar Prix de l'Arc de Triomphe in what was to prove his final racecourse appearance.

Horses as good as Sea-Bird, Mill Reef and Dancing Brave had won the Arc after their efforts at Epsom, but they had all had a mid-season break. The Longchamp contest had been a step too far for Nijinsky. Sea The Stars, though, did have the omen that his dam Urban Sea had won an Arc back in 1993 for Christopher Tsui's parents David and Ling. John Oxx too had won both a Derby and an Arc with Sinndar, although Sinndar had endured nothing like Sea The Stars' racing programme.

There was applause for Sea The Stars and his veteran rider even before they took part in the Arc and it proved a severe test for both. Sea The Stars was more lit up than usual and too keen to get on with things. Mick Kinane had to sacrifice position to settle him in behind other horses, which raised the risk of traffic problems down the straight. Coming into the straight Sea The Stars was hampered and momentarily lost his footing as Kinane angled for a run up the rail. It was going to take courage to get anywhere: he was going to have to find a killer punch. But then Sea The Stars had never ducked a challenge yet. The gap appeared, although it was rapidly being closed by the mare Dar Re Mi. Kinane asked, Sea The Stars responded with a blast of speed that took him through the gap and clear of Dar Re Mi and Stacellita. After that Kinane didn't have to ride a frantic finish. It was all over and he won with plenty in hand, two lengths clear of Youmzain, who was second for the third time in the race.

The best horse in the continent for years had won Europe's richest prize. It was a fitting ending for an extraordinary horse. Looks, temperament, ability, he had it all. And if some want to crab and say that he should have gone to America for the Breeders' Cup or that he should have stayed in training as a four-year-old to prove himself to be a true great then that is wailing in the wind.

After such a testing season in Europe it would have been asking too much even of a Sea The Stars to tackle the USA. A horse who had matured so steadily and visibly through his three-year-old career wouldn't necessarily have improved at four. And what else did he have to prove in Europe?

Career highlights:
2009: 2,000 Guineas, Derby, Eclipse, Juddmonte International,
    Irish Champion Stakes, Prix de l'Arc de Triomphe

3. FRANKEL

There are good horses, great horses and horses that set those little hairs on the back of your neck prickling when they run, even when they step into the paddock from the saddling boxes. Frankel's extraordinary victory in the 2,000 Guineas of 2011 pushed every other great performance I had seen on track to the back of my mind. Nothing so devastating had been seen on a British racecourse since Tudor Minstrel took apart his field in the same race back in 1947, yet Frankel was to produce an equally mind-blowing performance in the Queen Anne Stakes in 2012.

The style and power of Frankel's 2,000 Guineas victory would have been enough to make him Horse of the Year and earn him the highest rating since Sea-Bird and Brigadier Gerard but he ended his three-year-old season undefeated in nine races including a Sussex Stakes in which he conquered the top-class four-year-old miler Canford Cliffs. The versatility question – he had not raced outside Britain or over more than a mile – was the only one that stopped some from naming Frankel as the best horse they had ever seen. No one had any doubt already that he was a great one. On Frankel days at the racecourse you find the greats of the sport – ex-trainers like Mick Easterby and Mick O'Toole or current masters like Sir Mark Prescott and John Dunlop – joining the media and the rubber-neckers to make sure they get a good view of this racing phenomenon.

Trained in his resurgence by the ten-times champion trainer Sir Henry Cecil and owned by Khalid Abdulla, one of the most successful and sporting breeders we have ever seen, Frankel, a big horse with a massive chest cage and an extraordinary devouring stride, soon became a public hero. A son of Galileo and the first foal of the Danehill mare Kind, Frankel made his debut in a Newmarket maiden as a two-year-old in 2010 beating Nathaniel, who was later to win the King George VI and Queen Elizabeth Stakes and the Eclipse. Frankel then won a conditions race at Doncaster's St Leger meeting, stretching 13 lengths clear of his nearest pursuer. In the autumn he won the Group Two Royal Lodge Stakes at Ascot, opening up a ten-length gap on the field after moving from last to first with an effortless change of gear. In the Dewhurst he got somewhat over-excited after being bumped by another runner but eventually settled and won unextended by two lengths.

At three the big colt, the heftiest eater in the Warren Place yard, soon proved his wellbeing by winning the Group Three Greenham Stakes at Newbury from the talented and consistent Excelebration, who was to spend much of his career watching Frankel's backside from second place. The only worry was that Frankel, who had often fought for his head as a juvenile, still seemed a little excitable.

Then came the amazing 2,000 Guineas. Although there was a strong headwind at Newmarket, jockey Tom

Queally allowed Frankel to blaze away from the start and employed his huge stride to such effect that by halfway he was around 15 lengths clear. The other jockeys were hard at work in another race and those who tried hardest to keep in touch with Frankel paid for it by limping in at the tail of the field. The winning margin at the post was only six lengths but it could have been bigger if Queally had wished.

Urgings from many quarters to risk Frankel in the Derby going unheeded, his next allotted task was the St James's Palace Stakes at Royal Ascot and there Tom Queally did seem for once to let things get to him. Riding horses who possess maximum power but not necessarily the maturity to use it to best effect is not the easiest of tasks. On such occasions you are in the harshest of spotlights and any blemish shows. Every critic and fan has his own idea about how to ride a precious horse that has become, in a sense, public property. In the Ascot race Queally ill-advisedly rushed his mount up to his pacemaker at halfway and although that soon carried him clear of his rivals it left him vulnerable to a late attack as he tired in front. That late attack duly arrived in the shape of Zoffany and a tired Frankel finished only three-quarters of a length clear at the end. It was a year later before Cecil, who has faced the strain of battling stomach cancer for six years, confessed that he had never been so angry in his life: 'It was an absolute disaster. I can't bear thinking about it. I want to forget. The horse did very well to get through it.'

Everybody in racing then wanted to see the clash in the Sussex Stakes between the emergent Frankel and the established champion four-year-old miler Canford Cliffs, the apple of Richard Hannon's experienced eye and the winner of five Group Ones in his previous five races.

Tom Queally celebrates Frankel's victory in the 2,000 Guineas,
Newmarket, April 2011.

Again there was a dilemma for Frankel's trainer and rider, especially with Richard Hughes, the best tactical rider of his day, on Canford Cliffs. Although it carried the risk of setting Frankel up as a target and getting mugged on the line by a typical late Hughes swoop they elected to go out from the start and to use Frankel's stride to ratchet up the pressure steadily. They got it right. Halfway up the straight, as Tom Queally let out another notch and quickened again, it was Canford Cliffs who cracked. He hung left, his spirit possibly broken, although a minor injury was later detected. Frankel powered on to the line to win by five lengths: Canford Cliffs headed for the breeding sheds.

Frankel closed his three-year-old season with another exhibition, this time winning the Queen Elizabeth II Stakes at Ascot on the first richly endowed Qipco Champions Day. Towed along early by his pacemaker Bullet Train, he toyed with a top-class field including four Group One winners, accelerating away when he pleased and winning by four lengths from the dependable yardstick Excelebration.

Frankel fans had a shock early the next year when the colt struck into himself at exercise as he was being prepared for his reappearance. Rumours that a tendon injury meant his career was over spread like wildfire round the Aintree course on Grand National Day. Fortunately it proved no more than an interruption. On 19 May Frankel, who had performed an exercise canter for the Newmarket crowds on Guineas Day, reappeared at Newbury to contest the Lockinge Stakes. Looking magnificent in the paddock and seeming totally unfussed by the preliminaries, he drew gasps from the crowd when Tom Queally asked him to go on two furlongs out. He simply purred into another gear and left the ever-dependable Excelebration, now trained by Aidan O'Brien, five lengths behind him. It was a masterful performance, cool and authoritative, revealing not only that he had kept his huge stride and his speed but that he had become a more mature horse too. It was just what racing needed: the promise of a masterclass season ahead, with Frankel extending his repertoire to ten furlongs or perhaps even more.

Even Frankel's record, though, had not prepared us for the 2012 Queen Anne Stakes at Royal Ascot when ten horses, including his old rival Excelebration, took him on. He was calm in the parade ring, composed on his way to the start and settled well as his usual pacemaker Bullet Train made the early pace. More than two furlongs out Frankel eased to the front with his rivals already under pressure. He then stretched away with that huge stride to win his 11th consecutive race by a massive 11 lengths, more than doubling his margin over Excelebration in their previous three meetings. It was a massive demonstration of power and authority against a talented field, and what is so impressive about Frankel's surge is that it is so smooth. There is no explosion or moment of imbalance when changing gear: Tom Queally just lets out a notch and away Frankel goes, leaving the opposition behind him and still appearing to have plenty left at the finish.

Queally's hardest task at Ascot was pulling him up before he had completed a full honour lap. Said Frankel's jockey: 'He's been flawless in the past but I couldn't ask for any more today. It was a demolition again – he was awesome.' The British Horseracing Authority's head of handicapping Phil Smith said it was the most visually impressive performance he had seen in 40 years of rating horses and Timeform raised the big horse's rating to 147, two points higher than the mighty Sea-Bird, outstanding winner of the Epsom Derby and of the Arc in 1965.

Slowly we were learning more too about Frankel's home life. Handled so patiently by Cecil, Queally and work rider Shane Fetherstonhaugh, he had become the total professional on the racecourse, but interviews with his trainer revealed that there were still some rock star days as he smashed up his manger or tried to pull his rug over his head. Even on Queen Anne day after the race I noticed Frankel, still full of nervous energy, kicking over a water bucket and demolishing a geranium or two as the cameras clicked. But what was truly frightening was that his trainer averred that the horse was still improving.

Frankel's only other run before this volume went to press was in the Qipco Sussex Stakes. This time, with the Goodwood racecard decked out in Khalid Abdulla's colours of green with a pink sash, only two horses joined him and Bullet Train in a four-horse field in which he was the 1-20 favourite, but the story was the same. Frankie Dettori on Godolphin's Farrh and Paul Hanagan on Marwan Koukash's Gabrial were already hard at work when Tom Queally let out the notch two furlongs out. Once again Frankel's engine purred into overdrive, his stride lengthened and the field was left trailing by six lengths as the crowd applauded him home. Queally did not quite open the throttle as far as he had done at Ascot but Frankel's mastery was total. The crowds left Goodwood agog to see the superstar move up on his next outing to race over ten furlongs.

Career highlights:
2010: Royal Lodge Stakes, Dewhurst Stakes
2011: 2,000 Guineas, St James's Palace Stakes, Sussex Stakes,
    Queen Elizabeth II Stakes
2012: Queen Anne Stakes, Sussex Stakes

2. BRIGADIER GERARD

Named after Sir Arthur Conan Doyle's fictional military hero and owned and bred by John Hislop, who had himself won an MC after being parachuted into France with the Special Air Service, Brigadier Gerard was a son of the successful miler Queen's Hussar out of a non-winning racemare, La Paiva. Hislop was a famed amateur rider, a gifted racing journalist and a man renowned for his knowledge of the breeding industry, and he achieved his greatest success by bringing a mare he bought for 400 guineas to the local stallion who stood for £250.

The result of that mating, Brigadier Gerard, won his first race in Jean Hislop's colours, the Berkshire Stakes at Newbury, by five lengths. Sheilah Hern, wife of Brigadier Gerard's trainer Dick Hern, took a while to forgive her husband after she had asked him if she should include Brigadier Gerard in her Tote Jackpot entry. He advised against – and she had the other five winners! Brigadier Gerard, a 100-7 shot that day, was never such a long price again.

Some call the Brigadier, a bay colt who won 17 of his 18 races, the best horse we ever saw in Britain. He epitomised class, courage and consistency but he had to struggle in his early days to win due attention. It was not that he had disappointed as a juvenile in 1970 – he won all his four races as a two-year-old by comfortable margins and beat speedy customers like Mummy's Pet in the Middle Park Stakes – but simply that the highly talented My Swallow and Mill Reef were around at the same time.

In the two-year-old Free Handicap Mill Reef was rated 1lb better than Brigadier Gerard, My Swallow was rated

2lb better. So when it came to the 2,000 Guineas the Brigadier, at 11-2, was only the third favourite, as he had been for the Middle Park.

My Swallow was at that stage unbeaten in eight races. Mill Reef's only setback in seven contests had been his short head defeat by My Swallow in the Prix Robert Papin and those two principals had each tuned up with a preparatory race before the Guineas. My Swallow, trained in Newmarket by Paul Davey, set the pace for the first five furlongs but when Mill Reef was then ridden to reel him in the two locked in fierce combat.

Mill Reef, trained at Kingsclere by Ian Balding, had just got his head in front of his old rival when suddenly Brigadier Gerard came on the scene. In one scintillating burst of sustained speed he came up to the duelling pair, passed them and went away down into the Dip and up the final hill. Ridden as he was throughout his career by Joe Mercer, he won one of the epic Guineas contests by three lengths with Mill Reef in second, three-quarters of a length ahead of My Swallow. It gave a new ring to the meaning of authoritative and confirmed the judgement of his owners who had refused an offer of £250,000 for him.

Part of the measure of Brigadier Gerard's achievement in the Guineas is the style with which he won, part of it is to look at the careers of those he beat. Mill Reef was never defeated again in six races including the King George and the Arc. As well as the Prix Robert Papin, My Swallow won the Prix Morny, the Prix de la Salamandre and the Grand Criterium.

As a three-year-old in 1971 'the Brigadier', as he came to be known, followed his devastating success in the 2,000 Guineas by winning the St James's Palace Stakes at Ascot. This showed that he had the resolution to match his ability. The going was heavy and he lost his action in the deep mud. The talented miler Sparkler had scooted clear but Joe Mercer gave his mount time to get things together and they clawed back the margin inch by inch to win by a head.

Seen at first essentially as a miler, Brigadier Gerard echoed his sire by winning the Sussex Stakes over Goodwood's undulations by five lengths and confirmed how he liked the track by winning the Goodwood Mile that season by a ten-length margin. He won the Queen Elizabeth II Stakes at Ascot by eight lengths and ended his three-year-old season undefeated in ten races from five furlongs to a mile and a quarter by winning the Champion Stakes at Newmarket, although with the ground soft again he had to fight to beat Rarity by a nose.

The Brigadier carried on in the same vein as a four-year-old the next season. He extended his unbeaten run to 15 races. There were convincing victories in the ten-furlong Lockinge Stakes, Westbury Stakes and the Prince of Wales Stakes at Ascot in which he set a new course record. He then won the ten-furlong Eclipse Stakes at Sandown, slogging home in the rain ahead of the 50-1 outsider Gold Rod on soft going he did not relish. After that came the big test of tackling a mile and a half for the first time in the King George VI and Queen Elizabeth Stakes.

Luckily for the Brigadier it was a sub-standard field in 1972, but it still included four Classic winners including the previous year's Irish St Leger winner Parnell, who was bound to make it a test of stamina but who lacked finishing speed. Brigadier Gerard moved up within a length of Parnell as they entered the straight and went past him a furlong out to win, but the Brigadier, at the end of his tether, had veered towards the inside rail after passing

Parnell and had to survive a stewards' inquiry to keep the race. His class saw him through, but it had stretched his stamina and may have taken more out of him than was realised at the time, because then came the racing shock of the year.

In the Benson and Hedges Gold Cup (nowadays the Juddmonte International) over the extended mile and a quarter at York, up against the 1972 Derby winner Roberto and the runner-up Rheingold, the Brigadier tasted defeat for the first time. As described in Roberto's

Joe Mercer aboard Brigadier Gerard, Goodwood, July 1971.

entry, the American jockey Braulio Baeza produced the race of his life from Roberto who led all the way, shattered the course record and left Brigadier Gerard, who was also inside the old record, three lengths in his wake at the line. Jean Hislop commented rather tartly that Roberto must have been stung by a bee. Joe Mercer, Brigadier Gerard's regular partner, was more straightforward: 'A lot of people said Baeza stole the race but to my mind he didn't. I thought I would be able to go and pick him off whenever I wanted to. Sadly I couldn't.'

That sole defeat had no lasting effect on the Brigadier, who concluded his career by repeating his wins of the previous season in the Queen Elizabeth II Stakes (setting a new course record and winning by six lengths) and by beating Riverman in the Champion Stakes before he retired to stud with a £253,024 haul from 17 victories in his 18 races. He was accorded a Timeform rating of 144, the joint second-highest ever for a Flat racer behind Sea-Bird II, and the Brigadier Gerard Stakes at Sandown was of course named in his honour. In their definitive *A Century of Champions* published in the millennium year, John Randall and Tony Morris, today's leading Turf historians, made him their 'British Horse of the Century'.

Career highlights:
1970: Middle Park Stakes
1971: 2,000 Guineas, St James's Palace Stakes, Sussex Stakes, Goodwood Mile, Queen Elizabeth II Stakes, Champion Stakes
1972: Lockinge Stakes, Prince of Wales Stakes, Eclipse Stakes, King George VI and Queen Elizabeth Stakes, Queen Elizabeth II Stakes, Champion Stakes

1. ARKLE

It was said of W.G. Grace as a cricketer that he led contemporary sports writers to 'exhaust the language of
hyperbole'. It is much the same with Arkle: the ultimate
tribute to him is that they had to alter the rules of his
sport to accommodate the genius of the horse whom all
of Ireland knew simply as 'Himself'. The Irish authorities
introduced a system of dual handicaps for races in which
he was entered: one was to be used when he was declared
to run, the other for races he missed.

There have been other great horses on the Flat and
over jumps. Attempting to compare Arkle with Flat-racers
like Dancing Brave, Sea The Stars or Frankel is for me
akin to the preoccupations of medieval philosophers
with how many angels could be accommodated on the
head of a pin. Comparing Arkle with other great jumpers
like Golden Miller, Best Mate, Kauto Star (or even with
what his stablemate Flyingbolt might have become had
he not contracted brucellosis) is a little more meaningful although never conclusive. For me, though, Arkle
still reigns supreme, even if one of my most vivid early
racing memories is of forlornly cheering on England's
great hope Mill House against him on several occasions.

What made Arkle so great? Why did he become
the subject of songs and poetry? Why did he have post-
age stamps and tea towels emblazoned with his picture
and walls daubed 'Arkle for President' in Dublin? First
and foremost of course it was because of his results: this
supreme equine athlete won 22 of his 26 steeplechases
between 1962 and 1966. Those races included not just
championship contests like the Cheltenham Gold Cup in
which Arkle carried the same weight as his competitors,
but handicaps in which he carried huge weight burdens,

often 20 or 30lbs more than the top-class horses ranged against him.

Along with his three Cheltenham Gold Cups Arkle won the Hennessy Gold Cup twice, the Whitbread Gold Cup and the Irish Grand National, although he never contested the Aintree Grand National: his owner, Anne, Duchess of Westminster, a countrywoman who truly loved and understood her horses, always feared the risk of injury. As so often in racing, Sir Peter O'Sullevan put it best. Reviewing Sean Magee's polished and painstaking study of Arkle's life, he declared of the greatest steeple-chaser we have seen that he had 'an obit to die for'.

Results alone, though, do not make a horse capture the public imagination as Arkle did. Part of his appeal was the sheer sense of majesty he exuded in crushing his opponents and the exhilaration he imparted: he really seemed to enjoy his jumping. And while anthropomorphism, investing other creatures with human qualities and emotions, is a constant danger for any of us who love animals there really seemed to be a 'presence' about Arkle. The large pricked ears and enquiring demeanour as he strolled around parade rings made it look as though he was aware of his public and as if he revelled in the attention he received. At home too he was a gentleman. Tiny children could safely be placed upon his back, whereas his talented stable companion Flyingbolt would as soon kick your eye out as look at you, as their rider Pat Taaffe once noted.

Arkle, named after a small Scottish mountain overlooking part of the Westminster estates, was trained at Greenogue by the quiet man Tom Dreaper and ridden in every one of his steeplechases by Taaffe.

Before his chasing career began Arkle had not looked a world-beater. He had run third and fourth in a couple of bumpers (Flat races for jumping horses) and won two of the five hurdles he contested. But started over the bigger obstacles in the Honeybourne Chase at Cheltenham in November 1962 he immediately looked something special, skipping over the last fence and galloping 20 lengths clear of his field.

When he returned for the Festival in the spring, Arkle again moved into overdrive at the finish and scooted clear of his field in the Broadway Chase, two days before another great chaser called Mill House won the Gold Cup for England. Arkle finished the season unbeaten in two hurdles and five chases and won a race on the Flat and the Carey's Cottage Chase at Gowran Park to open his 1963–64 campaign. Ireland's favourite chaser, never beaten over fences in his homeland, then took his 100 per cent unbeaten chasing record into the Hennessy Gold Cup in November.

As a Gold Cup winner, Mill House was set to concede him 5lbs and Fulke Walwyn's big chaser took an early lead. Arkle was on his heels full of running at the third last when he slipped on landing and lost all his momentum. By the time Pat Taaffe had regained his rhythm Mill House was gone and Happy Spring had passed him too: they had to settle for third place.

That result left two racing nations yearning for the next clash of the titans in the Cheltenham Gold Cup of 1964.

In the Gold Cup Mill House was the odds-on favourite and only two horses, Pas Seul and King's Nephew, dared to take on the Big Two. Mill House was cool before the start, Arkle much buzzier. As Mill House led and Pat Taaffe sought to restrain his mount early on, the favourite seemed to be going the better, jumping majestically. Three out and the Irish contingent was getting a little uneasy. But then Taaffe pulled his mount out and asked

Arkle, who broke a bone in his foot during his final race
on 27 December 1966, recuperating in his box
in January 1967.

him to take the leader. They were together in a matter
of strides and jumped the second last that way. But then
Arkle simply engaged another gear. He jumped the last
ahead and sprinted five lengths clear up to the line. Mill
House was not just beaten but demolished. His trainer
Fulke Walwyn just couldn't believe that any horse could

do what Arkle had done to Mill House. Never a race so perfect or a triumph more complete, as the eloquent John Lawrence (Lord Oaksey) put it.

Just three weeks later Arkle showed how little the race had taken out of him by beating the tough mare Height O'Fashion by a length and a quarter in the Irish Grand National, giving her 2st 2lb over the three and a half miles. So superior was his talent reckoned to be that the Irish National Hunt Committee announced that in future there would be A and B handicaps drawn up for such races so that if a topweight like Arkle pulled out the resulting race was not a nonsense.

Mill House's follow-up to the Gold Cup was just as impressive. Humping a massive 12st 7lb in the Whitbread Gold Cup he went down by just half a length to Dormant, who carried three stone less. So despite what we had seen happen at Cheltenham, the Big Horse's admirers still hoped against hope that he could yet prove a match for Ireland's hero in the Hennessy, especially as Arkle was now set to concede him three pounds. Instead it was an even more complete triumph for Arkle. Pat Taaffe let him choose his own tactics: he chose to go head-for-head with the best jumper of fences around and take him on at every fence: … 'anything you can do' was the refrain. By the end of the back straight it was Mill House, not Arkle, who cracked and in the end as the Irishman came home clear he could finish only fourth.

Weight, though, can anchor any horse if there is enough of it. A week after the Hennessy Arkle raced again in the Massey Ferguson Gold Cup at Cheltenham, his 12st 7lb mark increased by a three-pound penalty for winning the Hennessy. Racing again so soon, over the shorter distance of 2m 5f and giving 32lbs to Flying Wild and 26lbs to Buona Notte, proved a step too far even for

Arkle, who led at the second last but could not find quite enough up the hill to repel the two boarders, even though he was closing again after the last.

After that Arkle won eight races in succession against the best that two countries could throw at him. In 1965, the year that Sea-Bird won the Derby, they included the Cheltenham Gold Cup in which he again beat Mill House, this time by 20 lengths, and the Whitbread Gold Cup at Sandown Park a few weeks later, in which he triumphed by five lengths. But for many one of the best races of Arkle's extraordinary career was the Gallaher Gold Cup at Sandown that autumn, in which the handicapper set him to concede 16lbs to Mill House. A seemingly revivified Mill House was racing fit, Arkle had not run yet in the new season and there were other good horses to face like Rondetto and John O'Groats, the first and second in the race the year before.

It was a measure of the extraordinary popularity of both Arkle and Mill House that the two were applauded out of the parade ring, down the Rhododendron Walk and as they cantered past the stands. Mill House was superb, flicking over along the railway fences and his fans began to hope, but when they turned into the final stretch Arkle strode by the leader as if he was not there. A shake of the reins at the last and he sprinted away up the hill for a devastating win that smashed Mill House's course record by an extraordinary 17 seconds. Rondetto took second and Mill House third and all three were applauded back in for their heroic efforts.

After that Arkle took another Hennessy Gold Cup, this time from the Scottish-trained Freddie, and won a King George VI Chase that was marred by the death of the talented young chaser Dunkirk, a two-miler whose heart was possibly broken by Arkle simply coasting up to him after his exhilarating jumping had taken Dunkirk a hundred yards or more clear.

Another victory in the Leopardstown Chase in March 1966 was taken as a given, but Arkle, more and more the handicapper's nightmare, was being asked in heavy mud to give the classy Height O'Fashion a full three stone. He did it, but for once Pat Taaffe had to use his whip in earnest and the margin was so narrow that it took a photo finish to confirm Arkle's success.

He won his third Cheltenham Gold Cup two weeks later against the weakest opposition he had ever faced at the Festival, with Mill House sidelined by an injury. Uncharacteristically, Arkle, who never fell, crashed through one fence but he still won by 30 lengths. What we did not know at the time was that Arkle, in his prime at nine years old, was to have only three more races, and he won only one of them.

In November 1966 he faced the starter in the Hennessy once again, bearing his customary 12st 7lb and up against Freddie, What A Myth (who later won a Gold Cup) and Stalbridge Colonist, the grey who had won 11 races in the 1965–66 season. Arkle led most of the way and beat off all the others but Stalbridge Colonist was being cannily ridden by Stan Mellor, who did all he could to make Pat Taaffe think there was no serious challenge. Carrying 35lbs less than the leader, Stalbridge Colonist was in fact going ominously well in his slipstream. Approaching the last, as the crowd began roaring Arkle home, Mellor pulled out and drove the grey into a sudden challenge. They battled all the way to the line but it was Stalbridge Colonist who had the momentum and he got the verdict by half a length.

Arkle was soon back on the winning trail, taking the SGB Chase at Ascot, and he went on once again to the Boxing Day highlight, the King George VI Chase at

Kempton. There tragedy struck. Arkle jumped the last well clear from Dormant but slowed almost to a walk on the run-in, was caught close to the post and beaten a length. He was clearly a stricken horse, and Pat Taaffe had felt for most of the race there was something amiss. Arkle had been 'hanging' outward for most of the way, never really taking hold of his bit and at one stage had nearly fallen. It transpired that he had broken a bone in his foot; in his final contest he had thus demonstrated a courage to match his brilliance.

Arkle's pedal bone mended and at one stage it was planned he should resume his racing career. But after a series of postponements the Dreapers and the Duchess of Westminster announced in October 1968 that the great horse was to be retired. Sadly it was not a long retirement. Arkle's pedal bone was fine but he began to suffer with stiffness in his hind legs. He was finding life more and more uncomfortable, often preferring to lie rather than stand, and in May 1970 he was put down to spare him further pain.

Arkle had, wrote John Lawrence, been bred for his job and taught to do it well by kindly men. 'He did it because he loved his own speed and strength and agility – and perhaps because he loved the cheers they brought him. He was, more certainly than any other thoroughbred I can think of, a happy horse who enjoyed every minute of his life.' Of how many human beings can we say that?

Career highlights:
1963: Broadway Chase, Power Gold Cup, John James Gold Cup
1964: Cheltenham Gold Cup, Irish Grand National, Hennessy Gold Cup
1965: Cheltenham Gold Cup, Whitbread Gold Cup, Gallaher Gold Cup, Hennessy Gold Cup, King George VI Chase
1966: Cheltenham Gold Cup

INDEX